W9-BKN-776

Boeing

BOEING

BOEING:
The First Century

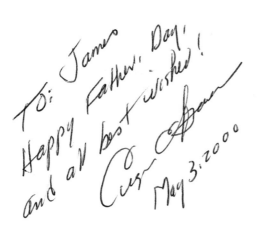

To: James
Happy Father's Day!
and all best wishes!

Cur Barn

May 3, 2000

Other books by Eugene E. Bauer

China Takes Off
University of Washington Press, 1986

Boeing in Peace & War
TABA Publishing Inc., 1991

Contrails
A Boeing Salesman Reminisces
TABA Publishing Inc., 1996

BOEING:
The First Century

Eugene E. Bauer

Introduction by
Wolfgang Demisch

TABA Publishing, Inc.
Enumclaw, Washington

Copyright © 2000 by Eugene E. Bauer

Published by TABA Publishing, Inc.
24103 S.E. 384th St.
Enumclaw, Washington 98022

All rights reserved. No part of this publication may be reproduced or transmitted in any form or by any means, electronic or mechanical, including photocopy, recording, or any information storage or retrieval system, without permission in writing from the publisher.

ISBN 1-879242-08-7

Library of Congress Catalog Card No. 99-094012

Cover design: Courtesy of The Boeing Company

Photos: Courtesy of The Boeing Company Historical Archives unless otherwise noted.

Book design, typography, and production coordination by Blue Heron Publishing, Inc., Portland, Oregon.

Printed in the United States of America at Central Plains Book Manufacturing, Inc., Arkansas City, Kansas.

Dedicated to my children,
Michael and Cheryl,
who suffered as a result of
my devotion to the job.

We must take the current when it serves,
or lose our ventures.

William Shakespeare

ACKNOWLEDGMENTS

I am deeply indebted to the late Harold Mansfield, who graciously consented to the use of numerous quotes from two of his books, *Vision*, and *Billion Dollar Battle*.

I extend special thanks to Clark McCann, Director of Advertising and Corporate Identity; and Sherry Nebel, Director of Media Relations—both of The Boeing Company—for their generous support in making the book possible.

I also extend special thanks to the staffs of Clark McCann and Sherry Nebel, in particular to Diane Moerer and Fritz Johnston—and to Lynn Hanks, Art Director, for designing the jacket. Further, and of singular importance, I thank The Boeing Company Historical Archives staff: Historian Michael Lombardi, who proofed the book for historical accuracy—and to Archivist Tom Lubbesmeyer, who enthusiastically searched out historical information and provided hundreds of photographs from which to choose.

Above all, I salute the management and employees of The Boeing Company, past and present—who in the final analysis, by their devotion to excellence—made the story of Boeing come alive over almost an entire century.

Grateful acknowledgment is given for use of short quotes from a number of publications.

An American Saga, by Robert Daley. Copyrght © 1980 by Riviera Productions Ltd. Reprinted by permission of Random House, Inc.

An analysis of Labor Relations News Coverage in the Boeing Company Paper and the Union Paper During the Strike of 1948, by K.L. Calkins, University of Washington Master's Thesis, TH 17015. All rights reserved. Reprinted by permission.

Aviation Week & Space Technology, Copyright © August 4, 1980, June 3, 1991, March 16, 1992, May 4, 1992, and December 23/30, 1996. All rights reserved. Reprinted by permission.

Business Week, Copyright © December 18, 1989, and March 1, 1993. All rights reserved. Reprinted by permission.

Boeing News, multiple issues. Reprinted by special permission.

China Takes Off, by E. E. Bauer, University of Washington Press, Copyright © 1986. All rights reserved. Reprinted by permission.

Clipped Wings, by Mel Horwitch, MIT Press, Copyright © 1982. All rights reserved. Reprinted by permission.

Forbes, Copyright © November 26, 1979. All rights reserved. Reprinted by permission.

Fortune, Copyright © September 25, 1978, September 28, 1987, July 17, 1989, August 28, 1989, February 17, 1997, and March 1, 1999. All rights reserved. Reprinted by permission.

Industry in the Pacific Northwest and the Location Theory, by E.J. Cohn, Jr., King's Crown Press, Copyright © 1954. All rights reserved. Reprinted by permission.

International Herald Tribune, Copyright © February 27–28, 1982, and September 12, 1985. All rights reserved. Reprinted by permission.

New York Times, Copyright © February 16, 1976, February 23, 1977, and February 15, 1979. All rights reserved. Reprinted by permission.

Ready All!, by Gordon Newell, University of Washington Press. Copyright © 1987. All rights reserved. Reprinted by permission.

Seattle's Economic Development 1880–1910, by A.N. MacDonald, University of Washington Ph.D. Thesis, TH 10295. All rights reserved. Reprinted by permission.

Seattle Post Intelligencer, Copyright © January 1, 1980, June 10, 1998, August 25, 1998, and November 18, 1998. All rights reserved. Reprinted by permission.

Seattle Times, Copyright © March 20, 1984, June 3, 1984, and October 24, 1989. All rights reserved. Reprinted by permission.

Sky Master, by Frank Cunningham, Dorrance & company, Copyright © 1943. All rights reserved. Reprinted by permission.

Technology and Change, by Donald Schon, Delacorte Press, Copyright © 1967. All rights reserved. Reprinted by permission.

The Grease Machine, by David Boulton, Harper & Row. Copyright © 1978. All rights reserved. Reprinted by permission.

Time, Copyright © April 7, 1980. All rights reserved. Reprinted by permission.

Twenty-first Century Jet, By Karl Sabbagh, Scribner, Copyright © 1996. All rights reserved. Reprinted by permission.

Wall Street Journal, Copyright © December 4, 1975, May 7, 1976, February 20, 1979, and October 9, 1980, Dow Jones & Company Inc. All rights reserved worldwide. Reprinted by permission.

Washington, Copyright © November, 1988. All rights reserved. Reprinted by permission.

Boeing, The First Century is also the distillation of countless conversations and meetings with other Boeing employees, managers, and executives over a span of 45 years, beginning in 1941 and continuing until my retirement in 1988. During this period, I had the pleasure of serving under five presidents, from Philip Johnson to Frank Shrontz.

Further, since retiring, I became additionally indebted to the many management personnel and other employees who either sat for interviews, escorted me around the various factories, or dug out material of value for my project. First, Phil Condit, an engineer's engineer with whom I worked in the seventies—who was named president in 1992—rising to chariman only five years later; then Frank Shrontz, an uncommonly talented manager, who led the Company through a tortuous reinvention process; and of course, Harry Stonecipher—unique industry leader from McDonnell Douglas—who shook the hallowed halls of Boeing into gripping reality a little more firmly.

Then there was Alan Mulally, Michael Sears, Jim Albaugh, James Jamieson, Larry Dickenson, George Torres, Marta Newhart, John Cashman, Craig Martin, Stephanie Mudgett, Ida Hawkins, Peter Conte, Jim Dagnon, Sean Griffin, Susan Bradley, Beverly Weiss, Roger Wynne, Dave Phillips, Lawrence Merritt, Tom Downey, Denny Kline, Pat King, Diane Gonzalez, Jim Keller, Jack James, G.M. Bunney, Lucy Slater, Volker Roth, Harry Fachet, Mark Smith, Bob Kruse, Roy Cantrell, John Winch, Becky DeArmond, Steve Pierce, Chi Yan, Viola Marshall, Al Gehri, David Cockerill, Mary Barr, Ray Bracy, Steve Morse, Latif Rahimane, Steve Douglas, John Bruns, J.B. Kump, Pamela Workings, Gale Kuznicki, Kristy Varnes, Christine Nelson, and L. Norm Yearsley.

No book of history would be complete without an insightful introduction, and for this I offer my most heartfelt thanks to Wolfgang Demisch, financial guru, who has his finger firmly on the pulse of the aerospace industry—which universally listens when he speaks.

Authors are never alone in writing a book. They need nurturing and enthusiastic support. For this support, I thank my wife Lori, who kept me believing in myself.

INTRODUCTION
by
Wolfgang Demisch

Aerospace is an American success story. Founded early in this century by strong-willed and capable innovators, the aerospace industry has become a key factor in national security, as well as a global engine of prosperity, linking the world's economy and its people.

The emergence of the Boeing Company, from its beginnings in a remote northwestern corner of the United States to its present preeminence as the world's largest, best financed, and most capable aerospace producer is almost an archetypal illustration of that process. Bill Boeing was a self-confident timber baron endowed both with the vision to recognize the potential of flight as well as the necessary drive and grit to achieve it. His Company prospered, driven by Boeing's own unrelenting high standards of excellence and his unceasing drive for economy. The strict ethos he inculcated was leavened by his mandate to *"Let no improvement in flying and flying equipment pass us by."* His firm demonstrated a powerful combination of innovative design with superior execution. These are still hallmarks of the Boeing process today.

Boeing - The First Century brings the development of this culture to life. The narrative fleshes out the evolution of the Boeing Company, from the early struggles for business of a fledgling enterprise to the cyclical booms and busts arising out of a business environment roiled by war, depression, and technological revolutions. It animates and gives immediacy to the relentless competitive struggle that shapes this industry, a struggle that begins as Boeing designers, marketers, and builders strive to develop the best among alternative options. The struggle also involves the competitors and the customers who must trade off conflicting economic, technical, and political pressures in their decision. This process, extended over a mosaic of many individual programs and products, blends into the larger story, the growth of Boeing into a world-class enterprise.

The firm's current success, notably global preeminence in civil aviation, plus leadership in space flight and strength in combat aircraft, remains bitterly contested. On the civil side, a formidable challenge has emerged from a renascent Europe, whose Airbus jetliners are now the clear alternative to Boeing's.

Recent Boeing manufacturing missteps have expanded Airbus's market acceptance. Longer term, however, the fundamental challenge is that civil aircraft technology is maturing. The cost-benefit ratio for new technology here, which had been positive throughout Boeing's existence, is now becoming negative. Boeing recognized this new reality when it withdrew from the joint-NASA program for development of high-speed jetliner technology.

Clearly, the dimensions of competition are shifting. Moreover, against a nationally sponsored competitor, price is an ineffective differentiator. Instead, Boeing must emphasize global partnerships, built around local content, technology transfers and offset procurements, which the nationally sponsored Airbus consortium will find difficult to match. Fortunately, Boeing's combat aircraft operations, formerly McDonnell Douglas, have had decades of experience with profitable foreign co-production of their aircraft, so that the process should be easily extended into the civil arena despite challenging pricing and labor content considerations.

The broader implication of this technology maturation is that Boeing is being driven to refine its markets. The creation of Boeing Airplane Services marks a first phase of Boeing's drive to assume greater responsibility for the support of the ten thousand Boeing and McDonnell Douglas jets now in global service. The support of this half-trillion dollar inventory is presently severely fragmented. A more centralized service system could be more efficient and more cost effective.

Another natural extension would be for Boeing to link with European or Asian aerospace firms. The removal of cold war barriers is opening the door to global aerospace firms. Boeing has the resources, the capability, and the presence to be the preferred partner worldwide.

A third option is for Boeing to strongly reinforce its existing thrust into commercial space and telecommunications market. Of course, telecommunications is a trillion-dollar sector dominated by national firms and technology enterprises with much greater capitalization than Boeing's. Still, Boeing has the space technology needed to be a contender. Such an initiative would fit well with Boeing's technology tradition and with the firm's motto, *"Bringing People Together."*

The costs and uncertainties that confront Boeing as it pursues its corporate renewal are now exacerbated by Boeing's shareholder demands. Now that it is one of the thirty firms which make up the Dow Jones Industrial Average, Boeing has become an important institutional holding. As such, Boeing's actions carry more economic and political weight, but also receive much closer scrutiny. Investments in risky new aerospace ventures or speculative longer-term research are correspondingly much harder to justify, even though they are Boeing's lifeblood. It is an indication of the difficulty leading companies face, that only one firm—General Electric—has been able to remain a Dow company throughout the span of Boeing's existence.

In that context, the difficulties Boeing has experienced during the last two years appear to have been a necessary wakeup call. Technology is Boeing's strength. The record that this book lays out so clearly shows that. Boeing has the talent, the toughness and the agility to flourish in the rapid-change environment endemic to technology enterprises. It is a misappraisal to see Boeing as merely an aerospace producer. The firm is a technology innovator, with a superior technology integration record and global marketing clout.

The investment community keenly appreciates that technology strength remains a central advantage of U.S. industry. The valuations granted individual equities are heavily weighted by the technology enterprise. The valuation placed on Microsoft, Boeing's Redmond neighbor, makes that clear. The challenge for Boeing's management is to mobilize the firm's massive technology resources. Given the ongoing transformation in air transport, the technology revolution in defense as well as the emerging fusion of space and telecommunications, there is no shortage of opportunity for Boeing in the new century.

William E. Boeing 1882–1956

Founder, Pacific Aero Products Company, becoming The Boeing Airplane Company in 1917, and The Boeing Company in 1961. First president, elected to chairman in 1922, continued as chairman until divesting in 1934.

PREFACE

Generations come and go, fading into the shrouds of history. Centuries live on, and are remembered fondly—or tragically—for all time. The twentieth century had its share of both euphoria and calamity. It will be remembered for its terrible wars and periods of uneasy peace—but more importantly, for its awesome strides in technology.

It was the century of antibiotics, atomic energy, automobiles, powered flight, radar, television, transistors, and xerography. It witnessed an explosion in electronics, spawning computers that exhibited the speed and adroitness to nearly challenge the human brain. Man rocketed himself to the moon and returned safely to the Earth, sent obedient satellites to the planets and the vicinity of the sun—indeed, dispatched a lonely robot that escaped the solar system itself—entering the vast, unexplored reaches of the space beyond.

In 1900—as the century opened—with a mixture of fear and hope, President McKinley sent American troops to China to quell the Boxer Rebellion, while the British dispatched Lord Roberts to South Africa to shore up their forces, bogged down in their fight against the Boers. The world wars to come were destined to leave their indelible scars.

Some fifty companies, most of them in Detroit, were experimenting with combustion-engine-powered automobiles. Henry Ford, in February, took a reporter from the *Detroit News Tribune* for a ride at the phenomenal speed of twenty-five miles per hour. The reporter was certain he was witnessing the dawn of a new era, and indeed he was. It had been more than 100 years since the first automobile—a single cylinder, steam-powered de Dion Bouton—appeared on the streets of Paris in 1769.

Still another new era, the age of manned flight—with more profound promise than the automobile—was growing on the horizon.

Airplanes began to bring people together—from all nations and from all walks of life—and before the end of the century, became a predominant force in shaping their lives. For the first time in history, the world was beginning to be linked as had been visualized by Wendell Wilkie in his *One World* in 1943.

From the time of the mythical, wax-winged Icarus, the lure of the skies had captivated man's imagination. Leonardo da Vinci, the first pioneer in the science of flight, who lived centuries before the days of mechanical power, was limited in his experiments to contrivances attached to the human body. Four hundred years later—after the invention of steam and gasoline engines—government incentives for a practical flying machine were offered. In 1894, Senator Lodge introduced a bill in the U.S. Congress to award $100,000 to the inventor of a machine capable of carrying 400 pounds.

Noted scientist, Samuel P. Langley designed, built and flew a model with a twelve-foot span, powered by a small steam engine. It flew two-thirds of a mile and achieved twenty-five miles per hour before running out of steam.

The Wright brothers had begun experimenting on a machine for powered flight in their bicycle repair shop in Dayton, Ohio. They built their own air-cooled, internal-combustion engine.

There were many who were certain that flying machines could never be successful, and in 1903, a respected American scientist, Simon Newcomb, published proof that powered flight was impossible.

In Germany, Count Ferdinand von Zeppelin was pursuing lighter-than-air vehicles. In 1900—after working with balloons since 1891—he flew his first hydrogen-filled airship near Friedrichshafen. Its two sixteen-horsepower engines gave it a speed of fourteen miles an hour. Zeppelins were destined to play a strategic role in World War I. When the Belgians entrenched themselves in the impregnable fortress of

Antwerp, zeppelins soon appeared in the skies—dropping bombs. Hydrogen-filled airships continued to be employed, until in 1937, the *Hindenburg*—after ten successful crossings of the Atlantic—was consumed in a ball of fire as it attempted to land at Lakehurst, New Jersey. Dirigibles were dead.

On December 17, 1903, the Wright brothers proved Newcomb wrong, when they maintained their manned craft aloft for twelve seconds, covering 120 feet of North Carolina beach at Kitty Hawk. Their success was more than a mere invention—rather the result of meticulous research and attention to detail in many disciplines—even constructing a crude wind tunnel.

In a few short years, new feats of flying were being announced, and improved craft were appearing. The fever had seized tinkerers, mechanics, engineers and scientists alike.

The number of companies engaged in the manufacture of airplanes proliferated—reaching twenty-four in World War I, but declining precipitously after the Armistice. At the end of World War II, only four major companies were producing airplanes for commercial service.

The same year that the Wright brothers first flew at Kitty Hawk, a young engineer with no knowledge of airplanes, came west to Seattle, Washington. His name was William E. "Bill" Boeing.

Bill Boeing was not an inventor in the strict sense, but rather a master at innovation—and an uncompromising perfectionist.

Starting from scratch in a primitive, isolated corner of the United States, how did Boeing manage to rise to the top and become the sole survivor as a builder of commercial airplanes?

This history of the Company scrutinizes its corporate culture from the beginning, and pinpoints the product decisions made by Bill Boeing and the eight subsequent presidents who followed him, who in spite of crisis after crisis, molded the largest and most respected aircraft manufacturing company in the world.

Further, the decisions of its major competitors are examined for their impact on Boeing's progress.

No attempt is made to discuss all the Boeing products. Such an undertaking would require several volumes.

The book draws heavily on *Boeing in Peace and War*, the 75 year history of the Company—written by the same author.

CONTENTS

PHOTOGRAPHS

CHAPTER ONE

An Era Dawns

Observers on the seventy-sixth floor of the Columbia Building in downtown Seattle, Washington, on the morning of September 30, 1988, barely needed to lift their gaze to witness the unfolding of a once-in-a-century panorama. Two giant airplanes were flying in formation above the waterfront.

Both were Boeing 747s—old *Number One*, which opened a new dimension in air transportation exactly twenty years earlier—and the *Dash 400*, culmination of advances in design and production over a series of twelve commercial configurations.

With no increase in body length, and only sixteen feet added to the span, the majestic new flying machine carried 400 passengers, twenty-seven more than the original—while increasing the range from 4,600 to 8,470 statute miles. New technology—much of it developed in Boeing laboratories—allowed reduction in crew size from three to two. Advances in avionics alone—changing from analog to digital instrumentation—cut the number of gauges and switches in the cockpit from nearly 1,000 to less than 400.

The Giants—1988

The original 747-100 leads the newest derivative, the -400 in the skies over Seattle, capping a twenty year domination of the world's international skies.

On the day of the flyby, Boeing had delivered 705 of a total of 877 on the order books, and the program had achieved that golden financial pinnacle referred to in the industry as a *cash cow*. Perhaps predictably, the 747 had run the course from unbridled optimism in 1968, to the brink of despair only three years later, before steadily climbing back out of the red.

When Presidents William M. Allen of Boeing and Juan Trippe of Pan American agreed by a simple handshake to a go-ahead on December 22, 1965, they put the corporate existence of both companies on the line. Boeing agreed to build the 747 and Pan Am agreed to buy twenty-five of them. There were no other orders.

Even though universally pessimistic about the 747, the world's airlines hedged their bets—rushing to secure coveted delivery positions—and within five months, fourteen carriers had pushed the firm order total to ninety-three. Almost overnight, Boeing had a $1.8 billion production backlog, an airplane on the drawing boards, and no plant suitable to fabricate the giant machine.

After clearing 250 acres of forest near Seattle, and constructing the largest building in the world, 5,000 employees were on the job by May, 1967. Vice President Malcolm "Mal" Stamper, a mid-century visionary in charge of the 747, named them *The Incredibles*. Caught up in the mystique of their fascinating new adventure, they wore Paul Bunyan stickers on their hard hats and lunch pails, and most refused to go home at the end of the shift.

Juan Trippe had prophesied that the 747 would be racing the intercontinental missile for man's destiny—as a powerful weapon for peace—as it transported millions of curious tourists to foreign lands. Mal Stamper confidently predicted sales of 600 airplanes by 1980.

The road to those achievements proved to be strewn with obstacles. In the fall of 1967, Lockheed had offered the L-1011 *Tristar*, and two months later, McDonnell Douglas began taking orders for the DC-10—beginning a cutthroat competition for the long-range market.

The 747 program was not the first big gamble by Boeing, nor was it the last—not even the costliest. But by any measure, it was the scariest.

With the U.S. economy heading for recession in 1970, some U.S. carriers began putting their 747s up for sale, while others left them parked in the hangars. Continental Airlines sold their entire fleet of six. The program epitomized the feast or famine nature of the airplane industry.

Bill Boeing, the Company's founder, was brought up by his Viennese mother after his German-born father died when he was eight years old. The family was wealthy, with large holdings of timber and iron ore in Minnesota's fabulous Mesabi Range. He had the advantages of education both in Switzerland and in the United States, where he attended Yale in the Sheffield Scientific School in engineering. At age twenty-two, hearing of opportunities in the timber business in the Pacific Northwest, a year before he was scheduled to graduate, in 1903, he headed west.

The scene had the stuff of legends. Coincidence, confidence, conquest, and courage merged to focus the talents and the vision of one man who attracted others of like minds. From the beginning, Bill Boeing laid down the exacting standards and the strict ethics that have pervaded the Company throughout its life.

Seattle was an unlikely site for an airplane factory. Tucked away in the remote northwest corner of the country, the area was a vast ocean of timber, lakes, rivers, mountains, and islands. In 1880, then in its twenty-ninth year, it was still no more than a good-sized clearing in the heavy forests that covered the Puget Sound area. The main settlement along Elliott Bay was centered on a patch about a mile and a half long, which stretched three quarters of a mile back from its eastern edge. Some houses had been built as far north as Lake Union, and a few had reached Lake Washington, several miles to the east. A. N. MacDonald, in a thesis, *Seattle's Economic Development*, portrays the stark panorama—"The town's outer edges with its numerous ten foot diameter stumps, relics from the giant virgin Douglas fir forest; slashings from those newly felled, and the occasional forlorn tree which had been left standing among the debris, impressed the observer with the community's newness, rawness, and bleakness."[1]

The milestone that first set Seattle apart from the many small settlements in the Puget Sound area, was the discovery of coal at Newcastle, only ten miles away. The second significant factor—which began to ordain Seattle as the future heart of the Pacific Northwest—was the merchant fleet of steamships which had been attracted to its natural harbor.

During the next thirty years, the period from 1880 to 1910, Seattle took off—exploding from an isolated frontier town to a substantial city—with 237,194 inhabitants. No thirty-year span in its history matches that period, which represented a sixty-sevenfold increase. In the nation at large, urban population had only tripled, and of the ten cities with similar populations in 1880, the highest—next to Seattle—was Los Angeles, with a twenty-sevenfold increase.

Land transportation evolved as the final key. In 1884, Seattle gained its connection to the east—via the Columbia River route, after the Northern Pacific Railroad completed its branch line north from Portland.

By 1910, downtown Seattle appeared as a modern city, largely rebuilt after twenty-six city blocks had been destroyed by the great fire of 1889. A Seattle housewife could buy Campbell's tomato soup, Ivory Soap, or

Post's cereal at the neighborhood store. Blatz's Milwaukee beer was available at the corner tavern.

In January 1910, America began to take its place in the new science of heavier-than-air flight, hosting its first international flying tournament in Los Angeles, however, the Europeans had forged ahead.

At the air tournament, Boeing was among the spectators. No one would have suspected the keen interest behind the thin-rimmed glasses of the tall, mustached man who appeared to be a college professor. His attention was riveted on a Farman biplane, a four-wheeled craft with two vertical tail surfaces and a wide cloth-covered horizontal surface installed considerably in front of the wings. The engine was attached behind the lower wing. As the aviator climbed from his seat on the wing and approached the crowd, Boeing led the excited group.

"Monsieur Paulhan, my name is Boeing," he announced. "I like your machine. I like the way you fly it." The Frenchman clicked his heels and did a quick bow. "Merci, Monsieur Boeing," he replied.[2]

Boeing inquired for details about the Farman airplane, and attempted to get permission for a ride on it. Paulhan was polite but evasive. The next afternoon, Paulhan completed forty-seven laps around the 1.6-mile course. The closest American, Charles Hamilton, had dropped out after twelve, and Glenn Curtiss at ten. Boeing, again in the forefront of the spectator group, asked once more about a flight. Still polite, Paulhan suggested he would take him—a little later.

Time ran out after many dignitaries were taken up, and Boeing never saw Paulhan again. The inviting wings on which he had visualized himself were dismounted, crated, and hauled away for shipment back to France. The bitter disappointment which Boeing felt, though carefully concealed, became a further fire for his own ambitions.

In 1910 also, at lower New York Bay, a young boy of ten stood with his father, watching an air race. The Statue of Liberty was one of the turning pylons. The planes were open kites with pusher engines, and the boy could see the pilots manipulating the controls with feet and hands. He could see the propeller blades flailing. On each lap the planes flew close over the awed crowd, and one plane crashed. From that day on, Juan Trippe yearned to be an aviator.[3]

The Los Angeles meet was recreated later in the year at Belmont Park in New York. Americans like Glenn Curtiss who was defending the Gordon Bennett trophy he had won at Reims the year before, were being followed with a national fervor.

In the crowd at Belmont was a young navy lieutenant by the name of George Conrad Westervelt. As an engineer and junior officer with the Navy Construction Corps in New York, he had obtained permission to represent the Navy at the meet. Although Paulhan did not attend, French aviators dominated the event; with Leblanc and Hubert Latham winning ten of the speed events, flying Bleriot monoplanes. The Gordon Bennett trophy was won by Claude Grahame-White of England. Ralph Johnstone, who flew to an altitude of 9,714 feet in a thirty horsepower *Wright Flyer*, was the only American to set a world's record. The astounding progress in aviation surprised the young officer, and he noted with concern the quickening pace of the Europeans.

Westervelt's next assignment was out west at the Puget Sound Naval Yard in Bremerton, Washington, as an assistant naval constructionist. Still later he moved to the Moran shipyard in Seattle. While there, he was introduced to Bill Boeing at Seattle's University Club.

Boeing purchased the Heath shipyard on the Duwamish River to build a personal yacht, and needing some nautical advice, invited Westervelt to visit his new enterprise. The two men, both bachelors, found many common interests. They cruised on Puget Sound on weekends, played bridge, and talked about mechanical things. Westervelt, known as blustery and argumentative, easily penetrated the aura of aloofness attributed to the straightlaced Boeing.

Airplanes became a common topic of their conversation, and the restless vision of Boeing was peaked when a barnstorming flier named Terah Maroney brought a Curtiss-type seaplane to Seattle.

On Independence Day in 1914, the two men arranged for a flight, the first for both, in Maroney's plane. Driving to Lake Washington, they found him waiting and ready to take them up. The plane sat facing a board ramp, its pusher propeller idling. The two straight wings were covered with muslin on both lower and upper surfaces. The plane was mounted on a sledlike float. The water-cooled engine was hung between the wings, its massive

The Red Barn—1916

The Heath building, modified to house the workers and the manufacturing facilities for early airplanes, the Red Barn was one of the central buildings in the subsequent Plant I complex. The Red Barn has been moved to the new Museum of Flight near Boeing Field, and restored as an historical monument.

radiator forming a vertical backrest behind the pilot's seat.

Boeing, anxious for the adventure, flew first, climbing up beside Maroney on the front edge of the lower wing and steadying himself with his feet on an open footrest that resembled a shoeshine stand. A mechanic in overalls pushed the machine out into the water. Maroney gunned the engine in short bursts. Both men adjusted their goggles, and Boeing took a firm grip on the leading edge of the wing with both hands.

The plane taxied in jumps and spurts, the noise of the engine shutting out all other sounds as the struts vibrated in the wind with increasing speed. The plane required a long takeoff run, and the water seemed to rush at them, with the wind beating on their bodies. Boeing gripped all the tighter. Abruptly, the ride became less violent. There was a bump and a jerk, a surge of power as Maroney poured on the gas, and the water dropped quickly away.

As the landscape tilted, Boeing realized they were banking and turning away from the lake. Looking down at the tiny buildings and the people who had been transformed to antlike proportions, he marvelled at his feeling of detachment and freedom. Relaxing momentarily on his perch as the plane leveled off at about 1,000 feet, he felt a certain mastery over the land below. Perhaps that was the moment that Bill Boeing decided to learn to fly.

Westervelt, who had waited eagerly on the ground for his turn, seemed equally impressed in the air. In the days that followed, there were more flights with Maroney. Boeing examined every detail of the airplane. "I think it would be easy to build a better one," he said, finally confiding his thoughts to Westervelt. "Of course we could," the young naval engineer replied.[4]

A local exhibition flyer, Herb Munter, came to Boeing's attention early, when in his careful, meticulous way of studying details, he was seeking the experiences of anyone he could find in the field. Thus, early in 1915, Boeing took Westervelt for a visit to Munter's shop on Harbor Island in the Duwamish River waterway. The shop consisted of a fifty-foot wide hangar of shiplap, built on sand that had been dredged up from the bay. Munter was working alone. Boeing inquired as to the type of craft Munter was building. "It's a *Munter*," he replied matter-of-factly.

In those days, each machine was a handcrafted article and no two were exactly alike. Boeing found that Munter was building his fourth airplane, the other three washed out in some stage of construction or testing. The first two had been built at home, based on a photograph of a Curtiss airplane in *Aerial Age*.

"Did you study engineering?" Boeing asked.

"No, I went to high school—nights."[5]

A plan was forming in Boeing's mind. The yacht he had commissioned Heath to build at the shipyard was a reality. Indeed, it was described as one of the finest and most technically advanced on the Pacific Coast. Now he thought about the possibility of building a pleasure airplane of his own—but only fleetingly.

The war in Europe, an area he had visited often, disturbed him. The possible role of the airplane as a decisive instrument was becoming sharply focused. In fact, aerial combat had already erupted, when on December 25, in 1914, British residents of Southend-on-the-Sea were roused from their Christmas dinners by the sudden hum of airplanes.

Running, gawking into the streets, thousands looked skyward to see two German planes which had flown up the Thames River, being chased by two British aircraft. The first air battle of the war had been joined, 9,000 feet above the ground at the breathtaking speed of seventy miles an hour.

Soon after the meeting with Munter, Boeing and Westervelt invited him to lunch. "We're going to get a group together to build some airplanes," Boeing announced. "Will you join us?"[6]

No one was more pleased at Munter's acceptance than Bill Boeing—who recognized him as a visionary—cut from the same cloth.

1. A.N. MacDonald, *Seattle's Economic Development, 1890–1910*, (Seattle: University of Washington, Ph.D. Thesis, 1959), 1.
2. Harold Mansfield, *Vision*, (New York: Popular Library, 1966), 8.
3. Robert Daley, *An American Saga*, (New York: Random House, 1980), 6.
4. Mansfield, *Vision*, 12.
5. Ibid., 13.
6. Ibid., 14.

Edgar N. Gott 1887–1947
President 1922–1926.

CHAPTER TWO

The Beginnings

With Herb Munter as the first employee of the yet-to-be formed Company, Boeing and Westervelt decided to build two airplanes, to be called the B&W. They would get the engines from Hall-Scott in San Francisco, build the pontoons and wings at the Heath shipyard on the Duwamish River, and construct the fuselage at a rented hangar on Lake Union.

Meanwhile, in Los Angeles, the "Flying Duke," a young barnstormer by the name of Glenn Martin, was starting a new company to build the Army's first training and bombing planes.

Introspective and reserved, Boeing did not always reveal his plans to those around him—but in his mind the next logical steps were forming—and sometimes he surprised his closest associates. Meticulous and thorough, he was bent on understanding every aspect of this new science that had taken a consuming grip on his life.

After corresponding with Martin, one day he abruptly informed Westervelt—"I'm going down there to learn to fly."[1]

Learning to fly was only one of Boeing's purposes in going to Los Angeles to meet with Glenn Martin. He wanted to see the many new innovations that Martin was incorporating—the Day Tractor design with the engine and propeller in front, building a fuselage in place of the box-kite structure; and installing the vertical and horizontal surfaces at the aft end—all forerunners of modern airplane design.

With aerodynamics still in the embryo stage, and with a paucity of wind tunnels, many of these innovations remained to be proved and refined in the air. Martin had only one trainer flying at the time, and when one of the five students crashed it, Boeing returned to Seattle, his training cut short.

Boeing had learned enough, and his creative mind was already racing ahead, contemplating improvements on the Martin plane. Thus, it was not too unexpected when he ordered a Martin *T.A. Trainer*.

Martin sent the crated parts to Seattle along with Floyd Smith, a pilot, who supervised the assembly of the airplane, as well as topping off Boeing's instruction in the air.

Boeing hired a mechanic, L.G. Stern, and seven men skilled in wood and fabric craftsmanship.

At about the same time, Boeing created a flying association, the Aero Club of the Northwest—a private club for friends. The B&W airplanes were to be built to serve the club.

One day while Munter was flying, he banked too steeply, stalled the plane, and crashed into the water. Munter was unhurt, and the fuselage was repairable, but the pontoon had to be replaced.

The Martin plane had been designed with a single pontoon in the center and sponsons near the outboard ends of the lower wing. Boeing quickly perceived the need for an improved landing platform and the B&W was designed with twin pontoons. Like everything associated with him, Boeing insisted that his pontoons be of the best quality. They were made of layered wood veneer, and riveted together, replacing the original plank construction.

When a German submarine torpedoed the British luxury liner Lusitania in May 1915—with the loss of 124 Americans—concern about the war was brought to the dinner tables of the average American family.

Boeing, fearing that America was falling behind the Europeans, and the likelihood that we would be drawn in, began a campaign of his own to

B&W—First Boeing Airplane—1916
Gross Weight, 2,800 lbs.; top speed, 75 mph; 125 horsepower.

highlight the impending danger. In November, along with certain unidentified acquaintances, he took the *Martin* off from Lake Washington and flew a bombing run over Seattle. Flying low over the downtown district, he dropped red cardboard bombs in the shape of artillery shells which carried a variety of warnings; America, citizens were warned, was unprepared to defend itself, and there was a critical lack of airplanes.

The military had suddenly become the dominant force in aviation, and the German zeppelins, which had begun to bomb London in June, would soon bow to the sweep of the new technology.

Boeing and his crew began construction of the B&Ws. After the pontoons, the wing ribs followed, however, shipyard techniques were woefully inadequate to build the fragile parts. Designed to saw timbers for ships, the yard did not possess a single jigsaw, so a subcontractor was brought in to make the lightening holes. The first product was rejected. The second, although of improved quality, was also rejected. Boeing sent one of his own men to supervise the work. This emphasis on quality became the hallmark of Boeing products.

Charles "Charlie" Thompson, one of the early employees, who hired in at the age of fifteen, recalls that Bill Boeing was particularly interested in the wood shops. "Once he came through and noticed a workman cutting lightening holes in wing ribs. The workman made a few nicks, which immediately caught Boeing's attention. He said they were unsatisfactory. The workman said they were good enough. Without a word, Boeing picked up the ribs and ran them through the saw, throwing the pieces on the floor."[2]

Although Westervelt contributed strongly to the design of the B&W airplanes, working steadily while Boeing was in Los Angeles for flying lessons, he never designed another, and was gone before there was a Company. In January, 1916, Westervelt was assigned to Navy fleet duties in the East.

Westervelt never drifted far from airplanes. Perhaps his most notable assignment was overseeing the construction of the first plane to fly across the Atlantic Ocean, the NC. Four of those flying boats were built, and on May 27, 1919, NC-4 landed at Lisbon, Portugal. He never returned to the West Coast, but lived long enough to see The Boeing Company lead America into the jet age.

During the first six months of 1916, Boeing's work force more than doubled in size, to twenty-three. With management duties increasing, Boeing brought in his cousin, Edgar Gott—with a degree in chemical engineering from the University of Michigan—as vice president.

On the bright Thursday morning of June 15, 1916, Boeing realized the first major milestone in his manufacturing efforts, as he proudly surveyed his new machine being readied for flight on the tranquil waters of Lake Union, the fresh varnish of the spruce struts gleaming in the sunlight. Its 125 horsepower engine and its span of fifty-two feet were identical to the *Martin* trainer, but it was lighter, with an improved aerodynamic wing section.

Boeing took the airplane to the Navy, but despite its approval, he was turned down for any orders. Disappointed but undaunted, he forged ahead—incorporating the Pacific Aero Products Company on July 15, 1916.

According to the articles of incorporation filed on that day, the new company would have ambitious objectives. It was to be a "general manufacturing business...to manufacture goods, wares, and merchandise of every kind, especially to manufacture aeroplanes and vehicles of aviation...."

The articles would also allow Boeing to "...operate a flying school and act as a common carrier of passengers and freight by aerial navigation."

1. Harold Mansfield, *Vision*, (New York: Popular Library, 1966), 14.
2. Charlie Thompson, interiew by Paul Spitzer, 28 August 1981, Boeing Archives.

CHAPTER THREE

The Crucible of War

The second decade of this century was one of the most significant periods in the history of American aviation. A number of farsighted, ambitious, and adventuresome young visionaries were experimenting with various innovations.

Two of those early pioneers were named Loughhead. The name was soon changed to Lockheed, the way everyone misspelled it anyway. When the Wright brothers flew, the Lockheed brothers, Allan and Malcolm, were fascinated teenagers. After studying the new science of aerodynamics, and tinkering with different designs, they succeeded in building—and flying—a wood and fabric biplane called the Model G. That machine caught the imagination of the Bay area when it flew over San Francisco early in 1913. By a stroke of luck and his flair for showmanship, Allan Lockheed made a profit by charging $1.00 a head to fly daredevil passengers at the 1915 Panama-Pacific International Exhibition. Those were heady times.

A year after the flight of the Model G, the Lockheed brothers joined up with another of the early pioneers, John Northrop, and they set up a business in an old garage in Santa Monica, California.

The Lockheed-Northrop team turned out handmade planes similar to the early Boeing models, but included a twin-engined two-seat monster known as the F-1. On April 12, 1918, the F-1 flew from Santa Barbara to San Diego, a distance of 211 miles—quickly claimed as a new American endurance record.

Even before the B&Ws flew, Boeing decided that a plane could be built along their lines that would be suitable for Navy training duties. Work was immediately begun on a new model, although the first dollar in profits was still to be made.

Bill Boeing, searching for additional talent, hired Tsoo Wong, a young Chinese recently graduated from MIT. Wong designed the Model C, which flew on November 23, 1916.

Wong had incorporated some new innovations as a result of wind tunnel testing. He put dihedral in the wing to improve stability, at the same time drastically cutting down the vertical fin, and eliminating the horizontal stabilizer—assigning its function to the placement of the wings—moving the upper wing to a position slightly forward of the lower wing. The elevator remained at the aft end with the tiny tail fin.

The new design troubled Munter, assigned to test the plane, and he was reluctant to fly it. The fin and rudder design didn't look right to him. With encouragement from Boeing, Munter took the plane off. Once airborne, he found difficulty in the turns. Shaken, he landed on Lake Union, storming back to announce to designer Wong that he would not fly the airplane again until something was done about the small fin and rudder. The plane was altered and improved and finally accepted by the Navy.

The war became a reality for America on April 6, 1917, after President Woodrow Wilson asked the Congress for a formal declaration. "The world must be made safe for democracy," he asserted. Less than two weeks later, on April 18, Pacific Aero Products was renamed—and the Boeing Airplane Company was born.

Soon Douglas Fairbanks and Mary Pickford were selling Liberty bonds, and school children were saving peach pits and dropping them in containers at grammar schools.

When the United States entered the war, the country was far down the list of air powers. The Army had thirty-five pilots, six flying boats, forty-five seaplanes, three land planes, seven balloons, and one rigid airship.[1]

At the time, France had 1,200 military airplanes, and Germany 1,000, in addition to fourteen zeppelins.

The Navy ordered fifty of the new Model C's. Boeing was determined to make the airplane better than anything flying for the Navy, and he recognized the crucial importance of the pontoons. He was certain that the riveted design for the B&Ws—itself an improvement over the *Martin*—was already obsolete.

One day early in 1916, Dr. Henry Suzzalo, president of the University of Washington, came into the old Tokyo Tea Room to visit the young Pocock brothers, George and Dick, who were to become famous builders of racing shells. With him was a gentleman they didn't recognize. George recalls the meeting, which had a major impact on his career:

"These are the boys I was telling you about, Bill," he said. We had a finished "eight" in the shop awaiting shipment to the University of California. Bill whoever-he-was got under the boat and spent some time on his knees inspecting it with intense interest. "This is the kind of work I want," he observed to Dr. Suzzalo, who by that time was at the door, tapping his cane and saying, "Come on Bill. I must go." Emerging from under the shell, Bill took out his card case, dropped a business card on the workbench, and said, "Come and see me as soon as you can." We looked at the card to see who Bill was. The card read *W. E. Boeing, Hoge Building, Seattle.*[2]

The Pocock brothers had commitments for some work in California, and it was near the end of the year before they returned to Seattle. So, early in January 1917, as George recorded:

"We went to see Mr. W. E. Boeing. He seemed glad to see us, and he said he would like us to build two sets of pontoons for his seaplanes. He said his plant manager, Jim Foley, would bring the plans and show us what he wanted. He did so, and it looked to be an interesting little job. After all, they were to be built of wood, and they weren't much different from small boats."

Foley asked what we thought they would weigh, since that was such a major factor. We told him "about 115 pounds each." He said, "If you can build them for that I'll buy you each a new hat." When we finished the first pair, one weighed 114 pounds; the other 116.[3]

The fifty plane order called for seventy-five pairs, including spares, and the Pocock brothers joined the Boeing work force.

George eventually became foreman of assembly, while Dick took charge of construction, and with a dozen men, were soon turning out a pair of pontoons a day. The total order of 150 pontoons was completed before a single C Model airframe was assembled—passing a legacy of perfection in manufacturing processes to those who came after them.

After the departure of Westervelt, Bill Boeing sought to increase his engineering staff, which he viewed as the key to a strong company.

In May of 1917, Louis Marsh was employed as a draftsman. Marsh had studied mechanical engineering at the University of Washington. And so began a steady stream of talent that flowed to Boeing over the course of its corporate life. *Indeed, the University of Washington was by far Boeing's largest single source for professionally trained people in the entire United States, and must be considered as a prime factor in Boeing's success.*

Later in May of the same year, both Claire L. Egtvedt and Philip G. Johnson joined the company. Egtvedt, then a senior at the University of Washington, entered the engineering department to work on design and stress analysis. He was one of three students recommended by the dean of the school when W. E. Boeing asked for the brightest students in the class. Two months after hiring in, Egtvedt was appointed chief engineer, with Marsh as his assistant.

Johnson, a fellow student with Egtvedt in mechanical engineering, also entered the drafting department, and soon became production manager. *(For many decades, drafting and engineering were inseparable, with engineers doing their own drafting).* These key men were continuing champions of integrity of product—the heart that Boeing had brought to the Company.

Notable also in 1917 was the hiring of a woman—a first for Boeing— and a first in the engineering department. Helen Holcombe was studying architecture at the University of Washington, and applied as a draftsman. John Foley responded in a positive manner. He sent a blueprint "to have duplicated and returned to us; and if the same shows up favorably, we will be pleased to advise you further in the matter."[4]

Holcombe departed for a time to return to her studies, came back in

1922, when a second woman joined the Company, and finally returned to architecture permanently. These women were the pioneers. By 1945, the 3,000-person engineering department included nearly 1,200 women.[5]

It was not long before Boeing won a contract to build fifty HS-2L Navy gunnery training planes. These were three-place flying boats, a Curtiss design that was in standard use by the Navy, equipped with Liberty engines. This airplane was the ideal next step for the expertise learned in building pontoons. The Navy commended Boeing for building the best HS-2 hulls at far less cost than at the other plants around the country. The giant Curtiss plant with over 14,000 employees required 2,400 man-hours to complete a plane. Boeing built them in 900.

The first American-built warplanes, Curtiss JN-4's, known as "*Jennys*," began to see action over France in May 1918. Two years earlier, American volunteers had flown British observation planes to locate the placement of men and artillery. At that time, there was still an air of camaraderie among the pilots on both sides, making a practice of waving a gloved hand and giving a nod as they swept by. Soon, the wave gave way to pistols and even shotguns, and when a German pilot mounted a machine gun on a Fokker, the war moved to the air in earnest.

World War I proved to be the crucible for the airplane manufacturing industry in the United States. American enterprise had performed an awesome task to tool for the war, reaching a plant capacity for producing 21,000 flying machines a year when the war ended.

Among the builders were Aeromarine, Burgess, L-W-F, Sturtevant, Engel, Springfield, St. Louis, Standard, Dayton-Wright, Curtiss, Fisher Body, Thomas-Morse, and Boeing.

At the time of the Armistice, there were twenty-four companies, employing almost 200,000 workers. Curtiss predominated, turning out 10,000 airplanes—from the smallest to the largest—and 15,000 engines.

The signing of the Armistice on November 11, 1918 signalled disaster. Within a few months, approximately ninety percent of the aviation companies had gone out of business.

The poorly financed partnership of Lockheed-Northrop was one of the casualties, missing the opportunities afforded by the war. The sale of two seaplanes to the Navy represented their total contribution to the war effort. The young venture folded and the Santa Barbara garage closed its doors. For the next eight years, Lockheed did not exist as a company.

Boeing's superior performance in the manufacture of the HS-2L gunnery training planes for the Navy was not sufficient to avoid the avalanche that overwhelmed the industry. At war's end the order was cut in half.

Hopeful for the future, during the fat years of 1917 and 1918, Boeing engineers had been busy creating a new design, the B-1 flying boat. The B-1 was destined to make history—as Boeing's first one-and-only. In an attempt to hold the engineering force together, a modification of the B-1, the BB-1 was created, but soon the engineering department was back down to two—Claire Egtvedt and Louis Marsh—who kept plugging along on new airplane designs. Faith in the future market flickered, but was kept alive.

In the factory, crisis followed crisis. Employment dropped to thirty. There was talk of closing the plant. It would not be the last time.

Intent upon holding a nucleus of the manufacturing force together, Boeing officials decided to manufacture furniture. Phil Johnson was placed in charge of the production program. Chief among the new products were bedroom suites.

Another was the Speed Sea Sleds, a scow-bowed boat with an inverted V-bottom and remarkable power and speed for the period.

George Pocock wrote of this experimental effort:

"Our first sea sled was a twenty-six-footer for Mr. Boeing's personal use. He was at that time courting his future wife, and we knew he was rather anxious to see this one completed so he could take her out joy riding. He used to come in quite often to the shop where we were building it and watch us work.

"One afternoon he was sitting on a bench, and seemed to be in such good spirits that I thought I would ask him a question which was uppermost in the minds of everyone working for him. I said, 'Mr. Boeing, it must be a problem to you to decide what to do with this plant. We know you are spending a great deal of money every week. The boys think every time you show up you have the key to lock this place up.'

"He replied, 'No it is no problem. I'm prepared to run like this with the people I now have on the payroll as a nucleus, for another two years, *and after those two years, we will never look back.*"[6]

In due course, the prototype sea sled was finished and ten were built. However, only three of them sold, the remaining seven sat, gathering dust until Prohibition took effect in January 1920. Fast rumrunners began bringing cargoes of illicit whiskey from British Columbia, and the speed of the Boeing sea sleds—forty-five miles an hour—provided a vehicle capable of outrunning the Coast Guard. The seven sleds were sold immediately—for cash.[7]

The furniture business expanded from its mainstay, Queen Anne bedsteads, to include phonograph cabinets, showcases, booths, library tables, and stools. They even bid on interior design and renovation. A notable example was a $1,500 proposal to modify Mrs. Nettles Corset Shop. At first, furniture and fixtures sold well. Then prices fell. Eastern manufacturers closer to the market, were able to outbid Boeing. Soon, there were 720 bedroom sets on the factory floor and no takers. At one point the factory manager reported a $100 cash balance after meeting the payroll. There was an outstanding note for $100,000 against the Company.

The fall and winter of 1919 were grey indeed, as the fortunes of the Company looked steadily worse. Bill Boeing was advancing money from his personal account almost weekly, and the specter of folding up the Boeing Airplane Company became his daily companion.

Historians were quick to remind people that there was no economic reason for Boeing to survive in the isolated Pacific Northwest.

1. Frank Cunningham, *Sky Master,* (Philadelphia: Dorrance & Company, 1943), 75.
2. Gordon Newell, *Ready All!,* (Seattle: University of Washington Press, 1987), 52.
3. Ibid., 55.
4. Boeing Letter, J. C. Foley to Helen Holcombe, Boeing Archives.
5. *Boeing News,* 26 April 1945, 5.
6. Gordon Newell, *Ready All!,* (Seattle: University of Washington Press, 1987), 60.
7. Ibid., 61.

CHAPTER FOUR

Postwar Progress

With thousands of hours of trial in the war, airplanes were ready to demonstrate their versatility and potential for peace.

In Europe, aviation history was made on February 9, 1919, when a commercial plane completed the first roundtrip between Paris and London. The aircraft, named the *Goliath*, took off from England, and three hours and thirty minutes later, arrived at a French airport near Versailles. A twin-engined craft, the *Goliath* had a top speed of ninety-seven miles an hour.

At home, on March 3, Bill Boeing and his hired pilot, Eddie Hubbard, completed the world's first international airmail flight from Vancouver, British Columbia, to Seattle. Flying a C-700 seaplane, they carried a mail bag containing sixty letters. On the way to Vancouver, they encountered a snowstorm and were forced down, staying overnight in Anacortes. On the delivery flight back to Seattle, headwinds caused them to put down for gas twenty-five miles from their destination, but measured against the odds, the operation was a success.

A new service—carrying mail—was becoming popular all across the

Model C—First Production Machine

Built for the Navy as trainers—1916–1918. Also established first regular airmail service between Seattle and Victoria, B.C. Eddie Hubbard and Bill Boeing with the first mail pouch.

United States, and in June, daily flights were inaugurated between Chicago and New York.

The following year, Eddie Hubbard, who left Boeing and purchased the one-and-only B-1, was awarded the nation's first international airmail contract, flying between Seattle and Victoria, British Columbia.

The B-1 was powered by a Hall-Scott L-6 water-cooled engine, producing 200 horsepower. It had a top speed of ninety-five miles an hour, could climb 3,500 feet in ten minutes, and land at a comfortably slow fifty miles an hour. With only slightly more than seventy-five miles separating the two cities, Hubbard could pick his holes in the weather. When the sturdy plane was retired from service eight years later, it had flown 350,000 miles and worn out six engines.

In spite of Eddie Hubbard's success in flying the mail with the B-1, Boeing's Washington, D.C. representative, Joe Hartson, was getting nowhere in his attempts to gain orders for the plane. However, he finally landed a contract to rebuild and modernize DH-4 de Havilland observation planes. The original wooden fuselage structure was replaced with a new and revolutionary Boeing-designed welded steel tubing structure. Boeing modified 298 of these airplanes for the Army, earning a profit on every unit.

The spark of creativity continued to burn brightly in the two-man engineering department, but Claire Edgvedt was concerned that there was no chance to embark on a new venture. He decided to confront Ed Gott with his dilemma. Gott had been appointed to president when Bill Boeing moved to chairman in May 1922. Going to Gott's office, Egtvedt found Boeing there also.

"We are building airplanes, not cement sidewalks," Egtvedt began. "If you want to build cement sidewalks, then you can do away with engineering. Just mix the materials, pour them into a form and collect your money. But if you want to build and sell airplanes, you first have to create them. That takes research and development and testing and engineering. Can't we hire a few engineers and try to build a future?"

Ed Gott seemed about to reply when Boeing spoke, nodding. "I think Claire is right."[1]

The Army had not called for any new pursuit plane competition. Anxious to get something moving, Egtvedt launched an intense review of the limitations of the current designs. He watched young pilots go through mock combat games, quizzing them for the important features of an ideal fighter. To a man, they called for a machine stripped for action. Light—maneuverable—fast, the attributes still demanded in modern fighters. Egtvedt pored over details. The possibilities excited him, and he became convinced they could build a machine good enough to sell itself.

When Egtvedt and Marsh were satisfied with their preliminary design concept, they went to Bill Boeing for approval. "What I'd like to do is go out on our own to build the best pursuit we can," Egtvedt said, "our own pursuit, using our own money."

Boeing was on his feet, looking over Elliott Bay toward the Olympic Mountains. Egtvedt kept up the momentum. "We should go to all the sources available," he continued, "here and abroad, to get information and data. We wouldn't be obligated to put in all the contrivances and devices that the Air Service thinks up. It would be designed for one purpose only—combat work."

Boeing didn't even ask how much the project would cost. He spun around. "That's exactly what we should do," he said emphatically. *"Do it on our own. Keep it secret. Develop the best pursuit that can be built. Then we'll take it back to Dayton and show them what we can do."*[2]

While the new pursuit design was incubating, the Company continued to seek business to keep the factory busy. When the Army called for bids on a sizeable order of MB-3A pursuit planes, a Thomas-Morse design, Boeing was ready.

Thomas-Morse had already completed and delivered fifty machines—and was well along on the learning curve. The order was a potential plum—200 planes—the largest ever placed.

Boeing officials did some plain and fancy figuring, submitted their bid, and held their breaths. The bid was considerably below the next lowest.

While the losers smugly watched to see Boeing go on the financial rocks, the Company dug in. The total order was delivered in a five-month span between July 29 and December 27, 1922—at a profit. *As Bill Boeing had predicted in 1919, the Company never looked back.*

In the back room of a barber shop on Pico Boulevard in Los Angeles, on June 21, 1920, Donald W. Douglas formed the Davis-Douglas Company. David R. Davis, a wealthy sportsman, had provided the financial backing to build a one-only, Liberty-engined plane for an attempt to be the first to fly across the continent nonstop. A rented second floor of an old planing mill served as the factory.

At the time, Douglas was the sole employee of the new company. Soliciting help from associates with whom he had worked at the Glenn Martin Company in Cleveland, he soon expanded the work force to six.

The year of 1920 was late when measured against many of the other pioneers in the fast-moving airplane industry. *Nevertheless this nucleus of six men grew to become one of the largest and most famous aviation companies in the world.*

Donald Douglas was well prepared for the task. An engineering genius, he abandoned his love for ships at an early point in his career, and embarked on aviation. Born in Brooklyn, Douglas initially followed in the footsteps of his brother, entering the Naval Academy at Annapolis in 1909. With his interest shifting from ships to airplanes, he resigned in 1912, prior to graduation, to begin his career in aeronautical engineering, a science, most of which had yet to be developed.

Enrolling as a student at MIT, the young Douglas was told he would require the full four years to graduate, despite his three years at the Naval Academy. Douglas replied stoutly, "I'll do it in two years." And he did.[3]

When Douglas graduated from MIT, Louis Bleriot in France, had already built more than 800 planes of different types.

Impressed with Douglas' ability, the faculty at MIT offered him his first job. Carrying a grand title, "Assistant in Aeronautical Engineering," the position paid an annual stipend of $500.

Remaining at MIT for only one year, Douglas aided Commander Jerome Hunsacker in the design of the first truly effective American wind tunnel, and in 1915 he accepted an engineering position with the Connecticut Aircraft Company, working on the first dirigible to be built for the Navy.

Meanwhile, out in Los Angeles, Glenn Martin had started a new company to build the Army's first training and bombing planes. Martin needed a chief engineer, and having heard excellent reports on a young man named Donald Douglas, invited him to join the Martin Company.

However, Douglas had itchy feet, and a year later moved back to the East Coast, joining the U.S. Signal Corps as its chief aeronautical engineer, to supervise the task of adapting heavy engines to light planes.

Martin also moved East, forming the Glenn L. Martin Company in Cleveland, in March 1918. One of his first recruits was Donald Douglas, who became chief engineer on the M-2 bomber program.

Douglas' yearning to go on his own intensified, and believing that financing would be easier in Los Angeles, he resigned and again headed West. The result was the Davis-Douglas Company.

The single airplane, the *Cloudster*, which Douglas designed and built, with the mission to be first on a nonstop flight across the United States, never came close, landing in Texas with a stripped timing gear. By the time the plane was transported back to Los Angeles and refitted for a second attempt, history overtook the program. Just as the *Cloudster* was ready to take to the air, Army Lieutenants Oakley Kelly and John Macready landed in San Diego in a Fokker T-2, the first to span the U.S. nonstop. The date was May 3, 1923, a day to remember—the idea of flying regular flights from coast to coast began to occupy the minds of many in the new industry.

Douglas was able to win an order for three torpedo planes for the Navy, the DT-1. However, he was fresh out of money to begin the project, and the government would not make a payment until the first plane was partially completed. Even with a $120,000 order in his pocket, he was helpless to proceed. Finally convincing Harry Chandler of the *Los Angeles Times* of the worth of the project, Douglas was able to borrow $150,000 from the bank—with signatures of Chandler and nine other prominent Los Angeles businessmen as collateral.

The Davis-Douglas Company was disbanded. In its place was formed the Douglas Company, and in 1922, the forty-two-man organization moved to a large, vacant building on Wilshire Boulevard in Santa Monica, an abandoned movie studio of the Herrman Film Corporation.

Orders for torpedo planes increased. At the time, General Billy Mitchell—in command of the United States air forces at the close of the war—had thrown down the gauntlet to the Navy, claiming that battleships were obsolete—sinkable by air-carried torpedoes.

By 1923, Egtvedt's visionary fighter had been transformed to reality. The XPW-9 pursuit, embodying a welded steel tubing fuselage and a number of other innovations, became the prototype for a long series of Army and Navy fighters. The Boeing-designed oleo landing gear struts represented a first for production military aircraft. The radiator was mounted in a tunnel beneath the engine, another first that was widely copied. With a Curtiss 425 horsepower engine, it had a top speed of 160 miles an hour, as compared to the MB-3A's maximum of 140. Its absolute ceiling of 22,850 feet compared to the MB-3A's ceiling of 21,200.

With the introduction of its PW-9 pursuit, Boeing began to carve out a reputation of leadership in military aircraft production. Modifications—through a D Model—continued to improve performance. A Navy version, designated as the FB, incorporated a hoisting hook, arresting gear, and improved landing gear for carrier operations, followed. A still later spinoff design, the FB-4, was an experimental model with a Wright P-1 air cooled 450 horsepower engine. It was not long before the Navy turned entirely away from water-cooled engines.

The Boeing philosophy, transmitted to Egtvedt and his engineering staff, and now firmly entrenched throughout the Company, was to keep reaching for a piece of untraveled sky.

Thus, still in 1923, with the PW program barely started, Louis Marsh and E.N. Gott journeyed to Washington, D.C. to discuss the Navy's requirements for a completely new trainer. A few months later, the NB-1 emerged—built entirely on speculation.

The NB-1 was the first Boeing plane to be powered by a radial engine—the Lawrence J-1 nine-cylinder 200-horsepower unit—which preceded the Wright Whirlwind.

The engineering staff continued to build, the University of Washington contributing the major share, including Jack Kylstra, later to become a project engineer, and Leslie R. Tower, making his mark as a test pilot.

Boeing's new successes seemed to assure the survival and growth of the Company. However, competition—always brisk— would become increasingly formidable.

1. Harold Mansfield, *Vision*, (New York: Popular Library, 1966), 24.
2. Ibid., 26.
3. Frank Cunningham, *Sky Master*, (Philadelphia: Dorrance & Company, 1943), 53.

Philip G. Johnson 1894–1944
President 1926–1933 and 1939–1944.

CHAPTER FIVE

Airmail Comes
of Age

In the summer of 1923, a smartly dressed young Army officer walked into the former Herrman film studio on Wilshire Boulevard in Santa Monica. He introduced himself as Lieutenant Erik Nelson, and asked to see "Mr. Donald Douglas." His mission was to discuss designing and building four airplanes capable of flying around the world. Douglas was away in the East, but a rush wire brought him back in a hurry.

After enthusiastically listening to the Army's proposal, Donald Douglas sat down at his drafting board and designed the *Douglas World Cruiser*, an airplane based partly on his successful DT series torpedo planes, but incorporating many new features. The DWC's were designed to operate either as land or sea planes.

Under the direction of Major General Mason M. Patrick, the flight had been planned for specific purposes:

> To demonstrate the feasibility of aerial communication and transportation between the various continents; to make the people of the world conscious that aerial transportation was able to meet any and all conditions under which it might be forced to operate; to arouse interest in aircraft as a vital force in the marts of commerce; to prove that planes could operate off the beaten path of regular established air routes and where no other means of transportation could operate efficiently; to show that aircraft could be kept going despite varied climatic conditions and that its days of "pampered flying" were in the past.[1]

The Army Air Service had been planning the flight for many months. It was to leave from Santa Monica, cover some twenty-two countries and approximately 25,000 miles, and return to Santa Monica in six months. Each plane had been named after a prominent city; the *Boston*, the *Chicago*, the *Seattle*, and the *New Orleans*. On March 17, 1924, the planes were ready, and after a two hour fog-bound delay they headed for Seattle. Difficulties on the first leg caused postponement, and the official start became the Sand Point Flying Field on Lake Washington. The date was April 5. Pontoons, installed at Seattle, remained on the planes until they reached Calcutta, where they again became land planes. Leaving Hull, England, the pontoons went back on for the hazardous, multi-hop trip over the Atlantic. After again becoming land planes at Boston, they flew to Santa Monica, landing amid an acre of roses on September 3. On September 28, the around-the-world flight was officially completed, when the planes returned to Sand Point in Seattle.

Two of the original four planes made the entire circuit. The *Seattle* hit a mountain peak near Dutch Harbor, and the *Boston* capsized and sank during towing after an oil pump failure had forced it down near the Faeroes on the leg to Iceland.

With the postwar slump fast fading into history, the country was in a vibrant mood. Calvin Coolidge, who completed the late Warren G. Harding's term, and was reelected in 1924, proclaimed that "the business of America is business."

Mail, carried by air, can properly be said to date from May 15, 1918, when Army planes flew between Washington, D.C. and New York City on an experimental arrangement with the Post Office Department. Later in the year, on August 12, the Post Office Department assumed complete control of the airmail program.

In 1925, after passage of the Kelly Bill on February 2, airmail was contracted to private operators. On November 7, Postmaster General Harry S. New announced the first route awards: Boston–New York; Chicago–St. Louis; Chicago–Dallas–Fort Worth; Salt Lake City–Los Angeles; and Elko, Nevada–Pasco, Washington. All five were operational by mid-1926.

Graduating from Yale at age twenty-three, Juan Trippe was a serious individual, who most considered would become a banker. On the contrary, he was determined to make a business out of aviation. In 1922, he organized Long Island Airways, capitalizing it at $5,000, putting up half himself, and selling stock for the rest.

When hard times caused the collapse of Long Island Airways, he charged ahead, forming Alaskan Air Transport, and continued to bid on airmail contracts.

When his Alaskan Air Transport failed to get a contract for mail, he formed Eastern Air Transport, and submitted a bid for the New York–Boston airmail contract. Unsuccessful again, he refused to quit, and merged with his competitor, Colonial Airlines. Upon signing, Colonial had no planes, no employees, no route system, and no landing fields. Trippe ordered four trimotors; two Fokkers and two Fords, announcing the order as the largest for commercial aircraft ever placed in the United States.

There was much to learn, and Trippe was on a fast learning curve. Day after day, he watched at the dirt airfield in New Brunswick, New Jersey as the airmail planes came in from the other side of the continent, and when they landed, he quizzed the pilots about their problems. One of the pilots he talked to was Charles Lindbergh.

Colonial Air Transport, still without its trimotors, commenced airmail service between New York and Boston on July 1, 1926, using single engine machines.

The Boeing fighter series, created in the tradition of building the best product, had put the Company on a sound financial basis. With an expanded engineering department, Egtvedt found it possible to do a substantial effort in preliminary design, creating the Model 40.

The single place "40" was completed in the summer of 1925. Powered by a 400 horsepower water-cooled, V-type Liberty engine, it had a cruising speed of 125 miles per hour, a range of 550 miles, and a service ceiling of 15,700 feet.

Eddie Hubbard had gone to California where flying was accelerating. Phil Johnson wanted to get him back, visualizing a mail and passenger airline around Puget Sound, including Victoria and Vancouver, B.C. Boeing was enthusiastic, directing Johnson—who had been appointed president in February, after the departure of Ed Gott—to invite Hubbard to rejoin Boeing. There was no immediate response.

Opportunities were again perceived by Allan Lockheed and John Northrop. They revived their operation in 1926, renaming it the Lockheed Aircraft Company, and moving their headquarters to Hollywood.

The result of their new efforts was an eye-catching, high winged monoplane called the *Vega*, which vaulted into international prominence, pushed by promotional pizzazz that was to become the Lockheed hallmark.

Promotion, in pure Hollywood style, was seized upon by Allan Lockheed as the way to proceed. He persuaded George Hearst of newspaper fame, to buy his first *Vega*, who entered it in the 1927 Dole race from California to the Hawaiian Islands. In spite of the catastrophic loss of the first *Vega* toward the end of the race, the sleek new plane had attracted worldwide attention.

A few months after Hubbard received Johnson's letter, he appeared in Seattle, bursting with an idea of his own. The United States Post Office, in November 1926, had announced plans to put its Chicago-to-San Francisco airmail route up for bids for private operation.

Johnson was away from the office, and Hubbard went to Claire Egtvedt. "This is the opportunity of a century, Claire. I've got all the figures on mileage and pounds of mail carried. If you can produce the planes, I know we can operate them successfully."

Egtvedt, taken by surprise, reminded his old friend that he was talking about a huge undertaking. "It's a lot of country. The distances are great, as you know. You'd have winter blizzards to contend with, and all that."

"We could do it."

"You'd have to fly at night. Are the beacons in, all the way?"

"Every twenty-five miles."

Thinking of the airplanes that would be needed, Egtvedt found himself tumbling fast. "We could modify the '40', I expect. Probably we could make room for a couple of passengers and still have space for the mail."

Egtvedt's mind raced, thinking how he could redesign the plane with a new Wasp air-cooled engine to replace the heavy water-cooled unit. He estimated he could save 200 pounds. After reviewing the performance details, they decided to go to Bill Boeing for approval.

Harold Mansfield describes that encounter:

After laying it all out for him, Boeing was silent. "This is something foreign to our experience," he finally ventured. They went over it all once more. When there was nothing more to say, Egtvedt and Hubbard departed. "It was a good try," Egtvedt said.[2]

But there was a disposition in Bill Boeing that did not show behind his stern look. It had strong roots, going back to the phrase he had inserted in their original articles of incorporation, and to the fact that he liked to finish what he had started. He knew he had the resources. By now his men had built a good reputation. If anyone could, they could do it. He found it difficult to avoid acknowledging this, as he tossed through the night. By morning the idea had taken control.

Boeing arrived at the plant early, eager to go over the figures one more time. The Post Office would allow up to $3.00 per pound for the first 1,000 miles and thirty cents a pound for each 100 miles beyond that. The figure Egtvedt and Hubbard had come up with was $1.50 per pound for the first 1,000 miles and fifteen cents for each additional 100.

"Those figures look all right to me," said Boeing finally, decisively. "Let's send them in."[3]

In January 1927, word came back that Boeing was the low bidder—extremely low. The nearest bid was $2.24, and the contract was awarded on January 15.

On February 17, 1927, the Boeing Air Transport Company was incorporated, the second step in fulfilling the original charter of July 15, 1916.

The plan called for building a fleet of twenty-five planes, to be ready on the line in five months—by July 1, 1927. The men bent to the task, the chance of realizing their dream within reach.

The redesigned plane, designated the 40A, had a fuselage constructed entirely of welded steel tubing, covered with fabric, replacing the combination steel and wood construction of its predecessor. The landing gear had been redesigned, adapting the new Boeing oleo shock absorbers to commercial use. The wings were redesigned with a new airfoil for improved performance. The plane was equipped for night flying. Accommodations for two passengers were provided in the fuselage behind the firewall, and the cargo capacity was increased to 1,200 pounds.

Everything was coming up roses in 1927. The 15 millionth "tin lizzie" Model T Ford rolled off the Detroit assembly lines; the "iron man," Lou Gehrig, hit three homers in one day and Babe Ruth hit sixty for the season; Al Jolson starred in the first "talkie" moving picture; Gene Tunney retained his heavyweight boxing title against Jack Dempsey in the famous "long count" match; and two army fliers, Lieutenants Lester Maitland and Albert Hegenberger flew from California to Hawaii, the longest ocean flight on record. However, history would record May 21 as the day in 1927 which overshadowed all other events.

On that day, a lanky, soft-spoken aviator landed his single place Ryan monoplane at Le Bourget Airport in Paris. Flying alone, Charles Lindbergh had completed the first nonstop flight from New York—and the future of air travel had suddenly become a subject of common conversation.

At Boeing, the race to build the mail planes finished with a hair-thin margin. On June 30, exactly on schedule, all twenty-five planes were gassed and waiting on the line, ready for the official start, the midnight transfer of the mail at Omaha to the new airline—the Boeing Air Transport Company. The next day, the line inaugurated passenger service.

Harold Mansfield beautifully captures the ambience and anxieties of that period in aviation history:

The first passenger to fly in the Model 40A was a courageous Chicago newspaper woman, Jane Eads, of the *Herald and Examiner*. She was the center of attraction at the Chicago airfield—in high heels, knee-length business suit, feather boa and felt cloche—headed for the clouds. At 9:30 P.M., on July 1, in the harsh white of arc lights, Pilot Ira Biffle helped Miss Eads up on the step pad of the lower wing and through the low door to the tiny cabin between the two wings. Biffle jazzed the motor twice and pushed out into the black.

Jane's heart palpitated as she began her role of trail blazer in the new form of transcontinental travel. The pilot, out of sight and out of hearing in the open cockpit behind, seemed far away. Alone in the night, behind the constant drone of the motor, Jane found companionship for a time with a thin crescent moon beyond the left wing. Now and then a sparkle of light drifted by in the black below. She wasn't sleepy. She turned the switch on the glazed dome light in the ceiling. It was cozy, the sea green of the little walls broken only by the sliding window on either side. She let in the cool air. This was fun, she thought.

Later the crescent disappeared and Jane began to feel rocky. The plane tilted and tipped, then dropped as in a hole. She wasn't sure if it was supposed to act this way. Then with a hard jolt she realized they were landing. At Iowa City she admitted, "I was scared."

They passed over Des Moines without coming down. A city without buildings, just strings of jewels. The flight over western Iowa was under a canopy of stars. It seemed strange that the sky should be lighter and more real than the earth below. The plane flew straight and steady into the western night. The changeless roar of the engine was strong, sweet music now to Jane Eads ears. How odd, how wonderful, she thought, to be settling for the night up here. She found the leather-cushioned seats just large enough to curl up on, kitten fashion, and it was peace.

The landing jolts of Omaha awakened her. Reporters were there to interview her. "I could fly forever," Jane glowed. "I love it." She transferred to a new plane, piloted by Jack Knight. Shoving off at 1:45 A.M., Knight wished her a "merry trip," and she called back gallantly, "Same to you—and a safe one."

Before morning the air grew choppy. Great flashes of lightning lit up the sky. The cracking streaks seemed to be breaking all around them. The plane was lifted and thrown about. Jane put her head on her knees and tried not to think about falling. Then it ended as suddenly as it had begun. There was a yellow fringe on the horizon behind, which grew and flooded the earth with a golden glow. She remembered how a pilot had told her he never knew why the birds sang so sweetly until he saw his first dawn from the sky. They came down at North Platte, then lifted again for Cheyenne, with the sun setting fire to the edge of the clouds on the horizon ahead. Out of Cheyenne, past the bald, rippling foothills, she could see in the distance the snow-crested magnificence of the Medicine Bow Range. Hugh Barker, the new pilot, pushed the mail plane higher and higher. Jane grew drowsy and her legs were heavy with the altitude and the bumping. The road seemed as rocky as it was below. They skimmed past Elk Mountain and into Rock Springs.

A veteran now of ups and downs and the vast, changing topography of the States, Jane flew on past the white flats of the Great Salt Lake country, the forbidding waterless gulches of Nevada, the ultramarine blue of Lake Tahoe, the yellow hills beyond. Suddenly the hills opened into San Francisco Bay. Twenty-three flying hours after leaving Chicago, Jane Eads put her feet on California soil, like an explorer who had discovered a new world—air transportation.[4]

The new airline made money. With public interest focused on air travel in the wake of the Lindbergh flight, the sky trail to California had come to stay. Finding that flying was not a certain way to the grave, more and more passengers purchased tickets.

Major differences developed between Trippe and the president of Colonial, and a after a vote by the stockholders, Trippe was bought out and left the airline.

He set out to form a new company, raising $300,000 and incorporating as Aviation Corporation of America on June 2, 1927. Trippe was managing director, with authority to bid on any airmail route he selected, and was authorized to invest into a newly formed New York corporation called Pan American Airways. Pan American did not own any planes nor did it have much money, but it had the inside track on the Key West–Havana, Cuba mail contract—soon to be awarded.

Trippe hammered out a deal with Pan American, in which his Aviation Corporation of America held a major fraction of the stock.

The Fokker trimotor, ready at the last minute, made the first official flight ten days later, on October 28, 1927, carrying a load of mail weighing 772 pounds.

The tiny airline with the prestigious name operated out of a three-room office suite at 100 West 42nd Street in New York City.

Although Havana was only ninety miles away, in hazy or rainy weather, pilots often had difficulty finding it. They had no navigation except the compass, and they measured wind direction and velocity by judging the amount of foam on the peaks of the waves 1,500 feet or more below.

By peserverance, involving pioneering efforts by Thorp Hiscock of Boeing Air Transport, and Hugo Leuteritz of RCA, who later joined Pan American, the two-way radio problem was solved—but the pilots had to accept the worst heresy of all—taking navigational orders from the ground.

With the support of Charles Lindbergh, everybody's hero, Trippe won the mail contract throughout the Caribbean.

1. Frank Cunningham, *Sky Master*, (Philadelphia: Dorrance & Company, 1943), 152.
2. Harold Mansfield, *Vision*, (New York: Popular Library, 1966), 27.
3. Ibid., 30.
4. Ibid., 31.

CHAPTER SIX

Charter Consummated

On the national scene in 1928, Herbert Clark Hoover, accepting the Republican nomination for President, promised "a chicken in every pot, a car in every garage." He was elected by a landslide in November.

The Boeing Airplane Company was beginning to enjoy an international reputation as a meticulous builder of both military and commercial airplanes.

A trip through the crowded factory buildings on the Duwamish in the early part of the year would reveal more types of airplanes than one could count on the fingers of both hands.

On October 31, 1928, the Boeing Airplane Company, jointly with Boeing Air Transport, Inc., and other individuals, purchased control of Pacific Air Transport, Inc., which had established a Seattle–Los Angeles mail and passenger route.

Model 80 series—1928–1930

Boeing's *Pioneer Pullman of the Air* carried 18 passengers and a crew of two, establishing the 27 hour, coast-to-coast Boeing Air Transport service over the mid-continent route.

Pacific, which began service in September 1926, flew two Fokker Universal cabin planes, five Travel Air biplanes, two Ryan monoplanes, and one Romair biplane—all equipped with Wright Whirlwind engines. A parent company was formed known as the Boeing Airplane and Transport Corporation—of which the Seattle factory was a subsidiary.

The parent company then reorganized on February 1, 1929, forming the United Aircraft and Transport Corporation, the largest organization of its kind in the United States. The new corporation included the Boeing Airplane Company; the Hamilton Standard Propeller Corporation; the Northrop Aircraft Corporation, Ltd.; the Pratt & Whitney Aircraft Company; the Sikorsky Aviation Corporation; the Stearman Aircraft Company; and the Chance-Vought Corporation. In addition to those manufacturing companies, the new giant included Boeing Air Transport, Inc., Pacific Air Transport Inc.; and Stout Air Services; as well as United Aircraft Exports, Inc.; United Airports Company of California, Ltd.; the United Airports of Connecticut, Inc,; and the Boeing School of Aeronautics.[1]

As constituted, the new corporation included everything from manufacturing airplanes, engines, and propellers to operating airlines and airports; a school—and even exports.

W.E. Boeing became chairman of the new corporation, and F.B. Rentschler of Pratt & Whitney became president.

Thus, not much more than a decade after he founded the Company, Boeing witnessed the fulfillment of his visionary charter.

Bigness was the criterion that seemed to attract widespread attention as airplanes quickly captured the imagination of an increasing segment of the public. Boeing was being looked to as the epitome of the biggest—and the best.

When the PB-1 was launched not long after the Model 40 mail plane prototype, it was the largest navy plane yet constructed in the world. Six times the weight of the B-1, this new giant carried a crew of five, and was equipped with two Packard 2A-2500 water-cooled engines, each rated at 800 horsepower. It boasted four-bladed propellers—one a pusher and the other a tractor, with two engines mounted back-to-back. The cruising range of more than 2,000 miles represented a spectacular advance, ideal for the Navy, which was beginning to focus on the vast two-ocean shoreline. New design innovations also appeared on the PB-1. The wings were of metal construction—fabric covered—with beams of welded steel tubing and ribs of aluminum alloy—the first use of aluminum in Boeing airplanes.

The bread and butter machines after the "40" series were fighter and pursuit planes for the military, however, the really exciting competition during this period was to increase passenger capacity in commercial models. The goal, set by Juan Trippe, was to at least double on each succeeding new design.

The last of a series, the 40B-4 carried four passengers. Then in 1928, Boeing claimed a huge chunk of future sky with the Model 80. Designed to carry twelve passengers with a new degree of comfort, the plane quickly became known as the "Pioneer Pullman of the Air."

Powered by three 425-horsepower engines, the "80" had reclining seats, adjustable to four positions; a lavatory with hot and cold running water; forced ventilation and heating; an insulated and soundproofed cabin; a small buffet; large windows of non-shatterable glass; dome lights; and wall lamps.

Juan Trippe was beginning to move mountains. In January, he hired the "Lone Eagle," Charles Lindbergh, as a technical adviser. Lindbergh became a welcome ambassador from the U.S. in Latin America. The previous December, he flew to Mexico at the invitation of that nation. Greeted

Model 80A Interior

by joyous crowds, he was entertained over the Christmas holidays by U.S. Ambassador Dwight Morrow and his daughters and then continued on a goodwill tour of South America. While greeting dignitaries, he also charted air routes and scouted for accessible landing sites.

Trippe had planned well. Having gained the aura of "flag carrier" for the U.S. in Latin America, he forged ahead. West Indian Airways, the principal Caribbean carrier, sold out to Pan Am. In quick succession, he acquired the airlines of Mexico, Peru, and Colombia, and organized an airline in Chile. Then, to finesse the Grace Steamship Company, who dominated trade with South America, he worked out a merger, creating Pan American Grace Airways—which became known as Panagra.

At a time when no domestic airline had yet managed to span the United States—first accomplished on October 23, 1929—Trippe was ready to push his planes out along ten thousand miles of routes. Soon he would be seeking bigger airplanes—and new engineering innovations—the Boeing hallmark.

It was not long until Boeing produced an improved version of the Model 80, announcing the 80-A, capable of carrying eighteen passengers and 898 pounds of cargo. The twenty-seven-hour coast-to-coast Boeing Air Transport service over the mid-continent route was established, and onboard stewardesses were employed for the first time. In all, sixteen airplanes of the Model 80 series were built.

Aviation marched with seven-league boots in 1928. In April, French pilots Costes and Le Brix landed at Le Bourget, completing a 45,000 mile around-the-world flight. Also in April, aviators Koehl, Hunefeld, and Fitzmau piloted a Junkers from Ireland to New York, in the first east–west flight over the Atlantic—flying into the teeth of the prevailing winds. In October, Harry Tucker made a new coast-to-coast record of twenty-four hours, fifty-one minutes in his Yankee Doodle monoplane, and in November a British flier hit 319.57 mules per hour in a seaplane.

In 1928, orders came in for the *Vega* from all sides. Lockheed was already living up to its modern motto: "There is a tide in the affairs of men, which when taken at the flood, leads on to fortune...."

The rush of orders forced Lockheed to seek a new location and they moved to a larger site in Burbank.

The *Vega* was followed by a parade of new airplanes; the underslung-wing *Sirius*, which Lindbergh used to fly from Washington, D.C., all the way to China in a series of carefully planned and publicized hops in 1931; the *Altair*, a two-seated airplane; and the *Orion*, with an enlarged, seven-seat cabin.

In every case, the introduction of an innovation was accompanied by heavy fanfare. Lockheed's location near the movie capital of the world was a magnificent bonus in its promotional efforts. They sought additional publicity from the achievements of the trailblazing aviators of the era; including George Wilkins, Amelia Earhart, Roscoe Turner, and Wiley Post, all of whom set and broke speed and distance records in Lockheed planes. The boast of the company in its advertisements, "It takes a Lockheed to beat a Lockheed," was beginning to cement a vision of invincibility in the Lockheed name.[2]

Caught in their own private enthusiasm, awash with favorable publicity, Lockheed concentrated too heavily on the headline-grabbing, but potentially low-profit, low-volume markets. In addition, left unattended was the reawakening military market of the United States government.

After a series of catastrophic events, both on a private and a national scale, which included the stock market crash of 1929, Lockheed, by then a struggling subsidiary of the Detroit Aircraft Holding Company, an early conglomerate, found itself bankrupt.

"'I have an idea, Claire,' said Eddie Hubbard, now operations vice president of the Boeing airline, when the two men were sharing a hotel room after the 1928 Los Angeles Air Races. 'Why shouldn't we go entirely to metal when we build our next transport? We have to line the mail compartment with metal anyway so the mailbag locks won't tear the fabric.'"

Stimulated by the idea, Egtvedt laid a piece of stationery on the dresser, drew the front view of a wing, long and slender.

"'If the body's going to be metal, the easiest way to make it is perfectly round,' he said sketching. 'Set it here on the wing. Here's an airplane with minimum drag.'"

"He had drawn a circle for the body, on top of the single wing. That was all there was to it, a low-wing monoplane.

"'It gets rid of all the wires and bracing on the wings.'

"To Hubbard, it looked too simple. 'Where's your landing gear?' he asked.

"'You could pull the gear up into the wing after you get off the ground.'

"'Do you think we could build that?'

"'It's only a question of whether we could afford the cost of working it out.'"[3]

Egtvedt felt that the corrugated-metal, "flying washboard" surfaces used for the body construction on the Ford and the German Junkers had to be eliminated. He wanted the skin to be perfectly smooth on the outside.

When Bill Boeing saw the sketch, he was impressed. He wondered aloud if they could get to work on it as a secret project, as they had done with the pursuit plane, and bring it out as a surprise.

Egtvedt listened, fairly jumping inside. He said he'd have the engineering department investigate.

1. First Annual Report to the Stockholders, United Aircraft & Transport Corporation, for the year ending December 31, 1929. Boeing Archives.
2. David Boulton, *The Grease Machine*, (New York: Harper & Row, 1978), 25.
3. Harold Mansfield, *Vision*, (New York: Popular Library, 1966), 39.

CHAPTER SEVEN

The All-metal First

The idea of an all-metal airplane was mind-boggling in 1928. Stress analysis for wings was still a relatively unsophisticated science, and no one knew how to reliably assign structural loads to the skin.

At Boeing, the chief engineer was Charles N. "Monty" Monteith, a graduate of MIT in aeronautical engineering; also a pilot, serving as instructor at Kelly Field, Texas; and chief of section in the Air Service Engineering Division at McCook Field—all of this prior to coming to Boeing.

Egtvedt's proposal had Monteith shaking his head. Highly regarded professionally, he had written the textbook on aerodynamics being used at West Point as well as at many universities. Reluctantly, he advised Egtvedt that it would be unwise to go ahead with the project.

Monteith was sharp, competitive, and eager to continue leadership in innovation, however he was painfully aware that engineers' mistakes bury them. In his textbook, he had written, "It must be as simple and as cheap as is possible to build.[1]

Monomail—1929–1930
First modern air transport.

In the airplane business, always at the cutting edge of technology, the conflict of boldness and caution haunted the waking hours of those who sought to create new designs.

As the days went by, the comfortable alternative to a low-wing mono-plane—a high wing, externally braced arrangement—became increasingly less satisfying to Monteith. Keenly aware that leadership—indeed survival—depended on innovation, he initiated a substantial preliminary design effort, gaining encouragement from Bill Boeing's unflagging confidence.

The low-wing, all-metal design, with its smooth, clean lines, quickly captured the imagination of the engineers, and the alternatives were abandoned.

Bill Boeing was elated—there was something almost magic about an idea that appeared at the right place at the right time. His words on that occasion have served to guide and inspire Boeing engineers from that day forward—almost a catechism for developing a winner every time.

"We must not dismiss any novel idea with the cocksure statement that it can't be done," he said in an interview. "We are pioneers in a new science and a new industry. Our job is to keep everlastingly at research and experiment, and let no new improvement pass us by. We have already proved that science and hard work can lick what appear to be insurmountable difficulties."

Monteith had become a disciple. He decided to go all out and make the best of it. According to Boeing's wishes, the project was kept secret until it was time to join the wings to the fuselage, accomplished at the airfield a mile south of the plant and in view of the public. Not at all like any airplane seen before, it had a slender, round, smooth body resting on a silver wing. Constructed almost entirely of durals, the first high strength aluminum alloy family, the *Monomail* had come alive. It was powered by a single, air-cooled 575-horsepower, Pratt & Whitney, Hornet engine.

In spite of all the innovations and sleek lines of the *Monomail*, the plane still retained an open cockpit, a concession to the pilots, obsessed with the idea that they must be on the outside.

The first *Monomail*, the Model 200, was not equipped to carry passengers, but had three cargo compartments with a total capacity of 220 cubic feet, providing for a normal payload of 2,300 pounds. In the second airplane, the Model 221, the center cargo compartment was converted into a passenger cabin with accommodations for six. Both models were later modified to carry eight passengers. The open cockpit remained.

With the *Monomail* taking its flying paces at the direction of Eddie Allen, famous test pilot and aeronautical engineer, it was quickly apparent that the next limitation to speed and performance was the propeller. The pitch of the blades could only be changed on the ground. After extensive experimentation, Allen chose a compromise setting, and the *Monomail*, one of the most revolutionary airplanes in history, made its maiden flight on May 6, 1930.

The year of 1930 was also notable for the maiden flight of another kind—the launching of the *Boeing News*. The January issue announced the aims and purposes of the new publication:

"Not many years ago the Boeing Airplane Company, housed in a small building with thirty employees, represented all of the Boeing aeronautical activities. The few men and women employed in this building were, of course, in intimate touch with all phases of the business.

"Today we have a far-flung organization, whose business includes the manufacture of airplanes, operation of the two longest mail lines in the United States, a subsidiary manufacturing plant in Canada, a flying school at Oakland, to mention only our major operations.

"It is my belief that the Boeing family has grown so rapidly, our activities are so varied, our personnel so separated, that the time has come when all of us should be kept informed about what the other groups are doing. That explains *Boeing News*.

"We trust that *Boeing News* will be informative and entertaining and serve a useful purpose in knitting our family of 1,500 employees into one group actuated by the desire to be of service to each other and to the public."[2]

The announcement was signed, "P.G. Johnson, President."

Boeing News became much more than a mere chronology of events. Indeed, it gave the employees a heightened feeling of participation, importance, and belonging.

In spite of the stock market crash on "Black Thursday," October 24, 1929, Boeing sailed along, riding a crest of production orders into the early thirties. They were good years. On the basis of Navy tests with the XF4B-1, a Boeing prototype, beginning as the Model 83, which featured bolted aluminum tubing in place of welded steel tubing, the Army ordered nine as the P-12. This was the first order of a 586 plane production run of F4B/P-12 machines.

The bolted aluminum-alloy construction was also incorporated in the Model 95, an airplane designed specifically to carry cargo and mail. Twenty-five of these planes were produced for three airlines: Boeing Air Transport, National Air Transport, and Western Air Express.

Progress in aviation continued around the world. In January 1929, Commander Richard E. Byrd explored 1,200 miles of the Antarctic by plane, and the U.S. Army craft, *Question Mark*, stayed aloft for 150 hours and 40 minutes—refueled in the air. Two decades later, it was Boeing who developed the first sophisticated aerial refueling system. Known as the "flying boom," the technology provided the U.S. Air Force Strategic Air Command essentially unlimited range for its heavy bombers.

On April 26, 1929, British fliers completed a record, nonstop, 4,130 mile trip from London to India.

At home on February 17, 1929, Universal Air Lines reported showing a film during a scheduled flight, and on July 7, Transcontinental Air Transport inaugurated what they called cross-country service, with passengers

Model 247 Series—1932–1935

First standard design for contemporary transport airplanes. It carried ten passengers, two pilots, and 400 pounds of mail.

traveling by plane during the day and sleeping on trains during the night. Then on October 23, the first coast-to-coast, all-air service began—from New York to Los Angeles in thirty-six hours—with an overnight stop.

The year was notable for other events. The Lone Eagle married Anne Morrow, Babe Ruth hit his 500th home run, Charlie Chaplin was runnerup to Janet Gaynor in the first Academy Awards ceremony in Hollywood, and in China, Canadian archeologist David Black discovered the 400,000-year-old bones of Peking Man.

The *Monomail* cruised at 140 miles per hour, and with increasing significance of aerodynamic drag on performance, the issue of the open cockpit eventually had to be faced.

The first 80A trimotors had provided for the pilots to sit inside an enclosed cabin, a situation which they strongly disliked. They wanted to be able to look out, lean over for a glance at the ground—to follow a fence line or a railroad track. The pilots complained so strongly that one of the tri-motors was modified to install an open cockpit atop the square nose.

The airplane, one of a kind, designated the 80B, did not last long. After a few trials at the higher speeds, the comforts of being inside the cabin began to outweigh the thrill of the open cockpit, and the airplane was converted back to an 80A.

The *Monomail* was not a celebrated airplane in terms of production, but was the spawning ground for still further advancements. It evolved to the twin-engined B-9 bomber, carrying two 30-caliber machine guns and four 600 pound bombs. A commercial version, the Model 247, followed.

With the stock market crash, the United States plunged into the Great Depression. Unemployment soon hit eleven million, eventually reaching twenty-five percent of the national work force. The Hoover Administration insisted that "prosperity was just around the corner."

With a landslide victory in November 1932, President Franklin D. Roosevelt promised a "New Deal" for the American people, announcing that "the only thing we have to fear is fear itself." At Boeing, the plant was busy turning out fighters—and looking to future products.

At noon on February 8, 1933, the silver-bright 247—a twin engined monoplane, fifty-four feet, four inches long and weighing 13,000 pounds—lifted from Boeing Field and winged out over Puget Sound on its first flight. Its retractable landing gear, first in the commercial industry, had been well proven on the *Monomail*. Soon it was to incorporate the controllable pitch propeller, developed by Frank Caldwell of Hamilton Standard.

The ten-passenger plane won instant acclaim. "They'll never build 'em any bigger," said a triumphant Monteith.[3]

The capability of the 247 was increased with a further series of improvements, finally evolving to the 247D. This model was the first twin-engined transport monoplane able to climb with one engine out, while fully loaded.

United Airlines—incorporated on March 28, 1931—a part of the giant United Aircraft and Transport Corporation, purchased a fleet of 247D airplanes, operating coast-to-coast and border-to-border. Spanning the U.S. became a matter of twenty hours—with only seven stops.

A total of seventy-five airplanes of the 247 series were manufactured, two purchased by the German airline, Deutsche Lufthansa in Hamburg.

The 247 design won Bill Boeing the 1934 Guggenheim Medal for successful pioneering and advancement in aircraft manufacturing and transport.

In this instance, first and best was not sufficient in the rapidly changing marketplace. The aircraft industry was sharpening its teeth. Technology, sometimes inching along, and at other times breaking its bonds with a sudden leap, was a constant companion—and a constant adversary. One could never be certain what competitors were hatching in their design rooms and wind tunnels.

Donald Douglas continued to expand his organization, and in 1929, they moved to a new building near Clover Field in Santa Monica. The Douglas Company became the Douglas Aircraft Company, an identity which it maintained for nearly forty years.

Trans World Airways approached Douglas to design an airplane with a larger cabin that would outperform the 247D. It was the right time for another leap in technology.

The product—ready for its test flight on July 1, 1933—was the twelve passenger DC-1. The six-ton, all-aluminum plane represented the hope for Douglas to wrest commercial supremacy from Boeing. The ensuing dogfight was still going strong forty years later.

The DC-1, a one-and-only, was improved and redesignated the DC-2 before it entered airline service. The plane immediately began an assault on aeronautical records. In March 1935, a DC-2 established a new transcontinental record of twelve hours and forty-two minutes from west to east, and in 1936, an east–west record, against prevailing winds, of fifteen hours and thirty-nine minutes, traveling at a speed of nearly 200 miles per hour.

Gambling in the airplane manufacturing business seemed to be the way of life. Douglas gambled on the DC series, setting the price far lower than the initial cost of production—counting on a learning curve which would reduce costs dramatically with a large production run. Further, the initial development cost of the DC-1 ($307,000), had to be recovered. With the planes selling for about $65,000 each, the first twenty-five netted a loss of $266,000.

The gamble paid off. The seventy-sixth plane raised the program out of the red, and by June 1938, some 132 DC-2 planes had been delivered. In the meantime, the DC-3, with a nominal configuration of twenty-one seats, was introduced.

With the DC series, Douglas achieved undisputed world leadership in the production of commercial airplanes. A total of 10,629 DC-3s were manufactured, including over 10,000 military versions, that were churned out of Douglas factories during World War II as C-47s, R4Ds, and *Dakotas.*[4]

A legendary flying machine, the DC-3 represented the single greatest propeller-driven airplane model that the world had produced. On December 17, 1985, the airplane celebrated the fiftieth anniversary of its first flight. At the time, aviation historians estimated that between 1,500 and 2,000 DC-3s were still flying with scheduled airlines, or serving the air forces of many developing countries.

In 1935, Donald W. Douglas received the Collier Trophy for development of the DC-2, and in January 1940, joined William E. Boeing in the select group of aviation pioneers to receive the Guggenheim Medal.

From the introduction of the DC-3 in 1936, until the start of World War II in 1939, U.S. air travel increased by 500 percent. DC-3s and DC-2s carried nearly 90 percent of all U.S. air traffic, and were operated by thirty foreign airlines.

In Burbank in 1932, with orders completely stopped, and the employment down to four, a federal receiver put Lockheed up for sale, valuing its assets at $129,961.

Allan Lockheed, excited by the opportunity to buy back the company he and his brother had founded, desperately sought to raise $100,000 for a bid, when to his dismay, he found that receivers had already accepted an offer for the astoundingly low figure of $40,000. The new buyer, Robert Ellsworth Gross, an investment banker with no knowledge whatsoever of flying or the production of airplanes, had purchased a bargain. Robert Gross invited his younger brother, Courtland, to join the company as deputy chairman.

Gross had a lot of catching up to do. For his $40,000 he had acquired floor space, a few boxes of spare parts, some blueprints, the total labor force of four people—and the Lockheed name. The goodwill in terms of world renown was probably worth tenfold what Robert Gross had paid for the company.

It was a good match. Gross had the knack for playing the market, knew how to keep his finger on the pulse of national trends, and immediately sensed a long-range future for commercial airplanes—which had come of age for mass travel.

Gross was in the right business to raise the capital that was so necessary to get on the track. He returned the *Orion* to production and began a blitz of the overseas commercial markets.

Swissair became Lockheed's first overseas customer, followed by many of Europe's emerging aairlines.

In a short eighteen months, Lockheed produced a challenge to its competitors, rolling out the all-metal, twin-engined ten-seater known as the *Electra* Model 10. As a result of spending over three times the $40,000 he had invested in the company—in research and development—Gross had accomplished his objective in one grand stroke. The new plane incorporated all the modern refinements: retractable landing gear, trailing edge flaps, and variable pitch propellers.

By the end of 1935, forty machines had been sold, half of them to the overseas market.

Robert Gross had the gut feeling to exploit new developments in the tried and true Lockheed tradition. The corporate complexion—and indeed the corporate conscience—was being indelibly molded to fit the personality of its boss.

The final leg of the "Big Three" in commercial airplane manufacturing had emerged.

In Seattle, with United Airline's competitors turning to the DC-3 and the *Electra* Model 10, there were no orders in sight for the 247D, beyond the initial seventy-five.

Boeing was suddenly reduced to third in commercial airplane sales.

1. Charles Monteith, *Simple Aerodynamics and the Airplane,* (Washington, D.C.: Army Air Corps, 1925), 5.
2. *Boeing News*, January, 1930, 1.
3. Harold Mansfield, *Vision*, (New York: Popular Library, 1966), 43.
4. DC-3 DAKOTA NEWSLETTER, Douglas Aircraft Company, 17 December, 1985.

Claire L. Egtvedt 1892–1975
President 1934–1939, Chairman 1939–1965.

CHAPTER EIGHT

Clipped Wings

The Boeing Airplane Company never flinched in the face of the trials of the marketplace. Bill Boeing had passed the torch of pride in the product to every level in the organization. It was left to the political and legislative processes to bring the Company to its knees—indeed coming within a hair-thin margin of forcing it out of business.

In 1934—just when Boeing sorely needed its strength to beat the new competition—the huge United Aircraft and Transport Corporation was ordered to break up. Three major entities remained: the Boeing Airplane Company, the United Aircraft Manufacturing Corporation, and United Airlines; separating airframe manufacturing, engines, and airline operations into individual companies.

Bill Boeing, disillusioned and bitter, sold his stock and retired from the Company. He was never to return to the aircraft business except for a short time during World War II as a consultant.

Inevitably, Boeing left a legacy of integrity and rock-hard ethics with those who followed him. His never-say-die attitude during his eighteen years

as the leader of the Company, was epitomized in a motto which was formalized from some of his earlier remarks:

> *I've tried to make the men around me feel as I do, that we are em-
> barked as pioneers upon a new science and industry in which our prob-
> lems are so new and unusual that it behooves no one to dismiss any novel
> idea with the statement that "It can't be done." Our job is to keep ever-
> lastingly at research and experiment, to adapt our laboratory results and
> those of other laboratories to production as soon as practicable, to let no
> new improvement in flying and flying equipment pass us by.*[1]

The Boeing Airplane Company, after the breakup, consisted of the par-
ent Company, incorporated in Delaware, and two subsidiaries: the Boeing
Aircraft Company in the State of Washington, and the Stearman Aircraft
Company in Kansas.

Boeing Aircraft Company of Canada, Ltd., remained as a subsidiary of
the Boeing Aircraft Company of Washington.

Claire Egtvedt, named president of the Boeing Airplane Company with
the departure of P.G. Johnson, inherited the smallest—and most fragile—
of the three new corporations. The first annual report of the restructured
company covering the four months from September 1, 1934 to year end,
recorded a net loss of $225,977 on gross sales of $1,116,627.[2]

Egtvedt wanted to build an experimental twin-engined bomber and a
matching transport. There was no money. In fact, when the legal separation was completed and the books rationalized, cash available for operations was down to $582,000, most of it needed to meet the payroll for the
remainder of the year.

After reaching an all-time high of 2,275 employees in May 1933, the
payroll dropped to 600 by late summer in 1934.

Some employees came in to offer a plan of spreading out the work—
one group on for two weeks and then off for two—thus preserving the core
of expertise. When the plan was adopted, many of them came to the plant
to work on their own time—with no thought of being paid.

This employee attitude was a notable example of the sometimes in-
explicable loyalty which Boeing employees felt for their Company. Bill
Boeing had left an organization behind that refused—as he had—the

P-26 Series—*Peashooter*—1932–1936

The P-26A was the first all-metal pursuit to go into production for the Army, rated as one of the fastest air-cooled fighters in the world. Top speed 234 mph, range 635 miles, service ceiling 27,400 feet.

notion that it could not be done.

With the dissolution of the United Aircraft Transport Corporation, Boeing was left without any foreign representation. Egtvedt invited Wellwood Beall, an exuberant young engineer who had been an instructor at the Boeing School of Aeronautics, to join the sales department. Beall, with degrees in both mechanical and aeronautical engineering from New York University, had made an auspicious entry into the industry, starting as assistant chief engineer with the Walter M. Murphy Company in Pasadena, California prior to his position at the Boeing school. A brilliant, pleasant-faced, outgoing individual, courting a thinly trimmed mustache, he was anything but the stereotype of an engineer—but destined to play a key role in the Company's future.

Egtvedt gave Beall the job of Far Eastern Sales Representative and sent him to China to sell the P-26 *Peashooter* to the Chinese Air Force. In July 1935, the Chinese purchased eleven airplanes. After coming off the production line, the planes had to be disassembled, crated, and shipped to China. It would be necessary to have a Boeing man on site who could not only reassemble the airplanes, but also train the Chinese pilots and mechanics. Beall found his man, Herbert D. Poncetti, known as Nemo, in Shanghai. Thus, Nemo became Boeing's first unofficial field service representative.

The impact and importance of *Boeing News* began to be felt as the company grew. Beginning monthly, the *News* was used not simply for informing but for influencing. While *Boeing News* worked hard at the job, it could not disguise the inequalities within the company at the time. The paper pointed out the harsh realities of managing a labor force in the feast-or-famine environment of the airplane industry. In 1933 there were many reasons for an hourly worker to look to a union for help. Hourly workers lacked the dignity and honor that salaried work enjoyed. Salaried employees had sick leave privileges, a broader insurance program, vacations, hot water in the wash rooms, and regular working hours. Hourly workers could be called to work whenever their services were required and sent home when they were not. For factory employees, Boeing had only a health contract with a local clinic and an occasional bonus on Christmas. In spite of the paucity of benefits, there was little effort to organize the workers. Employment was too tentative, hinging on production orders.

The National Recovery Act of 1933 gave Boeing factory workers the impetus they needed to unionize. Under its terms, the National Labor Relations Board (NLRB) was formed. Some employees, impatient for a labor union, wrote to the Seattle Regional Board in early March requesting a plant election. The Board called for such an election for March 15, 1934. The aeronautical workers American Federation of Labor union won all four of the shop employee positions on the five-man committee.

Notwithstanding this impressive beginning, labor organization at Boeing was still years away from gaining significant bargaining power.

Looking back from 1934, the late twenties and early thirties were halcyon years. For that brief period, the Company was national in scope, multiproduct deep, and growing with undiminished confidence.

Now, even *Boeing News* became a victim of the severe downturn. In November, it suspended publication.

However grim the near horizon appeared, there was hope. Integrity, innovation, and product excellence were destined to be rewarded. Boeing, and the Company he created, had built a blue ribbon reputation in the minds of the planners at Wright Field. Thus, it was inevitable that any new request for procurement would include Boeing on the bidders list.

Thus, in the spring of 1934, the lowest point in the Company's history since the days of bedroom furniture, Claire Egtvedt received a call from Brigadier General Conger Pratt, chief of the Air Corps Materiel Division at Wright Field in Dayton, Ohio. The general requested Egtvedt to attend an important meeting on May 14. The subject was secret.

After General Billy Mitchell proved in 1921, that a battleship could be sunk with aerial torpedoes, planners at Wright Field began pushing for more emphasis on bombers. The most enthusiastic of these new thinkers was a young lieutenant by the name of Leonard "Jake" Harman, who had become a Billy Mitchell disciple. The key in Jake's book was range.

The battleships that had been sunk by Billy Mitchell were close to the coast. In a real fight, they would be far out at sea, safely out of the range of airplanes—according to the admirals.

In airplane design, normally you took what range you could get, after determining how heavy a structure was required, and how large a power plant was available.

Harman thought perhaps the design process was being done backwards, suggesting that the baseline should be established according to mission requirements, instead of what was currently possible. His concept gained support with his superiors, and a list of desired future bomber categories was conceived.

Category One was a seventy-five foot wing span airplane with a gross weight of 15,000 pounds, represented by the Boeing B-9 twin, already in the inventory.

Category Two called for a 100-foot span and 40,000 pounds gross weight; Category Three, a 150-foot span and 60,000 pounds gross; and Category Four, 200 feet and 150,000 pounds gross.

In the fall of 1933, the Air Corps budgeted a project for a 5,000-mile range bomber in Category Three—reaching into the future as far as they dared.

General Pratt sent the proposal to Washington, recommending that Wright Field be authorized to put all its experimental budget into this single project.

In Washington, Air Corps chief Benny Foulois concurred with Pratt's recommendation, and took it to a meeting of the general staff, observing, "A plane with a range of 5,000 miles could protect Hawaii and Alaska." [3] The general staff agreed.

"The purpose of this meeting," General Pratt began on May 14, 1934 in the curtained, carpeted, brass-filled briefing room at Wright Field, "is to discuss a procedure under which the Air Corps will consider proposals for the construction of a long-range airplane suitable for military purposes— an airplane weighing about thirty tons, to carry 2,000 pounds of bombs a distance of 3,000 miles." Egtvedt caught his breath, glancing over to C.A. Van Dusen of the Martin Company, who appeared equally startled.

Back in Seattle, a special area was partitioned off in the engineering building. It was classified secret. Preliminary design studies were initiated immediately for a 150-foot wing-span, four-engine, giant monoplane. Project "A" was born.

Montieth was shaking his head over the project. A year earlier, he would have branded it as pure fantasy.

Decisions were made quickly in 1934. On June 28, a design contract was awarded and the project organized. Jack Kylstra was named project engineer. A wooden mock-up of the forward section, including the control cabin, was constructed.

Wright Field personnel became a common sight at the Boeing plant as they consulted and mulled over the design details.

Some of the proposed features taxed the imagination. The wing would have a passageway large enough to permit crawling out to the engines in flight. Wright Field even wanted a kitchenette with a hot plate and percolator.

Nevertheless, Project "A" was an experiment—nothing more. Its purpose was to learn how to build a maximum size airplane. The award called for a design study only. What the Boeing factory desperately needed was a hardware contract.

United Airlines, studying a Boeing design for an improved twin-engined machine, was concerned that the proposed airplane's performance was not sufficiently better than the DC-2s being flown by the competition. "Why not go to four engines?" they inquired.

The question reinforced a growing conviction in Egtvedt's mind that four engines were inevitable. Twenty-one years had elapsed since Igor Sikorsky, famous Russian aviator and airplane designer, had developed and flown the *Grand*, the world's first four-engined airplane. The date of that historic flight was May 13, 1913.[4] The *Grand* flew less than ten minutes on its initial flight, however from that day, four-engined flight was indisputable.

Progress demanded bold action. Competition was becoming keener, but there was plenty of blue sky still to be conquered...*let no new improvement pass us by....*

Events quickened. On August 8, 1934, a circular was issued from Wright Field with the specifications for the next "production" bomber. "Bomb load 2,000 pounds; desired top speed, 250 miles an hour; range 2,200 miles; a crew of four to six." Interested companies were requested to submit bids for the construction of up to 220 airplanes.

The word *production* danced in Egtvedt's brain. He began to envision a fleet of flying dreadnaughts, capable of defending themselves in the sky, as they carried bomb loads to distant targets.

Meanwhile, on May 19th, in Russia, the biggest airplane in the world, amidst much fanfare, made its first flight. The giant *Maxim Gorky*, with eight engines, had a wing span of 260 feet—64 feet greater than a 747— and a crew of twenty. When the pilot of an accompanying fighter plane decided to liven things up with a barrel roll, he came crashing down on the *Maxim Gorky's* wing, causing the huge plane to disintegrate in the air.[5] The world wrote the airplane off as a stunt.

Preliminary design of the four-engined transport for United was proceeding well, and a Model 299 bomber was in the concept stage. The circular said "multi-engine," possibly limited to two-engined machines in the minds of the Air Corps. Trimotors might also be a possibility. Egtvedt flew to Wright Field to inquire.

"Would a four-engined airplane qualify?" he asked. Major Jan Howard, the engineering chief, looked up quickly, squinted, then smiled. "Say now." He looked at the circular. "The word is 'multi-engine,' isn't it?"[6]

Back at the plant, work was kicked off on the four-engined bomber. The company's position was more tenuous than ever. They were operating in the red.

But there was a prospect of building 220 bombers. *The risk was loss of the Company.* All the resources of manpower and equipment—and borrowed money—would have to be sunk into a single costly experiment.

Egtvedt sought guidance from his friend and counselor, William M. "Bill" Allen.

Allen hailed from the almost unknown town of Lolo, Montana, in the Bitterroot Mountains thirty miles south of Missoula. The son of a mining engineer, he graduated from the University of Montana in 1922 with a B.A. degree. After receiving his law degree from Harvard University, he came to Seattle in 1925 to start law practice with the firm of Donworth, Todd & Higgins. His first assignment was legal advisor in the formation of Boeing Air Transport in 1926, and he quickly became the "Company lawyer."

Egtvedt, in the spirit of past Boeing innovations, wanted to build the airplane on speculation, fly it to Wright Field, and demonstrate its performance.

Allen was neither an engineer nor a pilot, but he had a way of focusing the central issue. "Do you think you can build a successful, four-engined airplane in a year?"

"Yes, I know we can," Egtvedt responded firmly, after only a moment's hesitation.[7]

On September 26, 1934, borrowing to the limit, the board of directors voted $275,000 to design and construct the Model 299, to be delivered to Wright Field for trials the following August. The entire Boeing work force was reorganized on a one-job, maximum effort basis.

The road was strewn with controversies and compromises—and innovations. Young Edward C. Wells, fresh out of Stanford University's engineering school, where he graduated with "great distinction," was the assistant project engineer.

By December, the major share of drawings were in the shops, and assembly was begun. Then they ran out of money. The board raised another $150,000 to finish the airplane. In mid-1935, the body and wings were ready to be moved to Boeing Field for final assembly. Everything was under canvas to protect Boeing's expensive secret until the opportune moment.

During that same period, Wright Field sent a contract to construct the giant Project "A" airplane.

The month of July at Boeing Field, was as tough a month as Boeing work crews had ever seen. Even Fred Laudan, the factory superintendent, checked in on first shift and out again at the end of the second shift around midnight. In the final week, shifts were not observed—the crews simply worked as long as they could stand up—to meet the July 28 flight date.

The curious, awed public had their first look at the shiny battle giant, arrayed with its five machine-gun turrets—with reporters immediately dubbing it an aerial battle cruiser.

Before sunrise, on Sunday, July 28, test pilot Les Tower checked out the airplane, and prepared for takeoff. Mansfield describes the event:

"A cluster of men stood at the edge of Boeing Field, shivering a little in the morning mist, their hearts and the soles of their feet catching the rumble of four idling engines at the far end of the field. The rumble grew to a burning, firing roar and the big form was moving toward them down the runway, racing past them. Les Tower lifted her slowly, surely, over the end of the field. As though timed by a stage crew, the sun popped over the ridge of the Cascades, its brightness glistening on the polished wings that streaked to meet it, and the 299 was a receding speck in the sky.[8]

Claire Egtvedt closed his eyes and smiled. Design engineer Bob Minshall turned to Ed Wells, who had been promoted to project engineer. "That's it Ed. Great work."

With the successful completion of the test flights, on August 20, 1935, at 3:45 A.M., the 299 was off for a nonstop flight to Dayton, Ohio. On board were Les Tower, engine man Henry Igo, and mechanic Bud Benton. Exactly nine hours after leaving Seattle, they were coming down at Wright Field. The plane had made the 2,000 mile flight in record time, averaging 252 miles per hour.

The 299 was not alone—a Martin B-12 and a Douglas B-18, both twin-engined aircraft were there also—but attention was focused on the radical new four-engined design.

Preliminary flight tests were excellent. The staff at Wright Field was eagerly following the progress—speed, endurance, time of climb, service ceiling, structure, design, power plant, armament, equipment, and maintenance.

One morning in October, with a takeoff that should have now been routine, the plane seemed to be climbing too steeply. Abruptly, it pitched straight up, falling off on the wing, dropping and straightening out—but

Model XB-15

Old Grandpappy, a one and only, stretched the imagination of designers to the limit. The huge, 139 foot span wing incorporated an internal passageway running from the cabin to the engines, permitting inspection—and even minor repairs—while the airplane was in flight. The same basic wing design was employed later for the Model 314 *Clippers*.

not enough. Billowing flame and smoke enveloped the plane as it hit the ground, with the fire trucks already speeding toward it.

Jake Harman, now bombardment project engineer, heard the sirens, and someone shouting "299." He raced out, hailed a field car, and rushed to the site. Fire trucks were pouring foam on the burning plane. Harman jumped onto a flatbed truck, yelled at the driver, Lieutenant Giovanelli, to back it into the burning mass. Pulling their coats over their heads, with arms shielding their faces, the two men dashed into the inferno and dragged out Major Pete Hill, the pilot, and Les Tower. Lieutenant Don Putt, the project test pilot, face gashed and burned, had jumped out the front end. Two other crew members scrambled out the back. Major Hill died that afternoon. Les Tower, who had been on board as an observer, was badly burned, but expected to survive. The rest had lesser injuries.

Examination of the wreckage revealed that the plane had taken off with the control surfaces locked. The tail surfaces were so large that locks were put in place on the ground to guard against whipping in the wind. Having forgotten to remove the locks before takeoff, the crew had doomed the plane.

Under the rules, the 299 was ineligible for the final judging—it had not completed all the tests.

Egtvedt was devastated. Boeing treasurer, Harold Bowman, back at the plant, gazed mournfully at the overdrawn bank statement. Les Tower rallied, but took the accident personally, blaming himself for not removing the control locks. The overbearing remorse took the fight out of him, and suddenly he was gone.

Rumors came from Washington that the 299 was too big for a human being to handle—that the Douglas B-18, a bomber version of the DC-3—would win. Egtvedt clung to Dayton and Washington in an all out attempt to salvage the program.

The 600 employees were already thinking about a bleak Christmas, when the news came that the B-18 had won the production contract. Now they were certain.

However, the 299 had gained many converts in the Air Corps and in Washington. A service order was placed for thirteen airplanes, plus a fourteenth for structural test. The new plane—the B-17—became the *Flying Fortress*.

Fabrication of the giant XB-15, the designation for the Project "A" design, continued—and was completed in 1937. *Old Grandpappy*, the one and only, was twenty-six feet longer than the Model 299, and had a thirty-six foot greater wingspan, at the time representing the largest bomber ever built. On July 30, 1939, the XB-15 broke the world record for weight lifting held by the *Maxim Gorky*.

1. Boeing Archives.
2. Report to the Stockholders, The Boeing Airplane Company, 1934, 6.
3. Harold Mansfield, *Vision*, (New York: Popular Library, 1966), 50.
4. Igor Sikorsky, *The Story of the Winged-S*, (New York: Dodd, Mead & Company, 1938) 86.
5. James Gilbert, *The World's Worst Aircraft*, (New York: St. Martins Press, 1975), 99.
6. Mansfield, *Vision*, 53.
7. Ibid., 54.
8. Ibid., 55.

Model 314 *Clipper*—1937–1941

The *Ocean Queens* were designed for Pan American for both transatlantic and transpacific routes. The largest airplane then flying, it carried 75 passengers, with 40 berths.

CHAPTER NINE

The Ocean Queens

The world was just about the right size for Juan Trippe, but he needed bigger airplanes to conquer its skies. Early in 1929 he reached an agreement with Sikorsky to build two giant four-engined airships, designated the S-40—each costing $125,000. A third was optioned.

In April 1931, the first S-40 rolled out and began flight testing. With a range of 1,500 miles, the 58,000-pound amphibian could cruise at 115 miles per hour, flying at 13,500 feet. Trippe named the new planes *Clippers*. Speed was reckoned in knots, and time according to bells. The fifty passengers sat in Queen Anne chairs upholstered in blue and orange, in a walnut cabin with blue carpets.

On Columbus Day, October 10, 1931, Mrs. Herbert Hoover christened the *American Clipper* with a bottle of water from the Caribbean Sea. A new era in ocean flying had begun.

On November 19, 1931, the S-40 *flying boat* took off from Miami on its maiden flight to Panama with paying passengers on board. Charles Lindbergh was at the controls.

A hot meal was served aloft, the first prepared in an American overwater aircraft galley. Passengers dined at real tables draped with linen tablecloths, using heavy silverware.

Lindbergh was pleased with the airplane—but not satisfied. The S-40 was based on the twin-engined S-38, upgraded to four engines. He wanted a completely new airplane. Contemplation as to the next step in design occupied most of his thoughts. Thus, high above the Caribbean, Lindbergh turned the controls over to copilot Basil Rowe while he and Sikorsky ate lunch, and drew sketches on the menu. He wanted a range that would take them at least from San Francisco to Hawaii.

Trippe had set his mind on crossing oceans. He searched the world for undiscovered islands suitable for landing spots; considered artificial floating islands; aerial refueling; and even catapults operating from ships in the open sea.

The Germans had already developed the DO-X, a huge flying boat with twelve engines. Built in 1929, it had accommodations for sixty-nine on a luxurious shipboard scale. In May 1932, the DO-X made a successful crossing of the South Atlantic to Brazil, then flew island-by-island to New York, where it circled triumphantly over Manhattan, returning to Germany via Newfoundland.

In spite of the apparent success, the plane simply had too many fuel gobbling engines to warrant continued development.

Still, Trippe was arrogant enough to rate nothing as insoluble, and five months before Lindbergh and Sikorsky made the sketches for the S-42, he had sent letters to all six prominent U.S. manufacturers, asking them to design a high speed, multi-engined flying boat having a cruising range of 2,500 miles against 30-mile headwinds and providing for a crew of four together with at least 300 pounds of mail. Four of the six manufacturers told him he was dreaming. But Sikorsky agreed to the proposal, and the Glenn Martin Company of Baltimore did likewise.

The S-42 was test flown by Lindbergh on August 1, 1934. Fully loaded, it averaged 157.5 miles per hour over a 1,242 mile course. The range was 2,540 miles—with no passengers.

By year end, Trippe had three Sikorsky S-42s and three Martin M-130s about to be delivered, and he kept staring at the globe. It appeared he would have to challenge the Pacific at its widest point—via Hawaii.

The following spring, the S-42 took off for Hawaii on a proving flight. On return, heavy headwinds nearly spelled disaster. The calculated maximum time the plane could remain in the air was twenty-one and one half hours. When it landed in San Francisco, it had been in the air for twenty-three hours and forty-one minutes. Testing with a gauge stick, the flight engineer found no measureable fuel, reporting, "Just about damp at the bottom. I don't think we could have made it once around the bay."[1]

In Baltimore on October 9, 1935, the first of the new Martin M-130 flying boats was turned over to Pan American, and on October 21, the airmail contract for flying the Pacific was awarded. Pan American was the sole bidder.

Trippe announced, "This flying boat will be named the *China Clipper*, after her famous predecessor which carried the American flag across the Pacific a hundred years ago."[2]

On November 22, 1935, the *China Clipper* inaugurated regular service across the Pacific.

Around the world, history was moving in giant strides. In Europe, the seeds of war began to sprout as Chancellor Adolf Hitler renounced the Treaty of Versailles. Heinrich Himmler, chief of the SS, took command of Germany's concentration camps. Mussolini's armies invaded Ethiopia, and in China, Mao Tsetung embarked on his 6,000 mile Long March.

At home, the United States officially recognized the Communist government of the Soviet Union, and the Roosevelt administration initiated a number of programs to bring the nation out of the Great Depression. A watershed year for legislation, 1935 brought forth Social Security—the single most far reaching socio-economic statute of the twentieth century. The National Labor Relations Act also became law—prohibiting employers from interfering with a worker's right to join a union, requiring management to recognize unions, and directing management to bargain collectively with them.

Egtvedt had been considering the possibility of doing something with a commercial adaptation of the XB-15, and he was acutely aware of the plant limitations for building big flying boats, which the market seemed to be demanding. Financing also presented a major problem. With stockholders expecting a profit, 1935 ended in a loss of $334,000—even worse than the year before. Nevertheless, construction of the fourteen flying fortresses simply demanded additional facilities.

Planning was initiated for acquiring a new plant site. There had been a persistent rumor that a California company had offered Boeing the lease of enough land for a new factory for ten years, free of charge. A pioneer truck farmer by the name of Guisseppe Desimone—an ardent Boeing fan— took the rumors seriously, and didn't want the Company to leave Seattle. He had settled on the rich bottom land along the Duwamish, the prime location for a new facility.

No land was for sale in the area. Farming had been good to the Desimones, and Guisseppe had enough land to part with "40 acres for Boeing and the future of the Pacific Northwest."[3] He sold the land to Boeing for $1.

In April 1936, the Company announced its intent to construct a modern assembly building on the site. This one-million square foot addition covered more than twenty acres. Named Plant II, it was occupied in February, 1941. The old Heath facility became known as Plant I.

Not long after Wellwood Beall went to China to sell pursuit planes, Pan Am flew the S-42 to Hawaii, and it was rumored that China and the U.S. would soon be linked by regular air service.

Beall, poised and confident with his invariably flashy bow tie and trim mustache, had been quickly accepted by his peers as a man of exceptional insight. He insisted that air service was at least ten years away.

But it was not long before Beall began to have second thoughts. When Pan Am put the first of their three Martin flying boats into service in the Pacific, he realized he was far off the mark. Taking a tour of the factory where the XB-15 wing was being assembled, even Beall was awed by its massive beams and trusses—more like a bridge than an airplane.

For one fleeting instant a vision of a giant flying boat flashed through his brain—much bigger than the Martins, and capable of carrying at least fifty, perhaps seventy passengers.

In the days that followed, Beall tracked the XB-15 progress and studied the details. Unable to contain his personal enthusiasm any longer, he went to chief engineer Bob Minshall, proposing that the Company get back into the flying boat business. He wanted to submit a *Clipper* design to Pan Am—utilizing the XB-15 wing.

"We've already discussed that," Minshall told him. "Claire and I talked with Pan Am about it." He showed Beall the letter from Frank Gledhill, the Pan Am vice-president and purchasing agent, asking if Boeing would be interested in submitting plans for a long-range four-engined marine airplane built around engines of 1,000 to 1,250 horsepower.

"Great. That's right in the XB-15 class," Beall said.

"I know. But we can't do it."

"Why not?"

Minshall spelled out the problems—money, facilities, manpower. "Look at the date they want the drawings. We're up to our necks now." Minshall looked tired. Responsibility was putting furrows in his round, full face.

"I'd like to work on it if that would help," Beall said.

"We've already written Gledhill that we won't be able to enter."[4]

Beall went away disappointed. The huge wing seemed so right for a flying boat, and the idea continued to haunt him. He could not put it out of his mind. He began making drawings at home on the dining room table.

The concept slowly came into focus. Night after night, Beall labored over his drawings. He took the sketches to Minshall, who was impressed. Egtvedt was in Dayton, but Minshall called him and got the green light to request an extension of the bidding deadline. Gledhill agreed, and Beall was assigned to the new program.

After some intense working sessions, the specifications for the airplane were established. The giant seaplane would be 106 feet long with a wing-span of 152 feet, and standing over 27 feet in height. The cavernous hull would accommodate seventy-four passengers and a crew of six. Grossing 82,500 pounds, the big ship would have a range of 3,500 miles.

In Pan Am's headquarters in the Chrysler Building in New York, and the Barclay Hotel, Egtvedt, Beall, and aerodynamicist Ralph Cram hammered out the cost and performance guarantees. On June 21, 1936, a $3 million contract for six Model 314 *Clippers* was signed, with an option for six more.

Back at the plant, hiring began to pick up. The Company found many of its new recruits in the waves of dispossessed farmers from the dust bowl who migrated to the coast. They were green—knew nothing about building airplanes—but they were eager and ambitious, willing to work hard for a few dollars. Boeing expanded its training program—always one of its strong commitments—to meet the need.

On September 23, 1935 the International Association of Machinists (IAM) issued a charter to a union local at the Boeing plant in Seattle. With the new National Labor Relations Act, now law, the number of union members grew. The union president, 68-year-old Milton W. Potter, with a committee of others, approached Boeing management that month to seek a wage agreement. After much discussion, a contract was negotiated. The Company asked the NLRB to certify that the union had a majority membership among eligible employees. The union was certified and the Company signed a *union shop* contract covering production workers.[5]

Another milestone was passed in April 1936, when *Boeing News* began publication again, with Harold Mansfield hired as editor and publicity manager. Mansfield, destined to play a unique role in Boeing's history, had served as a reporter for the *Post-Intelligencer*—Seattle's morning newspaper—after graduating *cum laude* from the University of Washington in 1934.

By 1939, the union founded its own newspaper, the *Aero Mechanic*, official house organ for Aeronautical District 751.

The first of the Pan American *Clippers* was approaching the zero hour for launching in late May, 1938. Most of its 500,000 parts were now in it. Fred Laudan himself, quick stepping, quick talking, was all over the plant and in and out of project engineer Ed Duff's office to see about final changes.

Edmund E. "Ed" Duff was not easily ruffled, even though he was fairly new compared to Laudan, having joined Boeing after graduating in mechanical engineering from the University of Washington in 1928.

Carpenters had to cut away the entire back side of the assembly building so the hull could be dollied out to the newly built dock where high derricks could attach its wings.

A national radio network had its microphone set up on the dock on May 31, the day for launching. Harold Mansfield reported from the scene:

Tide tables set an insistent deadline of 5:00 P.M. for the ship to hit the water, so there would be ample depth to get through the shallows and link up to the barge for the trip down the waterway and into the bay.

"This mighty triumph of American enterprise, this great Flying *Clipper* ship that will span the Atlantic and the Pacific carrying the flag of the United States to world supremacy in the air, is being lowered majestically into the water here in Seattle." The announcer spotted Laudan coming by.

"The vice-president and factory manager of this plant, Mr. Fred P. Laudan, is directing the operation. We are going to ask him to say a few words to our nationwide audience." An assistant grabbed Laudan's arm and coaxed him to the microphone. "Mr. Laudan, what does this occasion mean to you?"

The harried Laudan spared one glance from his ship. "To me? It means just one big headache." Hurriedly, an aide summoned him away.

Newspapermen from the East arrived for the flight. Jim Piersol, the *New York Times* reporter, and something of an aeronautical engineer, wore a skeptic's scowl. "The tail is too small for all that airplane," he said.

"Quit worrying," said Beall. It's been tested. It's based on the XB-15 and that's doing all right."[6]

"On Wednesday, June 1, Eddie Allen revved up the four 1,200 horsepower Wright Cyclone engines and began taxi tests. The following Tuesday, the *Clipper* was loaded to a gross of 77,500 pounds, just 5,000 pounds under its maximum, and ready for takeoff.

"At 6:17 P.M., the great roar of the Cyclones sounded across the water and Eddie Allen was moving toward the picket boats. The watchers raced ahead to stay parallel. Salt spray in the face and high excitement aboard, they bounced through the waves as the big-hulled flying boat raced past them, sailing high on the step. Ahead, the great hull skimmed the surface, lifted up, steady in the air, up and up into the northern sky. Yells of applause broke into the freshness of the wind. They watched the flying *Clipper* sail out of sight.

"After a thirty-eight minute flight, Eddie Allen landed on Lake Washington, where further testing was to be based. Beall caught up with him later in the evening. 'We had power to spare,' Eddie said, 'but when I got off the water I couldn't turn. There's just not enough rudder for that big body. When we got to 2,000 feet, I used power on one side for a wide ten-mile turn.'"[7]

The 314 went back to the wind tunnel. The tail was changed to a double, and finally a triple configuration.

The first *Clipper* was delivered in January 1939—late—a result of the extensive testing after the maiden flight.

On March 3, 1939, having flown nonstop from Washington, D.C., the first Model 314 was christened the *Yankee Clipper* by Mrs. Franklin D. Roosevelt at Anacostia Naval Air Station.

FDR on the *Clipper*

President Franklin D. Roosevelt celebrates his 61st birthday aboard a wartime *Clipper*.

There was no champagne at the christening. She used a gold trimmed bottle of water gathered from the Seven Seas by Pan Am.

Regular passenger service, New York to Marseille, was announced for June 28. A timetable was printed, and fares established: $375 one way, $675 round trip, and the first ticket was sold to W.J. Eck, who was from Washington, D.C., and had applied for ticket No. 1 ten years before.

The *Yankee Clipper* was the largest airplane then flying. Its propellers cut an arc fourteen feet, ten inches in diameter. It had a maximum range of around 4,275 miles at 150 miles per hour, and it could seat up to seventy-four passengers, or sleep forty in berths. It had two decks, both carpeted, the upper deck being used exclusively for the crew. The lower deck contained five passenger compartments, plus a dining room seating fifteen people, and a kind of honeymoon suite self-contained in the rear. There were dressing rooms for men and women, each with its own toilet, and the gentleman's toilet included—for the first and last time in commercial flight—a separate urinal. Commercial aviation would never know such luxury again.

The *Clippers* were also employed on the Hong Kong route and made the first connection to Africa. Pan Am excercised its options for a second contingent of six airplanes, designated 314As, with greater fuel capacity, increased power, and a passenger load increased by three—to seventy-seven.

During World War II, the total fleet operated as C-98s for the Army and as B-314s for the Navy. They carried priority passengers and priority cargo only. Admirals and generals flew—kings and queens of beleaguered nations flew—such as Wilhemina of the Netherlands and George of Greece. Roosevelt himself flew, becoming the first incumbent president ever taken aloft.[8]

1. Robert Daley, *An American Saga*, (New York: Random House, 1980), 156.
2. Ibid., 166.
3. *Boeing News*, 19 December 1986, 3.
4. Harold Mansfield, *Vision*, (New York: Popular Library, 1966), 63.
5. K.L. Calkins, An analysis of Labor Relations News Coverage…, (Seattle: University of Washington, 1968), 12.
6. Mansfield, *Vision*, 72.
7. Ibid., 75.
8. Daley, *An American Saga*, 335.

CHAPTER TEN

The Four Engine Era

The beginning of Boeing's third decade in July 1936, marked a major transition in airplane manufacturing. The four-engine era had been opened with the Model 299 and the giant XB-15.

The flying boats, result of determined pioneering by Juan Trippe and innovative response by industry, epitomized by the *Clipper* Queens, were soon to conquer the last bastion of angry ocean, the North Atlantic—and nowhere in the world would be out of reach by airplane.

In September, although only a nucleus of the worldwide organization which was to develop, a service unit was formed, with Wellwood Beall in charge. Nemo Poncetti, having returned from his assignment in China, was hired into the Field Service Section of the Service Unit. From the beginning, this organization dedicated itself to providing customers with the best service in the world.

Thus, early in its corporate life, service became one of the principal pinions upon which The Boeing Company flew. The others: integrity, quality of product, technical excellence, and attention to people as the key resource.

In 1936, powerful forces signaled dramatic change around the world. On March 7, German infantry goose-stepped into Cologne. The Rhineland—established as a demilitarized zone after World I—was reoccupied. Three weeks later, a plebiscite gave Adolf Hitler a 99 percent vote of confidence. In November, Japan's Kursu and Italy's Ciano met with Hitler in Berlin, where they signed an anticommunist pact pledging cooperation against the spread of Soviet influence.

In Spain, civil war erupted in July, when General Francisco Franco, leader of the Fascist troops, vowed to press on until he had installed himself in Madrid.

In Africa, Ethiopia's defense against Italy crumbled, and the capital of Addis Ababa, jammed with refugees, was about to fall. Benito Mussolini boasted, "Italy at last has her empire."

In Asia, Chiang demanded war on Japan, seeking to rally all of China.

In the U.S., Franklin D. Roosevelt won reelection by a landslide, defeating Alfred M. Landon in the greatest outpouring of voters in the nation's history.

The U.S. Army general staff met in Washington, D.C. to discuss bombardment airplane procurement policy.

The Air Corps had a quantity of twin-engined Douglas B-18s on order, and thirteen four-engined Boeing B-17s, with a fourteenth to be used for structural testing. In Category Four of the development list made up in 1933, the mammoth, 164,000 pound XB-19, more than two and one-half times the gross weight of the XB-15, was being designed by Douglas.

At the meeting, the merits of very large airplanes received intense discussion. The twin-engined B-18 was equal to any mission assigned to the Air Corps and was much less expensive than the proposed four-engined airplanes. Many felt that the planes were getting too big for the materials of construction. In the final report to the chief of staff, it was concluded that concentration on big bombers was inconsistent with national policy and threatened duplication of the Navy, which was assigned to protect the country beyond 200 miles from its shores. At this juncture, the future of the B-17 looked bleak indeed.

In Dayton, Jake Harman was still lobbying hard to get more bombers.

Colonel Oliver Echols, the Air Corps engineering chief, called him in. "Look Jake," the colonel said, "I have an idea. We aren't going to get any more than thirteen B-17s for awhile.

"We could make it fourteen if we made a flying airplane out of the one that is designated for structural tests. I doubt that we need those tests. Why don't we use that airplane to put in turbo-superchargers for high altitude?

"Harman thought it was an excellent idea. The engine turbo-supercharger, developed by Dr. Sanford Moss of General Electric with the aid of Wright Field engineers, utilized a turbine wheel driven by exhaust gases. The turbine was used to pump high pressure air into the engines for increased power at thin-air altitudes.

"What would turbos do for the speed of the '17?" Echols asked.

"Harman got out his slide rule and worked the numbers back and forth. 'At 25,000 feet, maybe 290 miles an hour.'

"Get hold of Claire Egtvedt and find out if Boeing will do it. I'll see if I can dig up the money."[1]

Bold innovation proved once again to be king of the industry. In one corner of the engineering department at Seattle, a few drafting tables were separated from the rest by a glass partition. On the door was a sign—*Restricted Area—Preliminary Design*. Ed Wells was in charge.

"Every so often, Claire Egtvedt would go down and lean over Ed Well's table. This time he had a new question. Did they have enough information on turbo-superchargers to put them on the B-17?

"Ed said he wasn't sure, but that he could get it.

"'Oliver Echols wants to equip the static test ship for high altitudes.'

"'How high?'

"'Twenty-five or thirty thousand feet.'

"'Not cabin supercharging?'

"'No, just engines.' But Egtvedt added when they discussed it further, that he didn't think they could always be partial to the engines. The people in the airplane needed air as well. Something will have to be done sooner or later about supercharging the passenger cabin."[2]

The modified airplane was called the YB-17A, and operating altitudes were increased to above 30,000 feet. The "17A" performed so well, validating the high altitude bombing capability, that thirty-nine of the new supercharger-equipped planes were ordered—designated as the B-17B.

Preliminary design, a small, select group, was the gestation center for new projects—shrouded in a certain aura of secrecy. All the manufacturers had them. At Douglas, experimental machines came out of an area called "The Holy of Holies," and at Lockheed, "The Skunk Works."

The latest new Boeing project was announced on George Washington's birthday in February 1937, when it was revealed that Transcontinental and Western Air Inc., had ordered six airplanes of a Model 307. It was named the *Stratoliner.*

Everywhere the coming four-engined transports became a subject for lively dialogue. A center spread Boeing ad in the March 15 issue of *Time* proclaimed: "The 4-Engine Era is here!"

With the boast, "Boeing has always built tomorrow's airplanes today!" the ad noted that the Boeing production line currently contained FOUR-ENGINED BOMBERS, FOUR-ENGINED TRANSPORTS, AND FOUR-ENGINED 'CLIPPERS.'[3]

Almost immediately, Pan Am announced they would purchase two Model 307s equipped for flying in the sub-stratosphere, and descriptive stories of the vast possibilities opened by this new type of plane, flowed from the pens of pundits.

With a gross weight of 42,000 pounds, the Model 307 accommodated thirty-three daytime passengers, in addition to a crew of four, and twenty-six passengers on overnight flights, with berths for eighteen, and reclining chairs for the remaining eight. The cargo capacity was 3,750 pounds, greater than the entire payload of the two-engined airplanes in service at the time. Powered by four Wright G-100 series Cyclone engines, capable of developing a total of 4,400 horsepower, the plane could cruise easily at over 200 miles per hour, attaining a speed of 250 at high altitudes.

The pressurized cabin, a spectacular first, augured well for Boeing to wrest the commercial leadership from Douglas.

The extra speed attainable at high altitudes—with sea level comfort for the passengers—and berths for night flying, made the airplane unique in the commercial field.

On December 31, 1938, Eddie Allen and a crew of four took the first *Stratoliner* into the air. Tests went well.

An electric atmosphere pervaded the engineering department—they had scored once again with a first in the industry.

There are times, however, when brains and guts are not enough. Technology plays no favorites, and the elusive edge of innovation can evaporate like the morning mist. Luck—a double-edged sword—can deliver fame and fortune, or can as easily, turn what appear to be golden opportunities into black despair.

The *Stratoliner*, ahead of its time and full of promise, was pushed too far in its test program. In March 1939, two representatives of the Dutch airline, KLM, were in Seattle to fly the airplane. They posed a very improbable flight situation, inquiring what would happen if two engines were out on the same side and the rudder was full-over for maximum yaw. When Boeing aerodynamicist Ralp Cram replied that there was no reason for that maneuver with such a big ship, Dutch engineer Albert von Baumhauer was not satisfied. They decided to try various angles of yaw, and measure the forces on the control column.

Later that bright Saturday afternoon, the sheriff's office called to report that a giant plane had crashed in the foothills of Mt. Rainier. During the test, the plane had approached stalling speed and gone into a spinning dive. An eyewitness reported that the plane had fallen out of the sky in pieces.

Sheriff's deputies had taken test pilot Julius Barr's body out of the pilot's seat; von Baumhauer's from the copilot's seat; chief engineer Jack Kylstra, Ralph Cram, Earl Ferguson, and five others from the remaining wreckage.

Robert "Bob" Minshall, chief engineer—newly elected to the board of directors—who was in charge, held his head and wept.

An old timer, Bob Minshall had joined the engineering department in 1918. He attended the University of Washington on a part-time basis, receiving a degree in civil engineering in 1923. Chief test pilot Eddie Allen, who was hired a few months after the maiden flight of the *Stratoliner*, came into Minshall's office shortly after the crash investigation was completed.

"'We have the opportunity here that exists nowhere else, Bob. We've come to the point where we need extensive research. Not just on the ground, but in the air—flight and aerodynamic research.'

Minshall was interested.

"'Now,' Eddie's finger shot up enthusiastically, 'you can't do that sort of thing in small airplanes. You have to carry all kinds of instruments and equipment. Here you are with a stable full of big airplanes. You're the ones to do it.'

"'Just what do you have in mind, Eddie?'

"'The day when you build an airplane and call in a pilot like me to test it is over. There should be a full-time, fully staffed department constantly carrying on this flight reasrch, and the same department should carry on a constant program of wind tunnel research. The two go hand in hand. They should be a part of designing the plane, not just testing it.'"[4]

Minshall discussed Allen's proposal with Egtvedt, and soon a department for aerodynamics and flight research was created, with Eddie Allen as the director.

Gathering a staff for his new department, in 1939 Allen hired George S. Schairer, a brilliant young aerodynamicist from Swarthmore College, who earned his masters degree at MIT. He was destined to leave his mark on Boeing airplane projects for the next thirty-eight years.

The thrust of the Model 307 program was blunted by the crash investigation. Only ten *Stratoliners* were built, five of them taken into the Army Air Corps as C-75s during World War II, where they pioneered the Air Transport Command's transatlantic routes.

Donald Douglas reached his quarter century mark in the aviation industry on July 6, 1939. A year earlier, he had developed a prototype for the DC-4, a four-engined commercial transport known as the DC-4E, which embodied many new advances in the state of the art. The DC-4 represented another giant step in commercial aviation. Roughly three times the size of the DC-3, the plane could carry forty-two passengers in a pressurized, sound proofed cabin. For the first time, the tail wheel was replaced with a nose wheel, providing a level platform for the plane on the ground.

Shortly after the announcement, forty airplanes had been ordered by domestic airlines—but none were delivered. After Pearl Harbor, with an urgent need for military transport, the Army Air Corps took over the orders, and the airplane went to war as the C-54 *Skymaster*. The thousands of hours of wartime flying proved the big plane, and assured Douglas of a continuing claim to the post war commercial sky.

The impact of the DC series on market share was boldly highlighted in the figures released from the Civil Aeronautics Authority in July 1939. Scheduled commercial aircraft in service and in reserve for the big three manufacturers were: Douglas, 183; Boeing, 45; and Lockheed, 42.

1. Harold Mansfield, *Vision*, (New York, Popular Library, 1966), 68.
2. Ibid., 68.
3. *Time,* 15 March, 1937, Centerfold.
4. Mansfield, *Vision*, 81, 82.

CHAPTER ELEVEN

The Flying Fortress

Boeing was in over their heads. The first nine
months of 1939 showed a loss of $2,600,000. Money would be needed—
quickly.

With the early *Clippers* posting a loss, the *Stratoliner* doomed, and General Echols reporting that the War Department in Washington had turned
down his request for funds for four-engined bombers for fiscal 1940-41, it
was difficult for officials at Boeing to find any silver lining in the dark clouds.

At Douglas, the DC-3 was being manufactured for both foreign and
domestic operators, with deliveries averaging six aircraft per month. The B-
18A was in production, with orders on hand for 217 airplanes. France had
placed an order for 100 DB-7s, an improved version of the 7B twin-engine
attack bomber built for the U.S. Army. A further refinement of the DB-7
design, the A-20A, was well advanced, and 123 airplanes were to be built for
the Army. Finally, the U.S. Navy had ordered 144 SBD scout bombers.[1]

Lockheed, with the eleven-passenger, Model 14, turned a profit in 1936—the first since 1929. With a continuing sure sense for image building, the company promoted the round-the-world flight of Howard Hughes in 1938. With a crew of four, Hughes established a new record of three days and nineteen hours. The world shrank, and sales boomed. The fourteen-seat Model 18 *Lodestar* followed. That airplane put Lockheed in the big time to stay, appearing in the war as the *Ventura* bomber.

Following his instincts, Gross sent his brother, Courtland, to England in 1937 to attempt to interest the British in a modified *Super Electra* to serve as a medium-range bomber. At the time, the British were sold on diplomacy as the solution to the demands of Nazi Germany, and Lockheed came up empty-handed.

Not one to be squeamish about customers, Gross took his offers to the Germans, again returning with no orders. The Germans said "no thanks, our aircraft industry is quite adequate." He even tried Japan, where he had better luck, concluding a contract on the eve of war in 1939.[2]

Undaunted by his limited success abroad, Gross turned back to the needs of the United States. His engineering department had grown both in numbers and in expertise, including a talented visionary, Clarence "Kelly" Johnson.

Johnson's first creation was one that captured the imagination of friend and foe alike in World War II, becoming one of the growing symbols of American air power, the P-38. It was dramatically different from any airplane that had ever flown. With a raised tail, twin booms extending from the two engines, all the way back to the tail, and only a central bubble for a fuselage, it was not only wildly beautiful, it performed. Quickly gaining the moniker of *Lockheed Lightning*, the plane went into mass production.

The British market did not evade Lockheed for long. In 1938, the British sent a delegation to the United States, visiting the major aircraft builders to determine how they could supplement their own industry.

According to a Lockheed legend, the five-day advance notice of the arrival of the British team gave them sufficient time, working around the clock, to build a plywood model of a bomber version of the Model 14 airplane.

Without fanfare, a production order for 175 machines was placed, for a contract value of $25 million. The airplane was named the *Hudson*. Orders added—and multiplied.

Work was also continuing on the Excalibur Project, a planned thirty-passenger answer to the latest version of the DC-3 and the *Stratoliner*. Des-

B-17 Series—*Flying Fortress*—1936–1945
The workhorse of the American bombing of Germany in World War II.

ignated the L-44, the airplane became the nucleus for preliminary design studies by Kelly Johnson for a still larger airplane. The audacious target was for transcontinental range and a speed of 300 miles per hour.

Multimillionaire Howard Hughes, who had gained control of Trans World Airlines, encouraged Lockheed to go forward, ordering nine while the airplane was not much beyond the doodling stage.

The product was the *Constellation*. When Pan American placed an order—for forty planes—Hughes increased the TWA order to forty. Thus, both Lockheed and Douglas had guaranteed themselves firm positions in the postwar commercial airplane market—even before the United States entered the war.

Angry currents flowed in Europe and Asia, with events marching to a quickened cadence. On September 5, 1937, the streets of Nuremburg were lined with storm troopers, as hundreds of trains converged on the city, bringing 600,000 German soldiers to hear their Fuhrer. On February 4, 1938, Adolf Hitler named himself as supreme commander of the German armed

B-17 Engine and Wing Line

Final Assembly, Boeing Plant II, Seattle, at peak production.

B-17 Fuselage Line

forces, and in March, followed his columns of tanks into Austria. By September, a four-power conference in Munich reached an agreement to divide Czechoslovakia, and German troops goose-stepped unhindered into the Sudetenland. Neville Chamberlain, prime minister of England, announced that the agreement "would bring peace in our time."

In March 1939, Madrid fell to General Francisco Franco, and the Spanish Civil War was history. In May, Hitler and Mussolini signed a "pact of steel", pledging mutual support.

After stunning the world with a nonaggression pact with Stalin on August 23, Hitler sent a mighty German force of 1.25 million men across the Polish border on September 1. Russian troops invaded from the east two weeks later. On September 3, 1939, Britain and France declared war.

In Nanking, Chiang Kai-shek and Mao Tsetung agreed to fight together against their common enemy, Japan.

At Boeing, it seemed inconceivable that the B-17 would not be ordered in large numbers. What was needed was an all-out effort to organize for mass production.

Lawyer Bill Allen went to talk things over with Claire Egtvedt. "'Why don't you try to get Phil Johnson back in the company?'" Allen suggested. Phil had been gone since the time of the breakup of the United Aircraft and Transport Corporation in 1934. "'The need now is production. That's Phil's long suit.'"[3]

In August 1939, Johnson came back as president, and Egtvedt became chairman. Recognizing the increasing significance of public relations, Johnson appointed Harold Mansfield to the new post of public relations manager.

With Mansfield, public relations took on a new importance in the Company, and the post eventually was elevated to vice presidential status under Harold Carr. In the entire history of the Company, there were only four men to hold this post, and all four were graduates of the University of Washington school of journalism. Following Mansfield were Carl Cleveland, Peter Bush, and Carr. When Carr retired, public relations was completely reorganized, and the title changed.

While the initial B-17B was yet to be delivered, scheduled for July 29, 1939, Boeing was requested to work out a license agreement with Consolidated in San Diego to start up a second production line. Consolidated responded by promising a new airplane—larger and faster than the four-year-old Boeing design. Herein lay the latent hazard that plagued all manufacturers of airplanes. As soon as new technology was committed to production and significant funds invested in hard tooling, competitors could offer riskless, incremental growth with zero investment. Those offers became known in the industry as "paper airplanes."

When the first $50 million of Roosevelt's rearmament program was authorized by Congress, the Consolidated program was given the green light, launching a direct competitor for the B-17—the B-24 *Liberator*.

Timing for the U.S. armed forces had also become crucial. With Congress routinely turning down appropriations for long range bombers as "aggressive"—with the potential of embroiling the U.S. in "Europe's war"—September 1, 1939 forced a complete rewrite of the rules of engagement.

A study ordered by Chief of Staff Malin Craig, to be delivered to his desk before his term expired—coincidentally on September first—made some sobering recommendations. The report hit the desk of General George Marshall, new chief of staff, the same day that Hitler's legions had begun the crushing defeat of Poland.

The report sounded a clear warning that naval forces and coastal guns were no longer sufficient to protect the United States. The bottom line spelled out the need for a flexible, long range air fleet. Marshall appointed General Frank Andrews—a strong advocate of the *Flying Fortresses*—as chief of operations on his staff.

The impact hit Wright Field like a tornado. Not only was the fire lit under B-17 procurement, but urgent discussion began on a "big bomber" which had previously been limited to the dreams of bomber enthusiasts.

The official notice reached Boeing on February 5, 1940. The circular requested companies to submit proposals within one month of receipt, for a 5,333 mile-range high-altitude, high-speed bombardment airplane, designated as the R-40B.

Although some were already viewing the B-17 as a stopgap airplane, the need had become urgent. In the fall of 1939, thirty-eight of a still newer version, the "C," were ordered for delivery in 1940.

Close on the heels of the "C" came the "D," with leak-proof bladders in the fuel bays and more powerful engines, now up to 1,200 horsepower.

The "E" came out in 1941. The 30 caliber machine guns were replaced with

50s. In addition, a Sperry ball turret replaced the belly gun position, and a powered turret was installed on top of the fuselage.

When Paris fell on June 14, 1940, General Echols told Boeing "All previous estimates are obsolete. We'll contract for 512 "E" models, but there'll be lots more later."[4]

Assembly lines were established at both Douglas and Lockheed. In 1942 the "F" model came out, and finally the "G." A new chin turret, pioneered on the "F," became standard equipment.

Although not destined to break into the big three in commercial airplane production, Consolidated was a giant in building military airplanes. Put together in 1923 from remnants of one of the largest manufacturers of World War I airplanes, Dayton-Wright Company—and one of the smallest—Gallaudet Aircraft Corporation, Consolidated was largely the efforts of one man—Reuben "Reub" Fleet.

On May 15, 1918, Major Reuben Fleet was put in charge of the U.S. airmail service. After the war, he served nearly four years as contracting officer and business manager of the Air Service Engineering Division, at McCook Field, Dayton, Ohio. Fleet brought a number of key people at Wright Field with him to Consolidated.

Under Major Fleet, the B-24 went forward at a feverish pace.

The March 30 contract called for first flight in nine months, before the end of 1939. The B-24 had innovations of its own, including a tricycle landing gear, first for a large bomber.

In 1943, Consolidated merged with Vultee, forming Convair, one of the largest integrated aircraft manufacturers of the World War II period.

Headlines extolling the exploits of the *Flying Fortresses* in raids over Germany, left the *Liberators* in their shadow—nevertheless, the airplane enjoyed the largest production run by far of any American aircraft. A total of 18,481 *Liberators* were built, more than half at the two Convair plants at San Diego and Fort Worth.

In 1942 the Seattle Division, for its B-17 record, and the Wichita Division, for its *Kaydet* trainer, gave Boeing the honor of being the first airframe manufacturer to be selected by the U.S. government for the joint Army-Navy "E" award for excellence.

Labor turnover was unusually high, primarily due to military induction and enlistments. To replace these men, the Company began early to employ and train female factory workers. In March 1942, about 2.6 percent of factory employees were female. Housewives came to work in droves, and by December 31, 1942, 42 percent of the factory work force in the Seattle plant were women. In 1943, the percentage peaked at over 50 percent.

Rosie the Riveter became the domestic hero of the war years, and a proud badge for women workers. At Boeing, 20 percent of all employees were riveters. Wearing colorful bandanas, they brought a new dimension to the work force, forming closely coordinated teams of two—riveter and bucker.

Engineering, a profession generally considered to be an exclusive arena for men, took a major upswing in female employees during the war years.

The "Forts" saw action in every theater of operations in World War II. Volumes have been written about their exploits—and their integrity.

The key to their phenomenal performance was the wing, which came through the entire series with no major structural changes.

As the power was increased, the body grew, armor and firepower was added; the loading on the wing simply went up.

Since stress analysis at the time was not sufficiently sophisticated to reliably include the wing skin as a load-carrying member, all the stresses were taken into account in the internal structure. In reality, the skin carried major loads.

Seemingly incredible events attested to the quality of design and manufacture that Boeing people had built into the *Flying Fortresses*.

On January 27, 1942, *Werewolf* limped home from a raid on Brest on one engine.

On October 17, 1942, *Flaming Jenny* returned to its base in England from a raid on northern France with flames raging from nose to tail, left outboard wing and number one engine gone—it had sustained more than 2,000 bullet holes.

In all, 12,726 B-17s were built—6981 by Boeing, 2,995 by Douglas, and 2,750 by Lockheed Vega.

1. Crosby Maynard, *FLIGHT PLAN FOR TOMORROW*, Douglas Aircraft Company, 1962.
2. David Boulton, *The Grease Machine*, (New York: Harper & Row, 1978), 29.
3. Harold Mansfield, *Vision*, (New York: Popular Library, 1966), 83.
4. Ibid., 91.

Rosie the Riveter

Rosie and her bucker, riveting B-17 wing front spars.

CHAPTER TWELVE

The B-29

In May 1941—the last commercial airplane on order, a Model 314 *Clipper*—was delivered to Pan American. Boeing turned its entire energies to the war.

With the factory going all out on B-17 production, the engineering department keyed to the R-40B superbomber. In order to have a prayer of meeting the 5,333 mile range target, drag would have to be reduced drastically.

Someone suggested putting water-cooled engines inside the wings—eliminating the nacelle entirely—with the propeller shafts sticking out in front. Ed Wells didn't like the design—there was no way to retract the landing gear, and the structure was poor around the engines. He arranged a brainstorming session with George Schairer and Wellwood Beall.

Schairer had an idea. "Had you thought of going at it the other way around? The wing itself is the biggest item of drag. Why not make the wing as thin as we can, and then go to work cleaning up the nacelles?"[1]

Subsequent studies showed that a thin wing would give them the range—and the speed went up dramatically.

There was only one problem, and it was major. Such a wing required a loading nearly double the thirty-five pounds per square foot that had long been considered the upper limit.

To achieve the required loading, the traditional truss structure was discarded. In its place, the modern wing evolved—spanwise spars at the leading and trailing edges—connected by chordwise ribs. The result was a structural box, which relied heavily on loading the skin.

With the German fighter force increasing its ferocity with every new battle, the Army Air Corps pushed for more guns, more armor, more bombs. The original target of 48,000 pounds grew to 85,000. Echols latest wish list would add still another 26,000 pounds.

Minshall suggested they work on an alternative smaller airplane in parallel, and Wells directed his engineers to start a new design. The more Wells looked at the alternative, the less he liked the big airplane. Finally he and Minshall went to see Phil Johnson.

"'We don't feel right about the big airplane,' Wells told the president. 'Maybe we should drop it and submit a smaller one.'

"Phil Johnson recognized Well's quiet sincerity. On the other hand, he knew what the customer wanted.

"'Now Ed' he said, 'if you *had* to make a good airplane out of this, could you do it?'

"Wells looked at Johnson. He thought for a moment, then answered, 'Yes.'

"Johnson smiled. 'Let's submit it and win the competition.'"[2]

On May 11, 1940, Beall took the latest design data to General Oliver Echols at Wright Field. Don Euler stayed, waiting for the result. Suddenly, Major H.Z. Bogert, acting chief of the experimental engineering section summoned him.

"We're giving you a contract to cover engineering and wind tunnel models and a wooden mockup of your plane. We're designating it the B-29.

"Push it. Cut the red tape. Move. We may want two hundred of them."[3]

Euler reeled from the office to phone the plant. Two hundred! They had never built a B-29.

In September 1940, developmental contracts were awarded to Boeing for the XB-29—and to Consolidated for the XB-32. Wing spans were 141 feet for the XB-29, and 135 feet for the XB-32. The huge Douglas XB-19, delayed in development—with new technology passing it by—was discon-

Model B-29—*Superfortress*—1942–1945
The B-29 was the air power of the Pacific in World War II.

tinued. The one and only XB-19 flew on June 27, 1941, serving as a flying laboratory for later innovations.

More changes—and more additions—went into the XB-29. The gross weight went up to 120,000 pounds, the wing loading to 69 pounds per square foot.

In a walled-off portion of Plant II at Seattle, the first XB-29 began to take form. Construction was under way in Wichita, Kansas, on a huge plant that would produce the planes.

The Air Corps hedged its bets to the end. Consolidated had been awarded a contract for three XB-32s and thirteen additional airplanes for service test, and later was awarded contracts for over 1,500 production airplanes. But after 114 were built, the contracts were terminated. Some of the planes were used for training, and before the end of the war, fifteen saw action in the Pacific.

More aerodynamic research and testing was conducted to develop the B-29 than on any previous Boeing airplane. The new wing gave the B-29 no more drag than the B-17, in spite of its much greater size. The flaps, which constituted almost 20 percent of the total wing area, were the largest ever used on any airplane up to that time.

The airplane went through eight major design changes on paper before construction was begun. When all the design modifications were completed, the range was increased to nearly 6,000 miles. The top speed was raised from 248 to 363 miles per hour, and the maximum bomb load increased from 5,800 to 20,000 pounds.

At Renton, on the south end of Lake Washington, near Seattle, a completely new plant was rising—not for B-29s, but for a strange new bird for the Navy. With submarines and surface raiders preying on shipping on both oceans, aerial reconnaissance was the only way to patrol the vast areas involved. The Navy wanted an airplane that could remain aloft for three days and nights without refueling in the air.

For that mission, Boeing designed the XPPB-1, an experimental bomber and patrol airplane, named the *Sea Ranger*. Three-fourths as large as the Model 314 *Clippers*, the huge flying boat had only two engines, and fully loaded, was unable to take off under its own power. To achieve the marathon missions, the plane was designed to be catapulted into the air.

Taking the empty plane up on her maiden flight on July 9, 1942, test pilot Eddie Allen reported excellent handling characteristics. However, the program was overtaken by fast moving events. Originally conceived as a successor to the Consolidated *PBYs*—the backbone of the naval air patrol fleet—its 158 mph cruise speed was its Achilles heel. Shortly after December 7, 1941, the Japanese attacked Dutch Harbor in Alaska. The slow moving *PBYs* were downed like sitting ducks—and the *Sea Ranger* was obsolete. The project was canceled, and the plane, renamed the *Lone Ranger*, faded into history.

Production workers continued under the contract originally negotiated with the Aero Mechanics Union in 1937. During the war years, Company–union relations were governed by the War Labor Board. However, at one point in February 1943, union members walked off the job in protest of the board's delay in granting a wage increase. It was the first work stoppage in Boeing's twenty-seven-year history. The union's half-day march to city hall in Seattle, achieved the desired results. The War Labor Board granted the increase.

At the University of Chicago, working under the top secret, $2 billion Manhattan Project, a group of physicists led by Enrico Fermi, achieved the first controlled nuclear reaction with fissioning uranium. The die was cast for the marriage of this awesome new weapon to the B-29.

The XB-29—first of the new breed—named the *Superfortress*—rolled out of the Plant II factory in September 1942. After packing it with measuring equipment, Eddie Allen and a crew of seven took the airplane into the air for its maiden flight. The date was September 21.

Eddie came back with an eloquent smile. "She flies," he announced.[5]

Manufacturing for mass production had already begun, and the newly completed plant at Renton, no longer needed for Navy airplanes, was assigned to the exclusive production of *Superforts*.

As flight testing continued, power plant troubles surfaced. In the first twenty-six hours of flight time, engines had to be changed sixteen times, carburetors were changed twenty-two times, and the exhaust system had to be redesigned. Allen felt they should discontinue flight testing until more laboratory and design studies were completed. But there was a war on. The weekly casualty lists were grim reminders. Testing continued.

On February 18, 1943, a day which found the Boeing executive staff gathered in the boardroom for their weekly meeting, an urgent call was piped to the anteroom. Ed Wells slipped out to answer it. He reappeared at the door, face ashen.

"The tower just got a message from Eddie. They're coming in with a wing on fire."[6]

The airplane was over Tacoma, about thirty miles south of Boeing Field when the fire started. They were able to extinguish it with the CO_2 bottle. Allen elected to return to the field. The wind was from the south, and he headed over Seattle to come in from the north. A second fire broke out when he was turning for the final approach. The fire reached the fuel tanks just as the plane neared the runway.

Losing altitude rapidly, and with one wing completely ablaze, the plane crashed into the Frye meat packing plant, a five-story, brick building adjacent to the field.

It was standard procedure on test flights to wear parachutes, and a moment before the crash, three men bailed out in a desperate—and futile—attempt to save their lives.

The remainder of the eleven-man crew perished in the fire—along with more than a score of people on the ground—primarily employees of the plant. Eddie Allen was still strapped in—at the controls—fighting the doomed machine to the last.

Father of three, at forty-seven, Allen was regarded as "the greatest test pilot aviation has ever had."[7] His first connection with Boeing was in 1927—flying the mail. He worked as a freelance pilot for many years, testing products of a number of leading airplane manufacturers. In 1939, he joined Boeing, however he was still loaned to others for critical testing. In fact on January 9, 1943, scarcely two months before the fatal crash of the XB-29, Allen had flown the Lockheed *Constellation* on its first test flight. "His hand on the controls cut first-flight insurance rates in half."[8]

The next day, at the McDermott building, a rented facility in downtown Seattle, where the B-29 engineering project was housed because of shortage of space at Plant II, the entire force increased its normal fifty-one and one half hour week to seventy-four. Certain features of the wing and nacelles were redesigned to provide internal ventilation, preventing the accumulation of explosive fuel vapors.

A memorial went up at Plant II, where Allen's dream began its first increment. A new wind tunnel, the first to be located at any Boeing plant, was dedicated on April 22, 1944. Appropriately, it was named the Edmund T. Allen Wind Tunnel and Aeronautical Research Laboratories.

In Wichita, Kansas, 200 acres of prairie had been transformed into a vast manufacturing plant, teeming with 29,000 employees: converted farm hands, housewives, and shopkeepers.

The first Wichita-built B-29 was in the air in June, 1943.

Early in the delivery program, the *Battle of Kansas*, an effort to work out the manufacturing bugs which developed as a result of getting parts from so many different places, was fought. In March 1944, the first combat ready *Superfort* was loaded. Earl Schaefer, general manager of the Wichita plant, was there.

"How heavy are you loading these?" he asked.

"135,000."

"135,000! Do you know the maximum gross is 120,000?"

"Yeah, we know. Your maximum on the B-17 was 48,000. We flew at 60,000 all the time in England."[9]

The planes were loaded to 135,000, and later to 140,000 pounds.

Early one morning late in March, Colonel Jake Harman took off for India, the first leg toward establishing bases in China, and on June 15, sixty-eight B-29s departed from handmade runways in Chengdu to bomb the steel works in Yawata, Japan.

By early 1945, massive firebombing raids were being made over Japan, with B-29s based in the Mariana Islands. In a single raid on March 9, 1945, 334 B-29s attacked the city of Tokyo, raining fire that appeared to nearly destroy the city.

Finally, at 9:15 A.M. on Monday, August 6, the *Enola Gay*, a *Superfort* piloted by Colonel Paul W. Tibbets Jr., released *Little Boy* over Hiroshima, wiping out more than four square miles—60 percent of the city of 343,000.

Less than 1,000 miles to the south, the U.S. Tenth Army was still landing soldiers on the Hagushi beaches on Okinawa. The thin Missouri twang of President Harry Truman came on the radio—announcing the cataclysmic event which had taken place at Hiroshima. Although they had no comprehension of the power of an atomic bomb, the soldiers knew intuitively that *Operation Olympic*—the landing of 1.5 million troops on the Japanese beaches, scheduled for November—would not occur. For a few brief moments their main concern was to avoid being killed by the flak falling all around—from the guns of supporting ships—which had erupted in a literal firestorm.

Three days later, *Fat Man* was dropped, destroying Nagasaki, and on August 15, Japan surrendered.

A total of 3,970 *Superforts* were built; 2,766 by Boeing, 668 by Bell, and 536 by Martin. That magnificent battle-plane took its place as a major instrument of both peace and war in a century in which mankind stared at oblivion—and oblivion blinked.

1. Harold Mansfield, *Vision*, (New York: Popular Library, 1966), 83.
2. Ibid., 90.
3. Ibid., 91
4. Ibid., 106
5. Private Communication.
6. Ibid.
7. *Time*, 1 March 1943, 56.
8. Ibid., 18 January, 1943, 72.
9. Mansfield, *Vision*, 137.

William M. Allen 1900–1985
President 1945–1968, Chairman 1968–1972.

CHAPTER THIRTEEN

Postwar Challenges

At Lockheed, the four employees of 1932 had blossomed to over 90,000 by the end of World War II. Production was equally impressive. Lockheed produced 2,900 *Hudsons* and 2,600 *Venturas* in addition to 10,000 P-38s.

When the war ended, Lockheed was the largest defense contractor in the Western world. Inevitably, in 1945, the company was one of the first to be dropped out of military production. Initially viewed as a disaster, the event was actually a fortunate one, putting Lockheed at the forefront in the postwar commercial market.

That enviable position was the result of timing, foresight—and plain luck. On April 17, 1944, fifteen months after Eddie Allen—on loan from Boeing—flight tested the *Constellation*, Howard Hughes flew the initial production model from Burbank to Washington, D.C. in a record time for a commercial airplane of six hours, forty-three minutes, and thirty seconds.

Pearl Harbor and the entry of the United States into the war had not halted, or even interrupted, the development work on the *Constellation*, as it had done on its major competitor, the Boeing *Stratoliner*. Thus, production of the world's largest, fastest, and most sophisticated airliner was continued during the war.

By the end of 1945, 20 *Constellations* had been sold to TWA, 6 to BOAC, and 5 to other airlines. Yet to come were orders for 105 more, valued at $75 million—sold to Pan American, Eastern, and American in the United States—and to both Air France and KLM in Europe.

Douglas was in an excellent position to challenge the Lockheed *Constellation* for commercial air transport leadership. Incorporating the latest technology developed during the war, and distilling the experience gained from millions of flying hours with the DC series, Douglas quickly brought out the DC-6.

A DC-5 had been designed at about the same time as the DC-4—and somewhat to the confusion of historians—was produced first.[1] Many of the systems and structural developments of the DC-3 were adapted to the DC-5, but the over-body, high wing configuration resulted in a greater empty weight, penalizing payload and range. Only twelve DC-5s were manufactured.

On November 24, 1946, the first DC-6, a beefed up, speeded-up, continuation of the "DC" line, was delivered to both United and American Airlines.

The DC-6 boasted a sophisticated cabin control system, providing for a 5,000-foot altitude environment, while flying at 20,000 feet.

By the end of 1944, Douglas had booked orders for 175 of their DC-6 model. Soon to follow were the DC-6A and B.

With Boeing bombers in the news for six years, at war's end, the Company was hardly viewed as a producer of commercial airplanes. As early as 1944, President Phil Johnson was hedging his bet that there would be an orderly return to civil air transportation. He ordered an engineering unit to look into a non-aircraft postwar line. Included in those studies were a low-priced automobile, as well as kitchen and bedroom equipment.

The Company had returned to profitability in 1940—earning $374,655—representing 1.9 percent of sales. Then, in 1941, with sales soaring five-fold, net profits leaped to $6,113,143.

This pleasant state of affairs was not to continue. In spite of unprecedented production, profits were extremely low during the remainder of the war years, with a disappointing trend. In terms of sales, the Company realized net profits of 1.35, 0.91, and 0.86 percent, respectively, for the years 1942–1944. The 1941 peak earnings of 6.3 percent, highest in the history of the Company, were not achieved again until 1980.[2]

Two new types of military aircraft had been completed during 1944: the XF8B-1, a Navy fighter plane designed specifically for long range carrier strikes against Japan, and the C-97 military transport, a double-decked aircraft for transporting troops and cargo.

The XF8B-1, a 20,000 pound gross weight machine with a top speed of 432 miles per hour and a range of 3,500 miles, was a very ambitious project. Known as the "Five in One," because it was to serve as a fighter, interceptor, dive bomber, torpedo bomber, or horizontal bomber, the plane never reached production in time to see service.

The C-97 was a hybrid. Utilizing the wing, power plant, landing gear, and the lower half of the fuselage of the B-29, a new, larger diameter, upper lobe was designed, creating an inverted figure-eight cross section. With a retractable ramp in the rear, and a crane hoist running the entire length of the upper deck, the plane was capable of loading outsize cargo.

The XC-97 set a new coast-to-coast speed record of six hours, three minutes and fifty seconds, averaging 383 miles per hour. The Army Air Force placed an order for ten service test models.

When the war ended, the Boeing Airplane Company did not even have a president. Phil Johnson died of a stroke in September 1944. Claire Egtvedt, in the office of chairman, resumed active management of the Company and started the process of finding a president. They offered the position to Bill Allen. In addition to his close association with the Company from the first day he joined its law firm, Allen had been serving on the board of directors for many years. He was the natural candidate.

Allen, in his modest way, declined, professing not to be qualified. Perhaps he felt the need for engineering expertise in a Company dominated by engineers.

In March 1945, the board urged Allen to change his mind. He finally gave a qualified consent, although the decision was made with great reluctance.

He made his own long list of things he would have to do if the board voted him in as president:

Must keep temper—never get mad.
Be considerate of my associates' views.
Don't talk too much—let others talk.
Don't be afraid to admit that you don't know.
Don't get immersed in detail—concentrate on big objectives.
Make contacts with people in industry—and keep them.
Try to improve feeling around Seattle toward Company.
Make a sincere effort to understand labor's viewpoint.
Be definite! Don't vacillate.
Act—get things done—move forward.
Develop a postwar future for Boeing.
Try hard, but don't let obstacles get you down. Take things in stride.
Above all else, be human—keep your sense of humor—learn to relax.
Be just, straightforward, invite criticism and learn to take it.
Be confident. Having once made the move, make the most of it.
Bring to the task great enthusiasm, unlimited energy.
Make Boeing even greater than it is.[3]

With history as the judge, Allen accomplished all of those things. He was an uncommon man—a leader among leaders. The people at Boeing developed an enduring faith in his ability to guide the Company.

The issue of president was not resolved until September 5, 1945. Seven men sat around the boardroom table on that day, busy with their first meeting since Japan surrendered. The main item of business was the election of a new president.

The Air Force was winding down its orders for the B-29. The C-97 had only a tenuous possibility for a long production run. Employment was already down to around 30,000 in Seattle, from a wartime peak of 45,000. By November, employment was expected to be cut again—by one-half. Experts in the industry viewed that figure as the critical mass below which the Company could not survive.

At the board meeting, the selection committee announced that William M. Allen was the unanimous choice for president. While he was being congratulated, Egtvedt's secretary appeared in the doorway, handing

Stratocruiser—1945–1950

A commercial version of the C-97 freighter, the twin-decked, 80 passenger Stratocruiser catered to comfort and class.

him an urgent note. It was from Bob Neale, factory manager. Word had been received from the Air Force that the B-29 schedule was being cut again, to fifty in the current month, then to ten a month until February. Neale reported that most of the fifty were already in the line, recommending that an announcement be made over the public address system before the four o'clock shift change, to close the plant.

"Egtvedt glanced at his watch. It was three-thirty. He looked at Bill Allen, shook his head, and said, 'Tell Bob that's okay.'"[4]

Allen realized he was in a desperate situation. He needed the team to stay alive, but the payroll was running at a half million dollars a day with no orders on the horizon. He knew intuitively that the potential was there in the guts of the company—the experience that his engineers had accumulated during the war. He decided he must hold that force together.

The C-97 was a logical start for a commercial derivative; however, Douglas and Lockheed had already established firm market positions, in fact satisfying all known customer demand. The price would have to be in the neighborhood of $1 million each to be competitive.

Boldly seizing the initiative, without a single order on the books, Allen put his engineers to work to convert the cargo carrying C-97 to a commercial airplane that would be competitive with the successful airplanes already in service.

Wellwood Beall forecast a breakeven at fifty planes by adhering to an extremely spartan engineering and manufacturing program. Convinced there was no other way to go, Allen ordered the plane into production. Then he instructed his salesmen to get busy and sell them. Within a month, Pan Am placed an order for twenty machines at $1.3 million each.

The product that evolved was the *Stratocruiser*, a luxurious, four-engined double-decked airplane that catered to comfort and class. In the Boeing tradition, it incorporated innovations that proved to be its best selling points. The unique lower-deck lounge—joined to the main deck by a spiral stairway—and berthable seats, piqued the imagination of the traveling public. The plane cost far too much to build—and sold at a loss—but accomplished its primary mission—holding the core of the technical and manufacturing force together.

It soon became clear that there would be insufficient work to keep the total engineering force busy for long. In the spring of 1947, the *Stratocruiser* design effort passed its peak. More than 300 engineers—about 16 percent of the force—hit the streets. It was the first general layoff of engineers in the Company's history. In the "one-company" city of Seattle, it meant they had to pull up and get out.

Boeing reported a loss of $327,198 for 1946, but the production run of fifty-six *Stratocruisers* lasted into 1950. Miraculously, they were all sold. However, the program did not turn a profit for ten years, finally nudging into the black on accumulated sales of spare parts.

1. Crosby Maynard, *Flight Plan For Tomorrow*, Douglas Aircraft Company, 1962.
2. *Annual Reports, The Boeing Company,* 1941–1980.
3. Harold Mansfield, *Vision,* (New York: Popular Library, 1966), 153.
4. Ibid., 152.

CHAPTER FOURTEEN

Labor Kicks
the Traces

Close on the heels of the ending of the war—
across the country—pent up demand caused a rush of work stoppages and strikes. In Chicago, 200,000 meat packers shut down 74 percent of the nation's meat supply in January 1946. Later in the same month, 800,000 steel workers hit the bricks. Elsewhere, General Motors, Ford and General Electric workers struck. The General Motors strike, lasting 113 days, was the longest and most costly in the history of the automobile industry.

Labor unrest at Boeing had been practically unknown. Other than the half-day work stoppage in February 1943, organized labor and management had enjoyed a harmonious relationship since the first contract with the Aero Mechanics in 1937.

The labor climate began to change in the fall of 1945 when workers were laid off as fast as the Company could process the notices.

A depression hit Seattle—32,000 workers had been laid off, there were

61,000 jobless in the State of Washington, and 62,700 veterans were expected home from the war.[1]

Employees were laid off in ascending order of seniority. The agreement provided that each could use his seniority to "bump" any other employee with less seniority on any job, at the same or lower pay, which the senior employee was qualified to perform.

Supervisors were uniquely affected, since most had risen through the ranks. The union protested that the Company could not demote supervisors into jobs covered by the labor agreement unless no employee already under union jurisdiction was available. Thus, since they could not displace union people, supervisors effectively lost their seniority rights. When the Company protested, the union requested arbitration, and King county Judge, Charles P. Moriarty ruled in the union's favor.

Bill Allen, on the job as president scarcely two months, was already being tested in his resolve to understand labor's viewpoint. On October 25, 1946, he had no choice but to lay off the 672 supervisors who had bumped union employees.

Allen asked the union to open negotiations for a new working agreement. In a letter to all shop employees, he wrote:

> *Experience since the termination of the B-29 and other government contracts has convinced the Company that the present labor relations agreement has become unworkable to such a degree as to seriously impede progress of the Company toward peacetime production and maximum acceleration of employment.*[1]

Conditions worsened. On November 15, the remaining supervisors did not report for work, and production nearly came to a standstill. Allen took direct action, sending a personal letter to each of the striking supervisors. Most of them returned to work five days later.

Later in the year, Boeing engineers in Seattle formed a collective bargaining organization, the Seattle Professional Engineering Employees Association (SPEEA), declining to call it a labor union, and signed an agreement with the Company.

In January 1946, A.F. Logan, Boeing wage and salary administrator, announced that amendments to the existing contract had been worked out and agreed to by both parties. One of the amendments, sometimes referred to as a new contract, providing for a fifteen percent increase in wages, was approved by the Wage Stabilizaton Board, a wartime agency that maintained jurisdiction in the unsettled, postwar period. This new contract was to "remain in force until March 16, 1947, or thereafter until a new agreement has been reached by the parties, either through negotiation or arbitration."[2]

Negotiations continued for over a year, and when the labor contract expired in March 1947, no new agreement had been reached. The Company held out for a change in the seniority system to allow transfer of qualified employees to other jobs on short notice.

K.L. Calkins reports: "The entanglement of the seniority system was like a footrace through a blackberry patch; it was hard to get anywhere without drawing blood."[3]

Allen viewed the problem in starkly simple terms—a necessity to maintain the direction of his work force. To the union, such a concession was like the threatening sword of Damocles.

Early in April, the union filed a strike vote request with the Department of Labor. Allen began an intense personal campaign to bring reason to the table. He appealed to the employees through *Boeing News*, stating "...the Company is not seeking to destroy seniority. Rather, it is seeking the first essential to job security—a successful, operating Company."[4]

Boeing then proposed to exempt 10 percent of the bargaining unit from the seniority provisions so that those employees could be transferred between jobs as their services were needed.

The union members essentially mistrusted the Company's motives, and when the proposal was put to a vote at a mass meeting on May 24, it was rejected by a 93 percent margin.

Immediately following the vote there were cries of "Strike!," and "Let's have a strike vote!" When union president Harold Gibson asked for those in favor of a strike to stand up, the entire audience seemed to rise as one man. The vote to strike passed by 94 percent; however, no date was established for it to begin.

Both sides had much to lose by a strike, but the union members gradually convinced themselves that a massive walkout would bring the desired concessions. They failed to recognize the determination of Bill Allen.

In California, workers at Lockheed agreed to a new contract for less money than Boeing workers were already receiving.[5]

In June 1947, the Congress passed the Taft-Hartley Act, an amendment to the Labor Relations Act. Under the Act, management was also allowed to file unfair labor practices complaints with the NLRB. Further, Taft-Hartley required a cooling off period of sixty days before striking, and granted the government power to enforce an eighty-day injunction against strikes which threatened national health or safety.

After the passage of Taft-Hartley, President Allen wrote still another letter to all employees, assuring them that the Company did not intend to use the new power of the law to seek undue advantage. Nevertheless, Allen let it be known that a strike would be viewed as a breach of contract—a violation of Taft-Hartley. Concerned at the turn of events, Harvey Brown, president of the parent union, the International Association of Machinists (IAM), directed the local union officers to continue negotiations and to explore arbitration.

When the union offered arbitration, the Company declined. The impasse continued.

Pressure grew. The Company was forced to live with the inefficient seniority system, and union members had not had a pay raise since March 1946.

In January 1948, Boeing submitted a new proposal, offering fifteen cents an hour pay raise, continuation of the union shop, and a modified seniority clause. Negotiations were completed in March and the new contract was put to the membership for a vote. Both parties had agreed to submit certain items to arbitration.

Neither side would accept the other's recommendations for an arbitration panel, and negotiations deadlocked.

Abruptly, the union council voted to give the Company a deadline to agree on an arbitration panel—4 P.M., April 16.

Without IAM sanction, there could be no strike, so the Company ignored the deadline. The current contract continued in force until a new one was "negotiated or arbitrated." To Allen, a contract was a contract.

Union members, heedless of cautions, were ready to strike. The situation was out of control.

Gibson called for help from International. "Don't let them strike. Hold them back," they told him. "I don't know if I can," he said.[6]

Garry Cotton, former Lodge 751 president who had advanced to a Grand Lodge representative's position, appeared before 400 shop committeemen. The issues with the company were virtually settled, he said. There was agreement on pay, vacations, holidays. The one remaining issue was seniority and it could be worked out without a strike.

"'The shop committeemen told him to go to hell,' recalled Gibson. 'So I stood up. I told them we weren't prepared for a strike. We weren't organized for one and we didn't need one. They started throwing union buttons on the floor.'"[7]

Gibson could not hold them. In an emergency meeting, the union's district council called a strike to begin one hour after midnight on April 22.

Allen was stunned. Then he was angry. He contacted IAM president Harvey Brown. Had the IAM sanctioned the strike? The answer was no. Allen wired Brown that the Company no longer considered Lodge 751 to be the bargaining agent for the employees. The union had broken its contract. Brown suggested that he send a committee from international to Seattle to discuss the matter, and Allen accepted.

The three-man executive council committee sent from the Grand Lodge called Allen when they arrived in Seattle to arrange for a meeting. When they told him they wanted Harold Gibson to sit in, Allen refused to meet. He was not going to confer with a man who had broken his word, and he began an active, intensive campaign to lure striking employees back to work.

The first plane to roll out after the strike started was a B-50 bomber, an improved version of the B-29. The rollout called for a plant celebration. The strike had been on for seven weeks. Prestrike employment had been nearly 19,000 and now was back to 5,000. Allen took the opportunity to invite all employees to the factory apron at Plant II for an important message on the state of the Company.

True to his starchily ethic philosophy, Allen did not ask for blind support. In an emotional appeal, he solicited employees to help the Company in its contest with the union, saying: "....I'm trying to accomplish a fair and honorable result. I only ask for your support if you think that this Company is doing the right and proper thing."[8]

When Federal Judge John C. Bowen ruled that the strike was unlawful, because the union had not given the required sixty-day notice, the hiring pace—and the bitterness—increased.

Then in July, the NLRB trial examiner, William E. Spencer, ruled that the clause requiring the agreement to remain in force until a new contract was signed must have limited duration, and therefore Boeing was guilty of unfair labor practices.

Boeing took legal exception to the Spencer ruling and requested a hearing with the full board. In the meantime, they announced that strikers would be rehired to fill available jobs only. Newly hired employees would not be dismissed.

With employment rates continually on the upside, the union, fearful that there might not be jobs for the strikers to go back to, moved to call off the strike. Boeing agreed to reinstate all those on strike who were under the jurisdiction of Lodge 751, and from whom it received applications within two weeks of the strike's end.

After spirited discussion of the conditions on the part of both adversaries, a vote was taken. Strikers voted twelve to one in favor of ending it.

By October, the striker reinstatement was complete, and employment was just over 19,000, slightly more than the pre-strike high. Also, in October, Boeing presented its appeal to the full NLRB, who, about a month later, upheld Spencer's recommendations. Boeing immediately filed an appeal to the Federal Court in the District of Columbia.

It was not until May 1949, that the three-judge Court of Appeals handed down a unanimous decision. Not only had Lodge 751 violated the Taft-Hartley Act, it had also violated its contract with Boeing—and lost its rights to bargain collectively for factory employees.

Boeing had already decided to manufacture future military aircraft at the government-owned plant in Wichita, with only flight testing to be completed in Seattle. The move signaled more layoffs in the Puget Sound area, and again there was talk, fear, and speculation that Boeing would move out of the city.

A hard-boiled review could not fail to conclude that a major manufacturing facility would have little chance to succeed in the Puget Sound Area. Cohn, analyzing those considerations in his location theory study of industry in the Pacific Northwest, stated that Boeing continued to exist there for no economic reason whatsoever, but simply "because an individual who happened to live in the Northwest evolved an original product which proved successful."[9]

However, one can argue that isolation actually worked to the Company's advantage. With its primary product uniquely capable of delivering itself to any place in the world, in the most rapid fashion yet devised, a major disadvantage of isolation from markets was negated.

In the case of labor, isolation militated toward an extraordinary loyalty—a loyalty which permeated the Company for most of its history. The 1948 strike was an exception, exacerbated by a series of unusual local and national conditions.

In January 1950, Lodge 751 was certified as bargaining agent, and on May 22, signed an agreement with Boeing. The contract was a clear victory for President Allen. Standing firm on principle, he had fought with every legal weapon at his command. Nevertheless, the bottom line was epitomized in one word—*fairness*. Allen had demonstrated that both sides— labor and management—were equal partners, and added significantly to his public personality as well as the esteem of his associates.

For the factory employees, loss of the union shop was a major blow. Although the union pressed for its reinstatement, they were never again able to retrieve that status. New employees could join the union or not, as they chose, but once having joined, they must remain members during the term of the contract.

On May 22, 1950—more than two years after the workers had gone on strike—a one year contract was signed with Lodge 751, ending the longest and most bitter confrontation in Boeing's history. Seven months later, in Wichita, Kansas, a similar contract was signed with Lodge 70. The strife was over, but the scars remained.

1. K.L. Calkins, *An Analysis of Labor Relations news Coverage...,* (Seattle: University of Washington, 1968), 24.
2. *Boeing News,* 21 March, 1946, 1.
3. Calkins, 33.
4. *Boeing News,* 24 April, 1947, 1.
5. Calkins, 38.
6. Ibid., 54.
7. Ibid., 55.
8. *Boeing News,* 10 June, 1948, 2.
9. E.J. Cohn Jr., *Industry in the Pacific Northwest and the Location Theory,* (New York: King's Crown Press, 1954), 44.

CHAPTER FIFTEEN

The Jet Bombers

What to do about a postwar bomber was a top priority. Ed Wells concluded that speed was the answer. Having watched the tests of Bell's experimental jet pursuit plane at Muroc Dry Lake, California, in September 1943, he directed Bob Jewett, chief of preliminary design, to work up a jet bomber, shaving the wings down to next to nothing to get maximum speed. Robert Jewett, an intense aeronautical engineer from the University of Minnesota, destined to lead the Company into missiles and space, put his senior designers to work on the project. In March 1944, they took the design to Wright Field.

"'Would you take speed as a substitute for guns?' Wells asked Oliver Echols.

"'Maybe so,' said Echols. 'If it's fast enough you might get by with just a stinger turret in the tail, and flak protection under the engines.'"[1]

In wind tunnel tests, as they increased the speed, air moving over the leading edge of the wings approached the speed of sound, creating the mysterious compressibility burble which became known as the "sound barrier."

George Schairer and his aerodynamics staff had been giving the subject considerable study. "We'll just have to beat it out in the wind tunnel," he concluded.[2]

The Army Air Force, concerned over the late start the United States had made in jet airplane technology, began pressing for proposals for quick construction of new experimental machines. Ed Wells took the position that Boeing should not propose a design until they learned how to make a successful one—rejecting the conventional approach of simply installing jet engines on a plane like the B-29. He concluded that something entirely new was needed.

While Boeing delayed, Wright Field went ahead with contracts to North American, Consolidated, and Martin for medium-range jet bombers utilizing conventional design.

In May of 1945, aerodynamics chief, George Schairer, as a member of the Scientific Advisory Board of the Army Air Force, had been at the Pentagon preparing to go on a special mission into Germany. The theory of high-speed flight was the hottest new subject, and sweepback seemed to some theorists as the way to achieve it.

The same day that General Gustav Jodl and Admiral Hans Friedeburg unconditionally surrendered the German armed forces to the Americans inside a little red school house at Reims, and Soviet soldiers hung the hammer and sickle atop the gutted Reichstag in Berlin, Schairer's group arrived at Reichmarshall Goering's Aeronautical Research Institute at Brunswick. They found drawings of a model with sweptback wings. German studies and wind tunnel testing had led to the design of the Messerschmitt ME-262 with a forty-five degree sweepback—already under construction when the war came to an end.

Wells created an entirely new group, selecting George Martin to lead it. Graduating from the University of Washington in 1931 with high honors, Martin began as a stress engineer. A visionary, and a relentless driver, he proved to be the right man for the job.

On September 13, 1945, the new team had a formal proposal ready for presentation to Wright Field. The proposed plane was radical in design—with a thin sweptback wing and six jets; four blasting from the top of the body, and two more from the tail.

The engineers at Dayton were more than skeptical—they were incredulous. "Why should the Air Force finance some wild idea George Schairer has?" asked one colonel. "Let's cut out this foolishness."[3]

The armament laboratory brought in some results of firing 50-caliber bullets into the burner section of a roaring F-80 jet engine in a wind tunnel test. The outcome was an uncontrollable blowtorch blasting from the side of the engine. That settled the body-mounted design.

Unable to salvage anything from the proposal, the Boeing team went back to the drawing boards. Wells recalled some data that Schairer brought back from Germany—experiments with engines mounted on struts under the wing.

In the face of cries of heresy from the aerodynamics staff, exhaustive tests were made in the wind tunnel. At least six positions were tested. The position in front and below the wing proved to be nearly ideal, and strut-mounted engines became another Boeing first.

There were still many sticky engineering problems to solve. The thin wing did not provide sufficient fuel capacity, and there was no good place to retract the landing gear. The retraction problem was solved by designing a tandem bicycle gear that pulled up into the body, with small, outrigger wheels retracting into the inboard engine pods. Adding internal body fuel tanks still did not give the Air Force the desired range, but the design was sufficiently interesting that they ordered two experimental models—the XB-47s.

The year of 1947 witnessed many first flights at Boeing. On June 25, it was the B-50; on July 8, the *Stratocruiser*; and on December 17, most spectacular of all—the XB-47 *Stratojet* literally shot off Boeing Field when test pilot Bob Robbins cut in a bank of the eighteen rocket assist (ATO) units, each of which instantaneously added 1,000 pounds of thrust to the 24,000 that its six engines were producing. (The B-47E, entering service in 1953, produced 43,000 pounds of thrust and carried thirty-three ATO units).

On February 8, 1949, an XB-47 crossed the United States in less than four hours, setting a new speed record of 607.2 mph.

The Air Force's reluctance was abruptly transformed into unbridled enthusiasm. They had an airplane that flew like a fighter, with a top speed of over 600 miles per hour—fastest known bomber in the world—and a range of over 3,000 miles.

With the addition of externally mounted wing fuel tanks, the range was increased to over 4,000 miles.

Boeing manufactured 1,371 B-47s at its Wichita plant, and both Douglas and Lockheed tooled up to raise the total to 2,040. The program was successful beyond Boeing's wildest imagination; however, it did not solve the most pressing requirement of the Air Force—a truly global jet bomber.

Even before the B-47 flew, Boeing had won the design competition for such an airplane. It was visualized to be twice the weight of the B-47, with wings swept back twenty degrees, and using turboprop engines. However, as the weight went up to gain range, the speed went dismally down. The Air Force wanted the speed of the B-47 with global range, and began studies on aerial refueling. The existing hose-and-drogue method would not be adequate to transfer the huge quantities of fuel required.

At Wichita, engineer Cliff Leisy was perfecting a "flying boom," essentially a telescoping pipeline that could be lowered from the tanker tail to the nose of the receiver—utilizing a combination elevator and rudder—known as a "ruddevator."

Immediately following the end of the war in Europe, the Soviet Union annexed the eastern half of Poland and northeast Prussia. In the Balkans and its occupied German territory, the Soviets set up Communist regimes, supplanting previous governments. On March 5, 1946, Winston Churchill, speaking at Fulton, Missouri, characterized the state of Europe in somber tones. "From Stettin in the Baltic to Trieste in the Adriatic, an iron curtain has descended across the continent," he declared.[4] The "Cold War" had begun.

The Soviets hinted in November 1947 that they had discovered the secret of the atomic bomb, and real peace in the world seemed more illusory than ever. When the Russians imposed a blockade on Berlin in 1948, the Truman-ordered Berlin airlift—which landed an airplane a minute at its peak—focused once again the need for modern, powerful air fleets. The U.S. Congress appropriated funds for a seventy-group air force, and the need to accelerate an intercontinental bomber became urgent.

Wright Field, with the prospect for inflight refueling becoming a reality, decided to fix the design at 300,000 pounds and settle on turboprop engines.

Ed Wells was not convinced. The turboprops were already two years

B-47 with Rocket Assisted Takeoff

The B-47 taking off from Boeing Field. The planes were equipped with rocket units for operations from short fields.

behind their development schedule, and an additional four seemed entirely realistic. He feared they could easily find themselves with an airframe and no engines. However, urgency in the Air Force was at fever level, and they were intent on awarding a contract for two experimental models. The possibility for Boeing to build a pure jet on its own funds was beyond contemplation.

When the Westinghouse Company revealed plans for a big new jet engine, the potential of jets appeared to be substantially better, and the turboprops comparatively worse. Wells went to Bill Allen. "We've come to the conclusion that the airplane should be jet powered," he declared.

Allen was startled. It would throw the program back, might bring a cancellation. "Isn't this pretty late to be proposing a change like that?"

"I know, Bill, but it just isn't the airplane we should be building."[5]

Ed Wells and George Schairer went to Wright Field to talk with bombardment project officer Colonel Pete Warden about changing to jet engines. He was sold on jet speed from experience with the B-47, but knew the push toward turboprops was strong. "Go ahead and work up a new design with jets," he said. "But we'll have to keep on with the turboprop airplane until we see what can be done."[6]

In July, 1948, the contract came through to build two experimental airplanes with turboprop engines.

Engineers at Seattle worked at maximum effort to put a proposal together for jets without jeopardizing the contract in hand for turboprops. They found they could get almost as much range, plus better speed without changing the wing or the sweepback. Utilizing a new jet promised by Pratt & Whitney, with a thrust of 10,000 pounds, they brought the speed up to 500 miles an hour. The plane would still be within the 300,000 pound gross weight target. Putting the proposal together, they headed back to Wright Field in October to sell it.

Colonel Warden looked over the data. He was clearly disappointed. "I think you need a faster wing," he said, "more sweepback—like the B-47. We've already compromised on range, with refueling. Let's not compromise any more on speed."[7]

Warden was greeted by a surprised silence. Then Wells, quickly sensing the gravity of the situation, responded firmly. "Let us see what we can do to get you some more," he said. Glancing at his watch, he noted it was nearly noon—Friday. Without hesitation, he promised, "We'll be back

The Chief Flies With Boeing Jet Bomber—1950

President William Allen prepares to board an early flight of the B-47, Boeing's sleek, six-jet bomber. It was a first of a kind for a Boeing president, and Allen's most cherished photo.

Monday morning."[8]

Boeing had sent its top team of engineers to the Field, armed with all the data on both turboprops and jets, complete with wind tunnel results. Wells and Schairer returned to their hotel rooms, where the rest of the team was waiting.

Wells unrolled the drawings. The twenty-degree sweepback suddenly

B-52 *Stratofortress*—1952

The eight-jet B-52 became the backbone of the United States Strategic Air Force Command, still in active service at the millennium.

looked conservative. "I think we'd better put this away and start again," he said. They looked at the drawings of a proposed medium range bomber they had brought along—thirty-five degrees of sweepback.

"Double this in size and you just about have it,"[9] Schairer noted resourcefully. Wells spread out drawing paper on the top of the bureau and began making a three-view sketch of the scale-up. Art Carlsen, project, and Maynard Pennell, preliminary design, worked up a weight breakdown. Bob Withington and Vaughn Blumenthal, from the aerodynamics staff, calculated the expected performance. Schairer laid out the lines of the new sweptback wing. By late that night they realized they had created an airplane. It had the range. The weight went up only a little, to 330,000 pounds. With a wing swept back thirty-five degrees, and a span of 185 feet, supporting eight engines, the speed went up to more than 600 miles an hour. *They had achieved Stratojet performance in an intercontinental bomber.*

On Saturday morning, Schairer rounded up some balsa wood, glue, and carving tools, and set to work on a model. Wells organized the engineering data and hired a public stenographer to put it into document form. By Sunday night, it was a clean, thirty-three-page, bound report—with scale model attached.

Pete Warden was beaming on Monday morning. "Now we have an airplane!" he exclaimed. "This is the B-52."[10]

Two experimental planes were built, and the first test flight was made on April 15, 1952. The first production airplane rolled out of the Seattle factory on March 18, 1954. In all, Boeing manufactured 744 of the giant *Stratofortresses*.

No one needs to tell the story of the exploits of the B-52. It wrote its own, providing the backbone of the Strategic Air Command of the United States Air Force for more than four decades, and was still in service at the end of the millennium.

1. Harold Mansfield, *Vision*, (New York: Popular Library, 1966), 147.
2. Ibid., 148.
3. Ibid., 157.
4. *Chronicles of the 20th Century,* (New York: Chronicle Publications, 1987), 609.
5. Mansfield, *Vision*, 174.
6. Ibid., 175.
7,8. Ibid., 180.
9. Ibid., 181.
10. Ibid., 182.

CHAPTER SIXTEEN

The Transition Years

In an uncertain, postwar world, new technology seemed destined to be directed preponderantly towards conflict, however no field of endeavor failed to feel the new surge.

Portents of dramatic change in business and industry were everywhere. One breakthrough was hardly digested, when another—promising to supplant it—stood poised on the threshold.

The war had spawned ENIAC—for Electronic Numerical Integrator and Computer—an extremely sophisticated calculator—invented by IBM. First utilized by the U.S. War Department in 1946, ENIAC worked 1,000 times as fast as any calculator ever devised—operated by a flow of electrons in some 18,000 vacuum tubes—and for the first time, all moving parts were eliminated, with electronic pulses replacing mechanical switches.

Scarcely two years later, Bell Telephone Laboratories announced the transistor, a lilliputian solid-state electronic device about $\frac{1}{200}$ the size, and requiring $\frac{1}{100}$ of the power of a single vacuum tube—destined to relegate ENIAC and its vacuum tube cousins to the trash heap of industry.

In a time warp of history, two quite disparate events in 1947 dramatically focused the pace of technology in the aircraft industry. Forshadowing a new era, on October 14, Chuck Yeager became the first human to travel faster than the speed of sound, flying a Bell X-1 rocket plane. Less than a month later, on November 2, Howard Hughes rang down the curtain on the glue and wood technology that had survived a half century, when he took the *Spruce Goose* to the air for its first—and last—flight. A 200-ton, eight-engined giant; with wings, fuselage, and empennage constructed entirely of wood—the world's largest airplane—the *Goose* had one of the shortest flights in history, rising seventy feet off the water before Hughes brought the big bird down to stay.

Turmoil and uncertainty threatened almost every aspect of the aircraft industry in the transition years of the late forties and early fifties. Strikes, material shortages, financial limitations, and locked-in government regulations were not the only concerns.

In July 1947, when President Truman signed legislation uniting all branches of the armed services into a single agency—creating the Department of Defense—a new face was put on the military procurement process. With the Cold War supplanting the heat of battle, United States defense agencies were in an unsettled state, as each postured to gain its perceived rightful share of the defense budget.

The world power balance shifted mightly when, on September 23, 1949, Truman announced that the Soviets had exploded their first atomic bomb. Following close on the heels of that sobering news, on October 1, 1949, Chairman Mao Tsetung proclaimed the birth of the People's Republic of China, a new Communist monolith.

In January 1950, Truman ordered the Atomic Energy Commission to proceed with the production of the hydrogen bomb, and proclaimed the beginning of NATO, as eight Western European nations signed the pact, escalating the Cold War yet another notch. Sixteen months later, a raging ball of fire destroyed the island of Eniwetok, when the world's first hydrogen bomb was exploded.

In May, French forces, feeling the sting of the attack of four well armed Viet Minh battalions, appealed to the Americans for aid.

In June, the U.N. and the U.S. agreed to send troops to Korea, and General Douglas MacArthur was named to lead the force.

Providing additional brainpower for the new postwar age, the U.S.

churned out millions of college graduates. More than half of the 2.5 million students who received degrees in 1947 were war veterans who had studied under the G.I. Bill. An unprecedented number majored in engineering.

Postwar factory manpower witnessed remarkable changes. Boeing was among the leaders in efforts toward equal opportunities for minorities, helping to secure women's place on the factory floor. Further, during the war, a team of recruiters combed the farms and cotton fields in the South, signing up black citizens to go to work in Seattle. As witness to the success of that program, in 1956, Bertram C. Williams and Gordon McHenry became the first two black supervisors at Boeing, and in 1961 Boeing was one of eight United States corporations that voluntarily joined John F. Kennedy's Plans for Progress program.

At Boeing, Cliff Leisy's "flying boom" project for inflight refueling was just entering production—with a high priority—to satisfy the Air Force requirement for global range for its jet bombers. The concept was fully proven, when, on March 2, 1949, a Boeing B-50 bomber completed the first nonstop flight around the world. Ninety-four hours and one minute after takeoff, the *Lucky Lady* landed at Carswell Air Force Base near fort Worth, Texas. The plane refueled four times in midair during its 23,452 mile flight.

The booms were quickly adapted to the Boeing C-97, which became the KC-97 series. The Air Force ordered the airplane as its standard tanker, assigning twenty planes to each B-47 wing.

The engineering study group that Phil Johnson initiated for postwar ventures quickly rejected the idea of building automobiles and refrigerators. Nevertheless, diversification remained a priority because of the vagaries of military procurement and the uncertain magnitude of the commercial airplane market. Engineering was going forward on a pilotless aircraft project, a ramjet engine, and a small gas turbine, all under government contracts.

The gas turbine engine seemed promising for both commercial and military applications, and the first contract was received from the Navy for turbines to drive generators for electric power aboard minesweepers. Later, the turbine was adapted to a Kaman helicopter and a heavy-duty truck. In 1955, Boeing created an Industrial Products Division, which centered its activities on the Model 502 gas turbine, and by year end, 500 units had been sold.

In spite of its success in numerous specialized applications, a mass market never developed for gas turbines and the project continued on a tentative, year-by-year basis.

On July 27, 1949, the world's first jet airliner, the de Havilland *Comet*, made its debut in the skies over Hatfield, England. The sweptwing *Comet* (20 degrees), powered by four jet engines tucked into the wing-body interface, was Britain's bid to gain world leadership in commercial aviation. With a comfortable five-year lead, they very nearly succeeded. Capable of carrying thirty-six passengers in a pressurized cabin at 40,000 feet, at speeds in excess of 500 miles per hour, it was almost twice as fast as any airliner in service.

In August 1951, an experimental Douglas *Skyrocket* plane broke all altitude records, climbing to over 72,000 feet above the earth by use of rockets—after being carried aloft by a B-29 bomber. The same month, the *Viking*—a pure rocket—reached an altitude of 135 miles above the desert of New Mexico. Aerospace was close to reality.

Rocket technology was opening up an entirely new field of missiles. Ground-to-air, air-to-ground, ground-to-ground, and air-to-air types were on the drawing boards in America's busy aerospace companies.

Boeing developed a ground-to-air pilotless aircraft (GAPA) under contract with the Air Force, and in 1946, were firing the needle-nosed missile by the dozens on the Utah salt flats. By 1949, with success achieved, and production imminent, the project was abruptly canceled. A Washington, D.C. decision had put all missiles of 100 miles range or less under Army jurisdiction, and the Army already had a missile of its own—the *Nike*.

Not to be discouraged easily, Bob Jewett and his preliminary design engineers presented their new electronic guidance system to the Air Force. The result was a joint proposal by Boeing and the University of Michigan for an advanced ground-to-air missile, which came to be known as BOMARC.

For BOMARC, far more than the guidance system had to be invented. Difficult new problems reared up as the requirements of performance stretched the limits of existing materials and manufacturing processes.

Utilizing a fuel and an oxidizer—stored in separate tanks—which ignited spontaneously upon contact, the new missile demanded a containment material with properties not yet achieved by industry. The Armco Steel Company had done laboratory testing of a new stainless steel called

17-7PH, which had demonstrated the corrosion resistance necessary to contain the red-fuming nitric acid oxidizer—while maintaining the high strength necessary for storage under pressure for long periods.

John "Fred" Baisch, a metallugical engineering graduate from the University of Washington, addressed the problem with the patience and intensity of a surgeon. The result was a tailoring of the new material by heat lot to each tank, essentially introducing laboratory controls into the manufacturing process.

BOMARC went into production, becoming the defensive shield around the northern perimeter of the United States—on instant alert during the Cold War period. Boeing was in the missile business to stay.

Working as a consultant for Pratt & Whitney during the war years, Charles Lindbergh was also in Germany immediately following the war, seeking information on jet airplane design. Back in the United States, he went to see Juan Trippe, and rejoined Pan American as a technical consultant. A survey was undertaken to determine if the time for commercial jet airplanes was at hand.

In November 1949, Wellwood Beall sent Trippe a letter in which he called attention to the jet progress in Britain. He pointed out Boeing's extensive experience in large military jet airplanes, suggesting the Company was well prepared with the know-how to design and manufacture an "outstanding type" of jet airliner. "All we need for an immediate go ahead is a customer."[1]

Trippe was not the customer Beall was looking for, and neither was any other airline. Commercial jets were being viewed by most experts as having no future because of their short range. Nevertheless, in October, 1952, Trippe ordered three *Comets*. He was one of the few who viewed jets as a way to reduce cost per seat mile, as a result of doubling the speed. Nearly everyone else saw the jets as a rich man's airplane—those willing to pay a premium for a super-fast, first class ride.

To Trippe, the *Comet* was an economic failure before it entered service. He ordered the three planes to cover himself, actually doubting that Pan American would ever take delivery.

The sleek new *Comet* did not make an auspicious start. Three units were damaged in runway accidents early in the program. Then two literally exploded in the air during proving flights.

The day of reckoning came on May 2, 1953, when the third *Comet*, first to carry passengers, crashed; and the airplane was grounded.

Parts of one of the earlier crashed airplanes were fished out of the Mediterranean Sea, and it was deduced that a small crack had formed in a window frame from the stress of the pressurized cabin. In turbulent air the flexing of the structure resulted in the crack instantly growing to several feet, rupturing the fuselage.

The reverberations of that crack investigation rolled through the engineering departments and the boardrooms of the aircraft industry around the world. Perhaps there was something fundamentally wrong with sustained, high-altitude, pressurized jet operations.

However, tragic accidents also continued to plague piston engine driven commercial airplanes. At this stage of design and manufacturing knowhow, there was still much to learn about producing long-lived airframes. At Boeing, the spotlight abruptly focused on the structures and materials departments to understand the problem of metal failure, and to devise a solution.

The commercial jet age was just around the corner, and it came at a landmark moment in history. Millions of Americans had returned from war to take up the tools of peace.

Perhaps more than at any time in this century, there was a freshness of beginning—an anticipation of unfolding opportunity. It was a time for testing—a time to be brave with a new kind of courage—a courage of faith in the creation of enterprise.

The Great Depression that had swallowed the dreams of our fathers was cloaked by a curtain of years. Its importance had faded and its sting had healed. Hope was in style. Self esteem was never higher, fear for the future scarcely considered.

The airplane industry stood at the cutting edge of a new era. Two decades lay ahead during which such amazing accomplishments would be achieved, that discussion of them in 1950 would have been branded as pure fantasy.

1. Robert Daley, *An American Saga*, (New York: Random House, 1980), 398.

Model 367-80 Prototype Jet Transport—1954

History recorded this airplane as the Boeing *$15 million dollar gamble*. Built entirely on Company funds, the airplane ushered in the jet age of commercial air transportation.

CHAPTER SEVENTEEN

Commercial Jets

The last *Stratocruiser* was delivered to British Overseas Airways Corporation in May 1950. Wellwood Beall went on the delivery flight, eager for a look at the British Comet. BOAC had ordered ten, and Europe appeared ready to tumble.

Boeing engineering studies for a commercial jet transport had been limited to designing a new fuselage, utilizing a B-47 wing. Dissatisfied with the results, George Schairer suggested taking a fresh approach.

After considerable study of the many options, a prototype concept evolved—a low winged machine with a nose gear up front and the main gear mounted in the wings, folding into the body. Four single engines would be installed in pods under the wings.

When Bill Allen attended the Farnborough Air Show the following spring, he was startled at the sleek, futuristic appearance of the *Comet*.

That night, at dinner with Maynard Pennell, chief of preliminary design, and Ken Luplow, sales engineer, Allen confronted them with some hard questions.

"How did you like the *Comet*?" Allen asked.

"It's a very good airplane," said Pennell.

"Do you think we could build one as good?"

"Oh, better. Much better."[1]

Back in Seattle, the romance of a jet transport seemed to be buried in the hard negatives of no U.S. airline demand for such an airplane, and no interest by the Air Force. To go ahead could well be a terrible waste of stockholder's money. The production order for the B-52 had not yet been achieved, and the only source of capital would be to incur more debt.

Allen directed the engineering department to take a look at a KC-97 with jet engines—for refueling B-52s. The Air Force turned a deaf ear—it would be cheaper to convert B-47s.

When salesmen Fred Collins and Ralph Bell pressed Bill Allen to order the construction of a jet transport prototype on speculation, he cut them down.

"Whose money are you spending?" he demanded.[2] He continued to push the Air Force to buy a jet-powered KC-97, to no avail.

Allen went through many weeks of soul-searching, thinking back to that September day in 1945 when he was made president. *Act, get things done, move forward.*

The time had come for a decision. Dictating a list of questions to his secretary, he called a meeting of his department heads. He told them to take plenty of time to reply to his questions. "We don't want to make a mistake," he said.[3]

Six days after the first flight of the B-52, on April 21, 1952, the second meeting—to answer Bill Allen's questions—convened. Jim Barton of cost accounting put the price of a jet prototype at $15 million—*equal to four times the total profit for the seven years since the end of the war.* Pennell reported the plane would meet the range requirements of a military tanker and would have three times the work capacity of the C-97. As a commercial airplane, the seat-mile operating cost would be competitive. Schairer said the same prototype could be used to demonstrate both a military and a commercial transport and could provide the performance data needed for production airplanes. Beall said Pratt & Whitney would have the engines. There was sufficient engineering and production manpower to do the job.

Allen went to the board, recommending a go-ahead. They concurred without a single dissenting vote.

Soon, interest began to focus on a plywood, walled-off area in the factory at Renton, where the new airplane, known as the 367-80 prototype, was taking shape. Incorporating a bold new feature, a completely sealed wing, the 367-80 was thousands of pounds lighter as a result of eliminating the old rubber fuel cells. The metal wing became the fuel tank.

The Air Force made no commitments, nor did the airline industry. The cost of the program increased to $16 million.

On May 14, 1954, at the shift change, precisely at 4:00 P.M., the hangar doors rolled open at the Renton factory and the new brown and yellow bird emerged from its secret nest to face the newsreel cameras. William E. Boeing was there. At age 72, he was witnessing the results of his vision— *Let no improvement in flying and flying equipment pass us by*. He could feel the enthusiasm in the electric atmosphere.

Trouble lurked in the background. When Alvin M. "Tex" Johnston, the test pilot, taxied the airplane a week later, he put her through some tough stops and turns. While wheeling into a final turn preparatory to takeoff, the left wing suddenly dropped, the left landing gear collapsing into the wing, and the left outboard engine pod coming to rest on the taxiway.

The rear spar trunnion attachment for the main landing gear had fractured. In retrospect, the timing was fortunate. Had "Tex" not given the airplane that last severe maneuver, he would have taken off, with a near certain failure of the gear upon landing—a potential disaster, and a serious setback for the commercial jet age.

The *Dash 80* was repaired and back in flight status in less than two months, and on July 15, 1954, commercial aviation witnessed a milestone of historic proportions—the maiden flight of the prototype for America's first commercial jet airplane.

Quiet happiness pervaded the scene. When "Tex" Johnston landed the plane at Boeing Field, and taxied up to the flight test hangar, chief engineer George Martin was waiting in shirt sleeves, hands in his pockets, a broad smile on his face. For today, his work was done.

A field car drove up behind Allen, and someone pulled him out of its path. "If it had hit me now I wouldn't have felt it," Allen said.[4]

Fallout from the trunnion fracture remained. Hogged out of a large steel block, representing the state-of-art of the steel industry, it had failed to measure up to the unyielding standards of the dawning jet age.

John "Jack" Sweet, chief metallurgist, another graduate of the University of Washington, put his staff to work to develop an entirely new material specification—based on exhaustive research—for steel forgings with multi-directional ductility as well as multi-directional strength.

When the steel companies read the requirements, they were incredulous. The reality of steel manufacturing did not square with producing a few hundred tons of special steel in an industry which operated in terms of 100 million tons a year.

Boeing persisted, gaining support from the entire aircraft industry—and the Defense Department. Ultimately successful, the resulting vacuum-melted steel exhibited excellent ductility in all directions, even when heat treated to tensile strengths 50 percent higher than the original *Dash 80* forging.

The giant B-52 was becoming a tremendous production effort, and Air Force interest in a jet tanker to refuel them accelerated. Sensing the inevitability of an order, in the summer of 1954 Allen authorized the start of engineering and tooling—at Company expense—for a production tanker, which for a short time, was known as the Model 717.

In March 1955, the Secretary of the Air Force announced that Boeing's new jet—renamed the KC-135—would become the standard tanker.

After Wellwood Beall returned from London, he became less and less visible in the Company's affairs. His problem with alcohol steadily worsened. In February, 1964 he made an ill-advised sales commitment while under the influence, and Allen called him in. At the time he was a senior vice president and a member of the board of directors. It was with great reluctance that Allen asked for his resignation. Shortly thereafter, he joined Douglas as executive vice president of operations.

His former colleagues at Boeing saw his hand in several Douglas successes over the next several years, and felt that Douglas's competitive position had been strengthened at Boeing's expense.[5] He retired in 1971.

The Lockheed *Constellation*, leader in commercial sales in the early fifties, was running out of options for improvements in range and capacity then being demanded by the airlines. The first generation of *Constellations* had pioneered transatlantic flights with a refueling stop at Gander, Newfoundland. The latest stretched version with more powerful engines, was able to dispense with the Gander stop on the eastbound leg, and by 1953, the *Super-Connies* were flying from New York to Amsterdam without re-fueling at Shannon, Ireland. But the westbound leg was another matter. Flying into the teeth of the prevailing winds proved to be beyond even the *Super-Connies'* capability.

Douglas delivered 753 DC-6 series airplanes between 1947 and 1955, far outdistancing Lockheed on numbers of airplanes in commercial service. Then, in 1956, Douglas shaded the glamorous *Connies* when the DC-7 was introduced. A total of 121 of the DC-7 models were purchased by the airlines, and Douglas again appeared to be firmly in control of the market. Jet airplanes had been relegated to the study category.

Lockheed was busy redesigning the *Super-Connies* with a new wing and turboprop engines. Delays in engine availability resulted in returning to piston power, with concurrent airframe and wing modifications. Rollout of the prototype—known as the Model L-1649A *Starliner*—was delayed until September, 1956, with first delivery to TWA in April, 1957. By that time the DC-7C had captured most of the market, and only forty-three production airplanes were built.

In July, 1955, when Boeing gave the go-ahead for production of the *Model 707*—the commercial version of the prototype—Lockheed, wary about airline acceptance of such a giant step as the jets offered, was already heavily committed in engineering and tooling for their entry into the race, the all-new turboprop L-188 *Electra*. The deadly pace of competition did not allow for second thoughts.

Just a month later, in August, "Tex" became an instant legend. As chief of flight testing, Bill Allen asked him to fly the *Dash 80* over the Gold Cup hydroplane races on Lake Washington, to show off the airplane. So "Tex," confident that he was not jeopardizing the airplane, came over the course at about 300 feet, pulled up and completed a 360 degree barrel roll at about 1,500 feet. Then, to the delight of the cheering crowd, estimated at 200,000—and an incredulous Allen—he turned the plane around and did it again. It was twenty-two years later before Allen was able to talk about that incident. Amazingly, not a word of the maneuver appeared in the local newspapers.

Thus "Tex" was destined to be remembered for his famous "barrel roll," long after his achievements as one of the premier test pilots of all time.

By the time the *Electra* flew in late 1957, the jet race between Boeing and Douglas was well under way. After about a year of working out design and production bugs, the *Electra* began commercial service with American Airlines early in 1959.

Even though the *Electra* matured later than Lockheed had hoped, and offered far less than the jets in terms of new technology, it had the advantage of significantly lower fuel usage.

Soon after the *Dash 80* flew, Juan Trippe sent Franklin Gledhill, his purchasing agent, along with Sanford Kauffman, from his engineering staff, to Seattle to look the prototype over. Of all the airlines, Pan American was the only one who had decided to bypass the turboprop technology entirely.

In Seattle, "Tex" took them up for a demonstration. In spite of the bare airplane—no soundproofing inside the fuselage—both men felt it was a fantastic improvement over piston planes. Nevertheless, jet technology was still short of what Trippe wanted. The plane, as configured, was not a truly nonstop transatlantic machine, requiring one stop westbound.

A crucial decision was imminent. The Pratt & Whitney J-57, although more powerful by one-third than any previous engine, still lacked the capability for a nonstop crossing. However, they were working on an advanced version, designated the J-75, which immediately riveted Trippe's attention.

Keeping his options secret, Trippe sent his team to the Douglas factory in Santa Monica to talk to Donald Douglas, and then to Lockheed to see Courtland Gross. He wanted them to know of his decision to switch to jets as soon as a viable design appeared, and he wanted them to compete with Boeing to drive the price down.

Donald Douglas at first refused. His DC-7 series was selling briskly. It would be the last major four-engined propeller airliner ever built, but Douglas did not know this, and he had orders for it carrying well into the future. The newest derivative, the DC-7C, was the result of a Pan American idea. Pressure from Pan Am had forced Douglas only a year before to lengthen the DC-7 wings by ten feet and to stretch the fuselage four feet. The result was a 20 percent increase in fuel capacity. The DC-7C could accommodate ninety-one tourist-class passengers, and was the first plane that could cross the Atlantic nonstop in all weather. Donald Douglas knew he had something good in this plane. Why should he allow himself to be pressured into a race for jet orders? He told Kauffman and Gledhill that a jet program would not be economic, and he mentioned a new study by the Rand Corporation which seemed to prove that jet engines burned too much fuel.

"'I've had an analysis made of that,' Kauffman told him, and he handed over some documents. 'Why don't you have your engineers make their own analysis.'

"Douglas found that his own engineers were anxious to build the plane and that their data coincided with Pan Am's. And so the Douglas Company, though far behind Boeing in development, decided to compete.

"Kauffman and Gledhill went to Lockheed, where they informed President Gross of the status of their negotiations with Boeing and Douglas. Would Gross like to build a jet also? Gross declined. Two factories competing was enough, he said.

"At this stage, it was entirely possible that Douglas would build a prototype to match Boeing's, and most airlines would refuse to buy either one. Apart from Trippe, the aviation world was terrified of jets."[6]

The explosion of the *Comets* in the air had brought into question the fundamental safety of jet airplanes. Operationally, too, jets seemed to promise disaster. Airports simply did not exist to handle this new type of plane. The engines burned kerosene instead of gasoline, and an entire new fueling infrastructure was required. Further, new hangars would be needed, as well as starting carts, and loading and servicing equipment—plus unknowns that had yet to surface.

With Boeing committed to the 707, and Douglas scrambling to complete the engineering for the DC-8, Pan Am was the only customer on the horizon, and Trippe decided he would purchase nothing less than a machine with true transatlantic capability and at least equivalent profitability to the DC-7C. His marketing studies told him he needed four more rows than the designs offered—equivalent to twenty-four more passengers. The bottom line was clear. Neither the 707 nor the DC-8 was large enough, and the engines were not powerful enough. Trippe decided to force the issue by playing the two manufacturers against one another by dangling the prospect of a large order.

By the spring of 1955, Douglas completed its DC-8 design—essentially the same plane that Boeing was already flying. The Douglas Board of Directors had authorized a production go-ahead with a minimum order of fifty planes. No orders came.

Trippe proposed building the bigger airplane in spite of the underpowered engine. He had confidence in the new J-75.

Boeing, having already invested $16 million, was totally committed. To change the size was beyond consideration.

Ralph Bell, Boeing sales director, lamented: "Our prototype is our biggest asset, but it's also our biggest obstacle. Douglas has a rubber airplane. It's easy to stretch on paper."[7]

For the moment, Trippe decided to concentrate on Douglas. Using the DC-2/DC-3 analogy, he coaxed Douglas to make the decision to redesign the DC-8 around the untested J-75. Douglas responded with a polite but firm no.

Trippe took his case to Fred Rentschler, chairman of Pratt & Whitney, and also a stockholder and member of the Pan Am board. A commitment to produce the J-75—and guarantee performance—would be the ace that he needed. Rentschler was adamantly opposed, pointing out that Pratt & Whitney had a perfectly acceptable production engine in the J-57 which matched the 707. Trippe responded by going to Rolls Royce, expanding his poker game to the international arena.

Trippe hardly hesitated in continuing to escalate the stakes. The Boeing prototype decision, which had gained the moniker "$15 million gamble," paled in comparison to the less publicized actions of the Pan Am chairman.

After an arm-twisting, pleading, promising campaign, arrestingly detailed by Daley,[8] Rentschler caved in, offering to have the J-75 ready by the summer of 1959—with the appropriate guarantees that Trippe had insisted upon. For that commitment, Trippe signed for around $40 million in engines. He would own the engines with no planes to put them on.

Taking his case to Boeing first, he announced: "If you won't build the plane I want, then I will find someone who will."[9] Allen, deciding that Trippe was bluffing, refused to budge. The 707-120 was there and he could take it or leave it. After all, Allen had another ace. With the KC-135 committed, the program was already guaranteed to be successful. It would be unnecessary to gamble further capital on a new fuselage and perhaps a new wing.

Playing the game to the hilt, Trippe went to Douglas—suggesting a turndown would force him to take his business overseas. The DC-8 was still on paper—no expensive tooling had been built. Douglas capitulated, agreeing to redesign a larger DC-8 around the J-75 engine. Trippe wrote an order for twenty-five planes, but requested the deal to be kept secret for a while longer, presumably to allow him a clearer field in dealing with Boeing. He wanted to be first with both so as to be guaranteed first in the air. Then, he ordered twenty of the smaller planes, leaving Boeing with the impression that it was the first order. This order was also kept secret, and Trippe signed both contracts on the same day.

Following an IATA executive meeting in New York on October 13, 1955, Trippe threw a party for the nation's airline executives, where he let it be known that Pan Am had just purchased $269 million worth of jets; $160 million to Douglas, and $100 million to Boeing.

In Seattle, Allen read about Trippe's deal in the newspapers. As it stood, Douglas would corner the foreign market with its big, longer-range planes, and would carve out a huge piece of the domestic market as well. Commercially speaking, the current 707-120 design was doomed before it ever entered service.

Allen phoned Trippe, offering to redesign the 707, and it was agreed that the Boeing-Pan Am contract would be renegotiated. Trippe would take six of the smaller 707s, inasmuch as Boeing was tooled up to turn them out reasonably quickly. These would suffice—with refueling stops—to open service on the North Atlantic months before anyone else did, and afterwards, they could serve Latin America. In addition, Boeing would build seventeen units of a bigger model, powered by the J-75.[10] The airplane was eight feet longer, with fifteen feet added to the span, and could carry up to twenty-four more passengers than the 120. The new design was designated the 707-320 *Intercontinental*.

Gaining the extra span was far from equivalent to starting over on the wing. It was accomplished by moving the zero wing station outboard from the airplane centerline, to positions on each side of the body, and designing a new center wing stub.

Some industry pundits not only called Trippe a gambler, they branded him as downright reckless. He had placed orders totaling $269 million on a net income of $10.4 million.

Airline delegations followed in lockstep to Seattle to fly in the prototype. Douglas won the second round when United Airlines ordered thirty DC-8s. It began to look as if Boeing had taken all the risks to prove the technology and Douglas was going to win the lion's share of orders simply by promising the improved version.

Pan Am Model 707 Christening

Mamie Eisenhower christening Pan Am's Boeing 707 *America*, as Juan Trippe looks on.
Photo by Hank Walker, Life Magazine © 1991 Time Warner Inc.

American Airlines ordered thirty Dash 320s. Eastern chose the DC-8; Continental and Braniff, the 707. And so it went, frantic, pell-mell into a new age of transportation. Airplanes would soon provide a doubling in capacity, with nearly twice the speed of propeller machines—promising to change the shape and size of the world.

In 1957, Donald W. Douglas, then sixty-five years old, moved to chairman of the board and Donald W. Douglas Jr. succeeded to the presidency. However, more than a change in president took place. A new team became responsible for the activities and the corporate conscience of the Douglas Aircraft Company. It would never be the same.

The first of the smaller Boeing model was delivered to Pan Am in mid-1958, and the inaugural VIP flight was made on October 19—from New York to Brussels. The plane was fitted out like a club car, with eighty-four seats.

The jets were an immediate financial success. During the first quarter of 1959, 33,400 passengers were carried on Pan Am jets, with a 90.8 percent seat occupancy, an all-time high. In the first five years of the Jet Age, overseas traffic doubled, and in 1963, Pan Am's net income after taxes was $33,568,000 on operating revenues of over a half billion dollars.

Later, Pan Am sold their DC-8s and standardized the fleet with 707s.

Early in 1956, Convair, then part of General Dynamics, a new, loosely organized nine-division conglomerate—of which Convair was the largest—saw themselves as a third contender in the great jet race. Reuben Fleet had long since sold his stock and left the company, and after the war, Convair enjoyed continued success with military airplanes, most notably the B-58, the first supersonic bomber. The company also developed successful twin piston-engined commercial transports; the 240, 340, and 440 series; of which over 1,000 were sold.

Encouraged by Howard Hughes, then still the controlling shareholder in TWA, Convair perceived market possibilities of as many as 250 jet transports of their own design, over a period of ten years—and predicted a rosy breakeven point at 68 aircraft. After securing letters of intent from TWA, Delta and KLM, and an engine guarantee from General Electric, the GD executive committee gave the go ahead for the Model 880, a sleek new jet similar in many respects to the 707/DC8s, but smaller and faster.

When KLM dropped out, Convair forged ahead, targeting United, who had expressed interest in a plane somewhat smaller than the DC-8s they had ordered, to handle their shorter domestic routes. They liked the 880—except for the five abreast seating.

President Allen, determined to do whatever it took to maintain leadership in the new field of commercial jets, directed his engineers to develop a model specifically to meet United's requirements. The plane was initially called the Model 717, a designation not to the liking of United, who chose to call it the Model 720. The -120 wing was retained and the body shortened by eight feet, with the width unchanged—still six abreast.

Convair and United had already agreed on eighteen of nineteen articles in a sales contract for the 880, when Boeing offered the 720. United chose the Boeing machine.

When the 880 rolled out on Christmas Day in 1958, it was already doomed. American Airlines, the last hope, decided to go for the 720B, a re-engined 720 with the newly developed General Electric fan. Convair, in desperation, offered to build a new model, the 990, with the fan engine. The 990 was to be the fastest jetliner in the world, cruising at 640 mph. American agreed to buy it—with suitable guarantees on speed, noise, payload and range, but insisted on trading in their old DC-7 airplanes. For Convair it was a double or nothing game, and they went forward on the 990. The first American 990 flew four months late, in January 1961. Since it was designed "straight to production," without a prototype, every airplane required major rework, and the guaranteed cruising speed was never achieved. A total of thirty airplanes were sold.

Boeing's 720B developed a life of its own, eventually being purchased by nearly a score of domestic and foreign airlines.

On February 3, 1959, disaster loomed for the Lockheed *Electra* when one crashed on landing in New York. Eight months later, a second *Electra* crashed at Buffalo, Texas, and the following year, still a third fell out of the air near Camelton, Indiana. In two of the crashes, engine separation had occurred in flight. All of the planes were called back to the factory for a radical restructuring of the wing and engine mounts.

It was a mortal blow for the *Electra*, and Lockheed dropped out of the commercial airplane business.

In 1959, Boeing offered an all-cargo version, designated the Model 735. The number did not stick, and was never used again, cargo planes simply being referred to as "C" models.

The enthusiasm with which the public accepted the new jet airplanes was unprecedented—and well earned. They brought a new dimension of vibrationless flight and a noticeably quieter cabin. It also became apparent that the jet engines were more reliable than their predecessors. Flight crews were quick to discover the new ease of operation. The 707 gained a reputation of being able to fly by itself—nearly dooming the program.

In February 1959, four months after the 707 began service over the Atlantic with Pan American, N712PA, the sixth airplane off the line, ran into trouble.[11]

Flying at 32,000 feet in quiet air, the flight was routine. The captain left his seat and strolled back into the cabin, chatting with the passengers. Suddenly, the airplane started nosing down. Losing altitude rapidly and increasing speed, its dive steepened. The captain, recognizing the problem, struggled to get back into the cockpit. He barely made it. With both him and the copilot straining at the controls, they pulled the plane out of the dive about 6,000 feet above the Atlantic Ocean. The loads on the wings were so great that the metal structure had surpassed its yield strength—and a few seconds more would have been too late. The only thing that saved the plane—and the commercial jet age—was the integrity that Boeing had built into the airframe.

When the airplane was returned to the factory for a complete structural and alignment check, it was found to be airworthy and fully qualified for continued flight. The report read in part, "The relative positions of the front and rear spar and the nacelles show that the wings are permanently twisted."[12]

Pan Am flew N712PA many more years, eventually selling it to a foreign carrier, where it continued in revenue service until October 30, 1984.

To meet the increasing demand for commercial jet airplanes, the Transport Division was formed in 1956. But by the end of 1959, the cutthroat competition with Douglas produced a financial crisis for the new division. The 707 program projected a massive loss of $200 million by the end of the year. Much of the increased cost could be attributed to the strict quality standards that Boeing had established.

The production runs for the B-52 at Wichita, the BOMARC in the new missile production center, and the KC-135 at Renton were creating sufficient profits to essentially subsidize the Transport Division, and provide the new investment needed to maintain the viability of the fragile entry into commercial jets.

Overall employment, which had reached an all-time peak at over 100,000 in 1957, was drastically reduced, and stood at 80,000 in 1959. It was feast or famine once again.

To meet the situation, Allen listed the principles that he felt must guide the effort ahead:

"In order to obtain business," he said, "we must earn the opportunity to compete for it. In order to compete we must have a better product to sell. In order to develop and offer a better product, we must have superior conception, design capability, and a demonstrated cost performance.

"In order to be superior in those fields, we must invest capital to sustain the people who will accomplish product and design, and we must put capital into research and development facilities and efforts. In order to have that capital we must either earn it through our profits, or attract it in the money markets."[13]

Those principles were being applied by putting 80 percent of earnings back into research and new facilities, latest of which was a Mach 20 hypersonic wind tunnel, the most advanced in the country.

1. Harold Mansfield, *Vision*, (New York: Popular Library, 1966), 191.
2. Ibid., 194.
3. Ibid., 196.
4. Ibid., 200.
5. Eugene Rodgers, *Flying High*, (New York: The Atlantic Monthly Press, 1996), 218.
6. Robert Daley, *An American Saga*, (New York: Random House, 1980), 403/404.
7. Private Communication.
8. Daley, *An American Saga*, 410.
9. Ibid., 411.
10. Ibid., 414.
11. *Aviation Week & Space Technology*, 9 February, 1959, 39.
12. W.F. Minkler, *Alignment Check—Airplane N712PA*, Internal Boeing Communication, CSPR-18, 10 February, 1959.
13. Private Communication.

CHAPTER EIGHTEEN

Military and Space

Speed remained the key to the future, be it commercial airplanes or weapon delivery systems.

After Convair won the competition for an advanced medium-range bomber—known as the B-58—a machine that could make a supersonic dash over the target area, the Air Force set its sights on a more ambitious goal—the capability of supersonic flight for the entire mission.

In 1953, Boeing won a study contract from the Air Force to brainstorm far-out ideas: a futuristic vehicle boosted to extreme altitudes by rocket and then allowed to glide to its target; nuclear-powered aircraft; ballistic missiles; and a supersonic bomber with speeds in the Mach 2 to Mach 3 range.

The supersonic bomber was given the top priority, and Thornton A. "T." Wilson, a rapidly rising young engineer from Iowa State University, was put in charge.

Wilson held an advanced degree in aeronautical engineering, and had just returned from a year's study at MIT as a Sloan Fellow in industrial management—a course that was then firmly embedded in Boeing's executive development plan.

By November 1955, competition had narrowed to Boeing and North American Aviation. North American, a war-spawned giant, manufacturing primarily military airplanes, was best known for its P-51 *Mustang*—the premium fighter of World War II—with a range capable of escorting B-17 and B-24 bombers deep into Europe. Both firms were awarded contracts to complete their design studies for a new strategic bomber designated as Weapon System 110-A by the Air Force.

Bill Allen spotlighted the effort. "This is a contract that Boeing must win," he said.[1]

To support the bid, research went forward on the combined effects of high pressure, friction, and heat; supersonic control; and manufacturing techniques. Proposing a giant step, Boeing chose titanium for the primary metal of construction. North American took a more conservative approach, choosing PH 15-7MO, a precipitation-hardenable stainless steel—cousin of the 17-7PH used in the BOMARC oxidizer tanks.

Specifically for the supersonic bomber, Boeing invested $30 million in a new, six-building complex near Plant II, completed in 1957—for research and engineering as well as the assembly of a complete prototype.

By the fall of 1957, the cards were on the table for the 110-A contract award. Ed Wells was noticeably nervous.

"What would we do if we lost?" Schairer asked him.

"There'll be hell to pay."[2]

On December 17, 1957, Convair fired the *Atlas*, first successful U.S. launch of a liquid-fueled ICBM. Schairer and Wells felt that another round of ICBM development was still to come—using solid propellant—which promised a major reduction in cost. Studies continued.

In May 1952, when Dr. Wernher von Braun, world's premier rocket scientist, suggested that it was not too early to begin the design of a space vehicle that could transport men to Mars, most of the world was not listening. No one had yet come close to orbiting a satellite around the Earth.

Incredibly, only five years later, on October 4, 1957, the Soviet Union astonished the world, successfully launching the first man made satellite.

Sputnik, at 184 pounds, caught the U.S.—planning its own satellite the following year—completely by surprise.

A month later, *Sputnik II*, weighing 1,100 pounds, carried a dog into space. When the U.S. finally launched its first satellite with an Army *Jupiter-C* booster on February 1, 1958, it paled in comparison—weighing in at 30.8 pounds.

In response to the Soviet achievements—with a touch of panic—the U.S. expanded its space efforts, passing the National Aeronautics and Space Act the same year, and creating the National Aeronautics and Space Administration (NASA).

On December 23, 1957, the 110-A competition decision was announced. North American would build the supersonic bomber. The use of titanium as the primary metal of construction was considered to be too great a step into the unknown.

Dismayed, but not disheartened by the Air Force decision, which seemed to be a step backward in technology, Boeing executives gathered in Allen's office. George Schairer presented the results of the solid propellant ICBM study to the assembled group. The case was impressive. However, there was as yet no Air Force definition—nor timetable—for a solid-fuel ballistic missile, so it was agreed to seek the impending contract for a boost-glide vehicle.

Allen formed an advanced projects team, with top priority, giving it authority to draft key people from the other divisions in the Company.

George Stoner, weapon systems manager on BOMARC, who had joined Boeing in 1941, was picked to head the team. Stoner had gained honors while working for his degree in chemistry at Westminister College in Pennsylvania, followed by several years of graduate study at MIT. He was eager to challenge the new frontier at the edge of the Earth's atmosphere.

While Stoner was gathering his team, on January 1, 1958, the Air Force sent a request for proposal for a dynamic soaring vehicle, with a Madison Avenue name—*Dyna-Soar*.

Stoner was quick to realize—and admit—that many companies were already well into critical aspects of the complex array of materials, manufacturing processes, guidance systems, and other key parameters. He set out to marshal an industry-wide team; finalizing on General Electric, Ramo-Wooldridge, Chance Vought, Aerojet General, and North American. His active imagination soon pictured a network of *Dyna-Soar* flights around the Earth, with multiple military uses, particularly global surveillance.

The greatest technological challenge was cooling the vehicle upon its return from the fringes of the atmosphere as it penetrated the oxygen-rich zone near the Earth.

Weight would be more critical than ever. No boosters were even in the design stage that were large enough to produce orbiting velocity.

By the law of conservation, the energy expended in the boost phase would have to be dissipated as heat during reentry. The nose and leading edge of the wing would reach temperatures in excess of 4,000 degrees Fahrenheit. Most metals melt at lower temperatures. Only ceramics and refractory metals—tungsten, molybdenum, tantalum, and columbium—remained as candidates. Ceramics were far too brittle for structural applications, and the refractory metals oxidized rapidly, requiring protective coatings to avoid burning up.

There were other choices. Active cooling, a concept chosen by the Bell-Martin team—the primary competitor—was only a matter of engineering. However, the resultant increase in weight demanded an even larger booster system. A third alternative was the use of ablative materials for the hottest surfaces. Nonmetallic in nature, ablative materials sublimed when heated, absorbing huge quantities of energy as they slowly gave up their mass. However, extensive refurbishment would be required after each flight.

Boldly, the decision was made to design the vehicle with refractory alloys, and go to orbit—Stoner opting for the system with the highest potential payoff—and the most difficult unsolved problems. The metallurgical community would have to invent new alloys, as well as coatings to protect them.

A cooperative program was initiated with the Wah Chang Company in Oregon, a primary producer of refractory alloys. Columbium was chosen as the most promising candidate for investigation. Metallurgical engineers Samuel "Sam" Elrod, and Ronald "Ron" Torgerson, from the South Dakota School of Mines and the University of Washington respectively, conducted the Boeing effort. The successful program produced two new alloys, C-103 and C129Y, both of which exhibited mechanical properties suitable for certain hot regions of the *Dyna-Soar* vehicle.

Equally difficult problems in many other disciplines were being confronted—and solved.

On June 23, 1958, the competition for *Dyna-Soar* was narrowed to the Boeing and Bell-Martin teams, each awarded contracts to develop their particular concepts.

Bill Allen was exuberant, intent on taking the final heat of the race. "We will undertake it with all the vigor and ingenuity at our command," he told the Air Force."[3]

Meanwhile, it became clear that *Minuteman*, the new solid propellant ballistic missile, would have a great business potential. Allen decided to enlarge the advanced projects proposal team into a Systems Management Office, headed by Ed Wells. For Boeing, this concept represented a landmark decision, emphasizing *program management* as the most important element in the complex world of missiles and space.

Dyna-Soar and *Minuteman* became the twin objectives of the newly formed group. T. Wilson, fresh from the 110-A effort, was chosen to head *Minuteman*—a huge national program—and preparations for a proposal required a new approach. The basic design had already been fixed, and the Air Force had divided the multi-billion dollar program into several packages: first stage booster, second stage booster, third stage booster, guidance and control section, warhead section, and finally, assembly and test. All but the last had already been committed to companies specializing in particular fields.

Many felt that the assembly and test portion alone would not provide enough work to be a worthwhile endeavor, but George Schairer disagreed.

"'If we're willing to go in and assist the Air Force in managing this,' he said, '...if we're willing to take the viewpoint that it's their program, not ours, and just help them do the job, I think there'll be plenty of business in it for us.'

"Wells agreed completely. 'The thing we've got to get across to our people is that we have to be responsive to the requirements. That means being responsive to the customer's view as to what the system should accomplish. They want to overcome the shortcomings of the liquid systems, *Atlas* and *Titan*, in terms of readiness, reliability, reaction time, and ability to be maintained over a long period without constant attention. Our job will be to bring an understanding of these needs, and how we can help to meet them.'"[4]

The result of that conceptual approach was the implementation of an effort that analyzed every aspect of the system—with even more emphasis on the management side than on the technical side. A 1/20-scale model was constructed and fired from an underground silo at the north end of Boeing Field. The Boeing proposal covered plans for hardened silos; underground control cubicles with their automatic equipment; a launch site installation system with missile handling devices; checkout and maintenance gear; the integration of the missile itself; a plan for management of the assembly and test plant; construction of installations; and plans for the research required to support each aspect of the program.

On October 10, 1958, Wells was working late—as usual—when he received a teletype from the commander of the Air Force Ballistics Missiles Division of the Air Research and Development Command, indicating the Boeing proposal had been evaluated as the best submitted.

Four days later, in Los Angeles, Bill Allen signed the contract.

The dimensions of the assembly and test portion continued to grow as it became evident that major aspects of the Boeing study were as yet unassigned by the Air Force, and the Company was the logical contractor to inherit them. The final result was that *Boeing was assigned overall responsibility for making Minuteman work as an effective strategic weapons system.*

With *Dyna-Soar* increasing its demands for the invention of new materials and technologies, Boeing created the Scientific Research Laboratories in January 1958. Conceptually similar to the Bell Telephone Laboratories, where the transistor was born, it employed 100 scientists—with an open charter. There were no fixed working hours—assuming that ideas were not captive to any particular time of the day or night.

The delay for the *Dyna-Soar* decision was agonizingly continued, but finally, out of the blue on November 9, 1959, Bill Allen received a phone call from General Beverly Warren of the Air Materiel Command. "Congratulations," the General began, "I expect you'll be glad to know that your Company has been selected as systems contractor for the *Dyna-Soar* program."[5]

Bill Allen was more than a little awed at the thought of the bizarre, sled-like wings of a *Dyna-Soar* glowing white like a meteor, as its pilot guided it down from space. Allen wrote a message to all Boeing management on the winning of the contract. "It is a project that captures the imagination. What we have won is an opportunity. What we do with the opportunity is entirely up to us."[6]

Allen's strong initiatives at the loss of the 110-A had paid off handsomely. Contracts for both the *Minuteman* and the *Dyna-Soar* had been secured. As a paradoxical footnote to history, the B-70 (110A) program was canceled before the airplane flew. North American built two units, the first making its maiden flight from Palmdale, California, on May 11, 1964.

The Ballistic Missile Command, antsy because of angry political forces—who had declared a "missile gap" with the Soviets—called for operational readiness to be accelerated by six months.

When the question reached Seattle, T. Wilson assessed the possibilities with his staff and the associate contractors. "With a mixture of perspiration and zeal, Wilson said it could be done."[7] The new schedule called for 100 missiles to be in place and operational by the middle of 1963, and 400 by 1964. On February 1, 1961, the "missile gap" began to recede into history as the first operational *Minuteman* made a perfect flight to its planned impact point 4,200 miles down range. The Air Force pronounced it an unqualified success.

Overnight, Boeing was faced with a production line that stretched across hundreds of sites in the north-central states of the United States, integrating the efforts and the products of a half-dozen major associate contractors. The final product was a launch complex—delivered underground—and ready to fire missiles.

Ernest H. "Tex" Boullioun, from the University of Texas, came to work at Boeing in 1940, almost by chance. Arriving in the Pacific Northwest on a motorcycle, Tex lost it in a poker game in Portland on his way to Seattle. Hitching a ride the rest of the way, he began his career at Boeing as an inspector. Tex, always seeking the heart of a problem, rose rapidly in the quality control department, and when *Minuteman* was ready for deployment, was in charge of installing the BOMARC missiles. Assigned to the same key role for *Minuteman*, Tex, along with Howard "Bud" Hurst, factory manager, a self-made man who started in the shops in 1929, devised the plan for implementation of *Minuteman*.

Instead of bringing the work past the workers on a traditional production line, they would bring the workers past the various installations, each special team accomplishing a specific task. That meant 8,000 men in the field, working in fifty to sixty holes at a time. Every task was broken down into eight-hour increments, so that skilled workers could put in a day or more and move on. Families lived in mobile homes, moving from base to base.

Ignoring those who said it couldn't be done, Boullioun convinced T. Wilson that it could, and they set up a control room in Seattle to track the operation on massive wall charts.

Busy days became the standard for the new teams—a special breed of employees called the *"Outplant Crew."* They went to the plains of Montana and the Dakotas, braving the blazing summer heat, bitter winter cold, and stinging winds.

In all, at the peak, Boeing put 33,400 employees on the program. The Company's work force in Seattle conducted engineering, subassembly and support activities. At Hill Air Force base, in Ogden, Utah, the missiles were assembled and dispatched to the six Air Force bases stretching from Montana to Missouri. Engineering support and test launches were the responsibility of a Boeing team at Cape Canaveral and later at Vandenberg Air Force Base in California.

Under the incentive features of the contract, Boeing consistently beat schedule and cost targets, giving the nation one of the best managed, mission-capable strategic systems in its history.

On September 24, 1964, *Minuteman II*, an improved missile with longer range and more accurate guidance, made a flawless flight from Cape Canaveral to a target in the South Atlantic.[8]

Four days after Christmas, 1970, the first squadron of new *Minuteman III* missiles was turned over to the air force at Minot Air Force Base, North Dakota. A total of 550 *Minuteman IIIs* joined the 450 *Minuteman IIs* already in place.[8]

Minuteman was one of the largest and longest programs in Boeing's history. In December, 1978, the last missile rolled out of the Ogden plant, twenty years after the initial contract award.

By spring 1961, senior project engineer Harry Goldie, a magna cum laude whiz-kid from the University of Washington electrical engineering school—and later, Cal Tech—who joined Boeing in 1949, was able to report to George Stoner that most of the major structural and aerodynamic design features of *Dyna-Soar* had been settled. The majority of his 1,600 engineers were turning to subsystem design: control, electrical power generation, hydraulics, and electronics.

Major problems remained. For example, there was a need for wires to go to sensors in the leading edges of the wings where they would be subjected to 3,000 degrees Fahrenheit. There were no suppliers—they turned away—laughing. Goldie gave the problem back to the project group. "We'll have to invent our own," he said, without batting an eye.[9]

The Soviets continued their lead in space, when on April 2, 1961, they startled an awed world with the announcement that a man had been launched into orbit and safely returned to earth. Yuri Gagarin, a 27-year-old air force major, accomplished the feat in a 10,395-pound *sputnik* called *Vostok*.

The following month, on May 5, the U.S. sent Navy Commander Alan B. Shepard, Jr., into space for a fifteen minute ride, landing downrange in the Atlantic Ocean. He flew in a *Mercury* spacecraft built by the McDonnell Aircraft Company in St. Louis, a pioneer in building space hardware.

Twenty days later, President John F. Kennedy asked the Congress to approve a multibillion-dollar program to send a man to the moon and return him safely to the Earth. Space efforts went into overdrive around the country, to achieve that goal before the decade was over.

With Kennedy's bold new initiative, the Air Force went to the House of Representatives with a request to increase the *Dyna-Soar* appropriations, speeding up the program by a full year.

The positive response from Congress for additional funds did not produce a speedup. Instead, Robert S. McNamara, Secretary of Defense, decided to withhold the funds and review all the options. He believed that the more sophisticated *Dyna-soar* would be late for the orbiting role, and favored ballistic launching of space capsules.

On December 10, 1963, Secretary McNamara announced his decision: *Dyna-Soar* was canceled. The program had already consumed $400 million dollars and years of effort. Abruptly, 5,000 Boeing employees, and thousands of others around the nation, were out of a job. It seemed that bad news always came around Christmas.

History will be unable to assess whether McNamara made the correct decision. It is altogether possible that the *Space Shuttle*—first launched on

April 12, 1981—might have been operational many years earlier, had the innovative *Dyna-Soar* technology been continued to maturity.

1. Private Communication.
2. Harold Mansfield, *Vision*, (New York: Popular Library, 1966), 227.
3. Mansfield, *Vision*, 237.
4. Ibid., 237.
5. Private Communication.
6. Ibid.
7. Ibid.
8. *Boeing News*, 5 October, 1978, 3.
9. Private Communication.

CHAPTER NINETEEN

The Impossible Airplane

Enthusiastic acceptance of the new commercial jets with their speed and quiet cabin comfort was unprecedented. Sales of 707s and DC-8s quickly spread around the world.

The Convair 880 and 990 airplane programs died an early death, and the combined cost of $425 million, written off at the end of 1961, represented the largest in corporate history.[1] The battle for dominance in the commercial jet market was left to Boeing and Douglas.

The red ink on the 707 program was not only due to the price war with Douglas. Major research and testing efforts had been mounted, and capital investment in facilities was unprecedented. Boeing had determined to produce a machine that was structurally safe for many thousands of hours.

Early in 1956, a huge water tank had been constructed at Plant I to simulate the airplane flight environment. An entire fuselage was submerged in the 20-foot wide, 20-foot deep and 130 foot-long-tank. Continued pumping of water in and out, on a regular schedule, simulated pressure changes as well as the gust cycles expected during thousands of flights.

A complete cabin pressure cycle could be accomplished in five minutes, during which twenty-five gust cycles were simulated. As the load and material performance history was developed, the design was continually improved. Final proof of structural integrity was made with the "guillotine," a device used to slash instantaneous incisions of varying length in the pressurized structure, providing a statistical validation of the behavior of cracks with continued cycles.

To test and qualify materials for windshields, a "chicken gun" was designed to propel the bodies of chickens against the windshields at jet speeds—simulating bird strikes.

Many other specialized test setups were developed for specific components and systems.

Demand for jets on shorter routes was soon a reality. Indeed, propeller airplanes were fast becoming an anachronism in the minds of the traveling public—long before the economics of jets justified them on short routes.

In May 1958, before the first 707 was delivered to Pan American, John E. "Jack" Steiner, was appointed to head a planning group for a Boeing short-range jet. At that time, Maynard Pennell—engineer extraordinary—who had cut his eye-teeth on the B-29, and headed the 707 program as senior project engineer—was in charge of preliminary design. Jack Steiner worked for Pennell as an aerodynamicist. The two men had great respect for each other's ability, sharing a common vision—the maturation of the commercial jet airplane business.

Both had graduated from the University of Washington; Pennell with a degree in aeronautical engineering in 1940, and Steiner majoring in both law and engineering. Ultimately turning exclusively to engineering, he graduated at the top of his class, and with borrowed money, headed for MIT with plans for a doctorate. In New York, at a meeting of the Institute of Aeronautical Sciences, he met and sought career advice from George Schairer. Schairer put him to work writing a thesis on the hydrodynamic stability of flying boats while he earned his master's credits. In 1941, Steiner began his life-long career at Boeing.

It was a fortunate coincidence that Steiner and Pennell had come together at a propitious moment in history. It was Pennell, perhaps more than other, who led the thrust into the commercial jet age.

When Steiner was given the short-range jet assignment in 1958, the plane had a number—the 727—but not much more. Thirty-eight design variations had been tried, and it was beginning to look like an endless journey. To keep the airplane as small as possible, they had concentrated on two-engine versions, but two engines under the wings posed a serious load-and-balance situation, and two on the back added excessive structural weight to the fuselage.

The world market was judged to be 500 airplanes in the short-haul category; however in 1958, the Lockheed *Electra* was still a strong competitor, with a short-field capability that looked impossible to match with jets, and Douglas was working hard on a short-range jet called the DC-9. As a further complication, there were no jet engines available of the right size.

"If we're serious about offering a short range jet," said Harry Carter, chief of market research, "we're going to have to come up with one that can operate as economically as the turboprops—and into the same short fields."

"That's O.K.," said Jack. "If we don't have a few problems we'll die of comfort."[2]

Steiner viewed all of those negatives as simply problems to solve.

Before the year was out, Douglas was discussing the DC-9 with airlines in Europe. The concept was a scaled down DC-8 with two engines in pods under the wing—a configuration Boeing had already rejected. The Boeing strategy remained to design a still smaller airplane, so as not to interfere with the sales of the 720, smallest of the existing family.

The public, enamored with jets, still had an aversion to anything less than four engines, perceiving them to have greater safety.

Discussions with the airlines did not provide much to go on. Uncertainty as to what the next step should be was predominant. United, a bellwether of the industry, used Denver as a hub on its transcontinental flights, and a one-stop airplane would have to be good for mile-high Denver. Performance requirements for a twin, with one engine out, would be very difficult to meet. With United favoring four engines, and hedging its bets with turboprops, it was apparent the *Electra* was the horse to beat.

Boeing found TWA receptive to a twin—but only lukewarm. In a phone conversation with Bob Rummel, TWA engineering vice president, Steiner listened intently, when Rummel, half joking, said, "Why don't you compromise on three engines and make a good airplane?"[3]

Boeing's interest in a three-engine airplane stood at zero. There were more problems than with the twin. Where to put the third engine—if indeed the right-sized engines were available—or even on the drawing boards?

With so many unknowns, a prototype seemed imperative. The finance department put a thundering no on the suggestion.

Even without the added expense of a prototype, the necessary price of a 727 appeared to be in the $3.25 to $3.50 million range—with production of 200 units needed to break even. There was no such market in sight. United and TWA together might be good for 80—still a big if with *Electras* selling for $2.1 million, and British *Viscounts* for $1.27 million. A market analysis showed a price between $2 and $2.5 million would be required for a 727 to be competitive. *The project seemed to be clearly impossible.*

The team studied a preproduction airplane in lieu of a true prototype, with sufficient lead time ahead of the first production unit to avoid investment in two sets of hard tooling. Dave Breuninger of manufacturing estimated a cost of $6 million to build such a machine.

"What's the alternative?" Jack asked. "Build the first airplane with the regular production tooling? Flight test it concurrent with production?"

"That's right."

"It will cost more if we have to make changes then; that's exactly what you want to avoid."

Breuninger smiled. "You have to get it right the first time."[4]

After still another review, engineering could not find anything that made sense, and was beginning to harden on the four-engine concept, a machine slightly smaller than the 720. It was reported that Douglas had reached the same conclusion on their proposed DC-9. The sales department balked, insisting on a truly small airplane. Bob Rummel of TWA was still pushing for three engines.

By 1959, the marketing department presented a depressing outlook. "The market is not yet ripe for exploitation," their report read. They added that whether the airplane was built by Boeing or Douglas, it would probably have to be priced well above the figures used in the study, and close to the price of the 720. "In short, it appears that a small jet is not economically possible."[5]

Sales engineer Art Curren, genuinely disturbed, brought Steiner a factory workload forecast. "It drops off too damned abruptly for comfort the end of '62," he moaned. "We're in a really bad hole in '63 and '64. If we're going to sit in on the poker game, we've got to put up or shut up."[6]

After discussions with Joe Sutter, head aerodynamicist, Steiner concluded that what was needed was an entirely new design formula—discard all the warmed-over variations and start fresh—in the Boeing tradition.

Sutter, described by his department head in the University of Washington school of aeronautical engineering, as "my brightest student,"[7] had been digging into boundary layer control and other ways to increase lift, exactly what was needed to provide superior performance on short, high-altitude landing fields.

William H. "Bill" Cook, with a master of science from MIT, and chief of the technical staff, agreed. He devised a research plan to test a series of alternatives in the wind tunnel and fly the most promising concepts on the 707 prototype. A particularly provocative idea was the use of multiple flaps.

With new urgency, Steiner and Pennell got Bill Allen's approval for a two-month, all-out evaluation program, culminating in a go-no-go recommendation to the corporate offices.

Abruptly, Ed Wells reported that United Airlines was prepared to sign a letter of understanding with Douglas by the first of July—only thirty days away.

Wells—quiet, thoughtful, competent—seemed always to have the correct advice. "Don't panic," he said.

"Let's project the potential through the next ten to fifteen years," Wells told Steiner. "We have to realize that the important thing is how many we can sell altogether. The profit comes from staying in the market, not with the first ones you build....We have to look beyond the present. We ought to be in a position to sell whatever is in the best interest of the customer. Try to get there by just cutting costs, and you may not get there at all."

"You aren't concerned about the cost problem?"

"Of course. My point is let's not compromise on getting the product we can sell."[8]

In late June, the puzzle was complicated further when Eastern indicated their preference for three engines. American was adamant on two, and Douglas publicly announced its decision to build a four-engined DC-9.

Taking stock, Steiner concluded that Douglas was ahead with their four-engined version, with a tie-up with Pratt and Whitney for engines. In England, de Havilland was ahead on a three-engined design, and a three-engined airplane seemed to be common ground that just might get all the major airlines together. But there were no engines of the right size. Schairer proposed that Boeing write its own specification for an engine, rather than wait for something to come along.

Rolls Royce was building the engines for the newly announced three-engined de Havilland *Trident*. Steiner needed more power, urging Rolls to design a larger one. Desiring to get into the U.S. market, Rolls agreed.

The team considered a three-engined airplane with two mounted on the wings and one in the tail. A breakthrough on the lift problem had been achieved, and when the test results were all digested, the aft-mounted engine design looked surprisingly good.

With no time to work out an exotic boundary-layer control, the technical staff had concentrated on multiple slotted flaps, finalizing on a triple-slotted trailing edge flap system, with a flap on the leading edge. The combination provided a small, efficient wing for high speed, but also with high lift for short runways.

Just when it appeared that the technical problems were yielding to solution, the tooling estimate of 1.5 million man-hours shot up to 5 million. A 727 production decision was still on hold.

When British European Airways signed a contract for twenty-four three-engined *Tridents* at the end of August 1959, with all mounted aft, and a "T" tail, Pennell decided that the Trident was the competition to beat. All efforts were directed to designing a better machine. Location of the horizontal tail was the crucial parameter.

Teaming with European partners was reviewed and rejected—and time ran. Engines mounted on the tail called for still another extensive wind tunnel testing program.

By May 1960, Joe Sutter had the results. The low tail came out negative and the "T" tail was in. Finally, the 727 had a configuration. The "T" tail, with sweepback, provided an unforeseen benefit, having the effect of lengthening the airplane, which increased the latitude for load-and-balance. Concurrently, the horizontal stabilizer was smaller, trading off for the heavier structure required for the aft-mounted engines.

Sales and marketing fretted that the public would view the airplane as simply a copy of the *Trident*. However, with the British plane already committed to the factory, Boeing had a unique advantage. Sitting in the catbird seat with a "paper airplane," it was no great task to design a superior product. That's exactly what happened. Engineering design for production—no prototype—was committed on June 10, 1960.

The Rolls engine looked good to Steiner and the company had willingly worked with Boeing at their own expense, but Eastern wanted to switch to a new, larger, Pratt & Whitney engine which they viewed as a more rugged design, with more opportunity for growth. Steiner worried about the modifications required for the airframe—and the increased cost.

Eddie Rickenbacker, president of Eastern made the final decision—choosing the Pratt & Whitney. With this change, plus a loading stairway in the tail, and other additions requested by the customers, the price was set at $4.2 million, a price that once seemed inconceivable from a sales point of view. But the latest design was a far different machine, with much greater earning potential.

Cash requirements were estimated to build up to $130 million prior to the first delivery. Now, the very survival of the Boeing Airplane Company was again on the line.

Allen went to the board in late August with a recommendation to go ahead with the 727 if orders could be achieved for 100 airplanes. The board approved.

Steiner took to the road to try to gain a commonality compromise among the airlines. United and Eastern agreed to the latest configuration. Allen proceeded to hammer out contracts. The best he could do was forty planes for Eastern and forty for United—twenty of which were subject to cancellation—with a deadline of December 1.

As the deadline approached, the order list was stuck at eighty, with twenty still subject to cancellation. Allen fretted. The board left the decision to him. *Act—get things done—move forward.* The buck could not be passed.

Deciding there was no turning back, Allen pushed the button, and on November 30, 1960, one day before the deadline, he signed contracts with United and Eastern, for a total of $420 million—then the largest single transaction in commercial aviation history.

Five hundred engineers were now on the program and more were being added at the rate of 120 per month. Manufacturing had to gear up a completely new production line, with hard tooling. Everything was aimed at the rollout, scheduled—and achieved—on November 27, 1962. *The impossible airplane was a reality.*

Wells and Schairer wanted to be doubly certain of the structural integ-

Model 727—1963–1984

The "Impossible Airplane," which became a best seller. Here, the final airplane of the 727 series rolls out of the factory.

rity of the 727. They recommended the testing of two complete airframes, rather than the traditional, single static test unit. The second airframe would be subjected to fatigue testing, simulating flight conditions for the complete life of the airplane—considered at the time to be twenty years.

"With all the investment we're putting into it the only way we can come out on the program is by having enough sales," Wells told division manager John Yeasting, in advocating the admittedly expensive precautionary steps. "We'll be in a much better position to get these, if we're on the soundest possible foundation. We'll get our money back in the long run, if we get our changes in early."[9]

The extra testing meant painful additions to the budget, but Yeasting approved them, as did Allen. The whole case for the airplane rested on it being right.

Prior to first flight, the company had invested over $150 million, and five customer airlines were committed to a total of $700 million.

After the airplane completed its test flights, its performance was the harbinger to its outstanding commercial success. It was simply a far better airplane than any offered by the competition.

Mansfield captures the mood at Boeing after the proving flights. "Jack Steiner and Joe Sutter went to Dick Rouzie, director of engineering. 'We're in trouble. We've made a mistake,' Jack said.

"Rouzie was accustomed to trouble, having been with Boeing since 1928—fresh out of Purdue University in mechanical engineering—but he was worried, until he saw Jack's grin.

"'We've got a lot better performance than we're supposed to have.'"[10]

The airplane was achieving more than 10 percent better fuel mileage, promising millions of dollars in fuel savings.

As demonstrated throughout Boeing's history, its strong, patient, intense engineering efforts had once more been the key. The triple slotted flap system devised by Bill Cook and his staff, stood out as a technological breakthrough.

The first 727-100 was delivered to Eastern airlines on October 29, 1963. The 727 spawned a family of airplanes, responding to the customers needs. The last unit—and last of the 727 family—was a -200F freighter delivered to Federal Express on September 18, 1984.

A total of 1,831 units were sold, a record for commercial jet airplanes. The 727 found a niche of size and performance in the commercial transport world with no worthy competitor, becoming a *cash cow* for Boeing for many years.

One day, when Jack Steiner visited the production line at the factory, a big sign, always there, caught his eye. "STOP. Do not enter unless you are interested in making a QUALITY PRODUCT in a SAFE MANNER."[11] Steiner stopped—and entered.

1. *Fortune*, January, 1962, 65.
2. Harold Mansfield, *Billion Dollar Battle*, (New York: Arno Press, 1980), 8.
3. Ibid., 19.
4. Ibid., 24.
5. Ibid., 29.
6. Harold Mansfield, *Vision*, (New York: Popular Library, 1966), 248.
7. Private Communication.
8. Mansfield, *Vision*, 251.
9. Ibid. 297.
10. Harold Mansfield, *Billion Dollar Battle*, 140.
11. Ibid. 174.

CHAPTER TWENTY

Supersonic Airplanes

A commercial supersonic airplane was a certain economic impossibility for any private company. At a minimum, developmental costs would have to be borne by the government. Nevertheless, industry's goal was speed—and the economic realities were only vaguely defined—as enthusiasm for this new frontier grew.

Technical problems of staggering proportions remained. Aerodynamically, a supersonic wing fell far short of the desired lift-over-drag ratio of the subsonics, translating to a requirement for vastly more powerful engines. Severe sweepback helped in the L-over-D ratio, but the resultant delta wing left no good place to locate the landing gear or the engines—and produced an unacceptably high landing speed.

Titanium, the best candidate for construction of an airplane traveling three times the speed of sound—because of the 600 degree Fahrenheit operating skin temperature—had barely passed the pure metal stage. High strength titanium alloys— still in the laboratory—remained to be proven.

One square inch of finished 0.040-inch-thick sheet of commercially pure titanium cost five cents in 1964, compared to one-fifth of a cent for clad aluminum alloys of the same thickness. The new titanium alloys would cost considerably more, and scrap—unlike aluminum—was not reclaimable.

Following the failure to win the B-70 supersonic bomber business, Boeing accelerated its research efforts toward future supersonic vehicles.

However, in spite of new enthusiasm in preliminary design, Bill Allen worried that a supersonic effort would drag Boeing down. With the 707 deeply in the red, and the 727 only a gleam in John Steiner's eye at the time, a supersonic transport seemed to be pure fiscal insanity. Nevertheless, Allen saw the inevitability of the next wave of technology, and he shifted top corporate executives into positions to create the managerial posture necessary to step up to this new challenge. The time seemed to be right—and North American, Douglas, Lockheed, and Convair all began moving in the same direction.

Companies in both Britain and France were also studying supersonic transports, clamoring for government subsidies.

At the Paris Air Show in 1961, Sud-Dassault of France displayed a model of a *Super Cavarelle* designed to convince the world that the French were in a position to produce a seventy-passenger supersonic plane with a range of up to 2,000 miles.

The French revelation put added urgency on the British efforts, and after some sparring to set up a joint program—with no progress—the two governments intervened, and in March 1962, an agreement was formalized and approved.

On the engine side, there was remarkably little conflict, with Bristol-Siddeley holding the upper hand with its already proven *Olympus*.

The airframe and systems were another matter, with little visible common ground. Again, the governments intervened, the two companies agreeing to work out design problems as they went along. By 1965, both firms were ready to cut metal on two identical *Concorde* prototypes—one assembled in France and the other in England. The airplane would be a more conservative design—all aluminum—for Mach 2 speeds.[1]

Researchers at NASA's Langely Field laboratories had been working on ideas to solve the wing problem. In early 1959, John Stack, director of research at Langely, called Schairer. "We have a new invention we're show-ing to industry. Can you send someone back?"

"Sure, what is it John?"

"We have some new ideas on variable sweep."[2]

The idea of changing the sweep of the wings in flight had been tried, when Bell, under an Air Force contract, had built and flown a fighter. Chang-ing the sweep proved to be only part of the solution. To preserve stability, the Bell machine's wings were not only hinged, but also mounted on tracks, moving backward and forward along the fuselage. After demonstration of that complex mechanism, industry interest cooled considerably, but Stack refused to abandon the idea. With additional wind tunnel tests, he dem-onstrated that there was indeed a correct place for a fixed hinge point.

At Boeing, efforts focused on a pivot mechanism—linchpin of any fam-ily of variable-sweep airplanes—military or civilian. The result was a unique bearing design capable of transmitting heavy loads for thousands of cycles.

Preliminary design studies for variable sweep in tactical fighters had also been going on since 1959. Vaughn Blumenthal, another of the legions of engineering graduates from the University of Washington—in charge of the fighter effort—was invited to a briefing at Wright Field in early 1960, to discuss the design of a variable sweep fighter. When the companies in attendance were asked if they were ready to take on such a project, the only one to volunteer was Boeing. Blumenthal expressed an eagerness to begin. "We can start immediately," he said.[3]

Recognizing the broad potential of a wing pivot design and sensing the opportunity for capturing the crucial edge in the expected fighter compe-tition, Ed Wells authorized construction of a full scale-mockup. The new technology would make all existing fighter airplanes obsolete.

The Company was confident and growing, and in Morton, Pennsylva-nia, on March 31, 1960, the Vertol Aircraft Corporation, with 2,300 em-ployees, was acquired, becoming a Boeing division, adding helicopters to its line of products. There, three new models were showing promise; the big *Chinook*, of which the Army had ordered ten; the *Sea Knight*, that had just won the Marine Corps competition; and a civilian version called the *Model 107*, that had been sold to New York Airways.

In recognition of the increasing diversity of the product line, the Boeing Air-plane Company became The Boeing Company on May 3, 1961.

When Wright Field released a request to study a proposed experimental tactical fighter—to be called the *TFX*—and to utilize variable sweep wings, Boeing was far ahead of the industry in the technology.

Election years were the worst possible times for fast action on pending government programs. Thus, the formal competition decision for the *TFX* hung in the balance all during 1960. Finally, Secretary of Defense Gates decided to leave the decision to Robert McNamara, new Secretary of Defense under President John F. Kennedy.

McNamara ordered a study to find out if the Navy and the Air Force requirements for a fighter could be integrated.

More than a year later, on October 1, 1961, the Defense Department requested formal proposals on the *TFX*, calling for a design which would satisfy both the Navy and the Air Force. For Boeing the delay was deadly, their technological lead quickly evaporating. Efforts were redoubled, and in February 1962, Boeing was chosen as one of the finalists—along with a team headed by General Dynamics.

A source selection expected in May was postponed until June—pending further study. The net result of all the delays was to make the two airplanes almost identical, throwing the decision into the political arena.

In early November, rumors drifted out of the Pentagon that Boeing had won—in all probability the largest single defense program of all time. With four years of dedicated effort behind them, Boeing expectations were still understandably high. On November 24, Secretary McNamara announced that the General Dynamics team was the winner. Boeing—and Seattle— were stunned.

Henry M. Jackson, Senator from the State of Washington, called President Allen, highly concerned. He had learned that the Boeing bid was lower by $100 million, and that all the evaluating groups had recommended Boeing. Jackson wanted to call these facts to the attention of Senator John McClellan's Senate investigating committee, of which he was a member. Allen hesitated, fearing the request would be attributed to Boeing and would color future relations with the Department of Defense. He cautioned his staff not to become involved, leaving the hearings to the political process.

The hearings did not reveal any irregularity or evidence of influence. However, they did reveal sharp differences of opinion. The operational people favored the Boeing proposal, but the Secretaries reported that the evaluation scores were so close that either product was considered acceptable. In sum, the final decision rested on one man—Secretary McNamara—who professed to have two criteria: commonality and cost. According to his analysis, Boeing had shown 60 percent commonality, and General Dynamics, 85 percent. Nevertheless, Boeing had proposed to do the job for $100 million less—on a fixed price contract.

Paradoxically, the technological innovations incorporated in the Boeing design—resulting in superior performance—were considered by McNamara to be too risky, and he simply did not believe the cost figures would hold for follow-on requirements. The General Dynamics design had avoided such new features as inflight reversible thrust and the incorporation of significant amounts of titanium in place of heavier steel parts. It was an unusual turn of events—where superior technology, so crucial to military superiority—failed to win.

Bill Allen was called to testify. He was reluctant, but Ed Wells felt the technical questions needed clarifying. They both testified on April 24, 1963; Allen stressing Boeing's low cost bid, which he pointed out was based on jet bomber and transport experience as well as the BOMARC, itself a complex supersonic interceptor, and Wells explaining the extensive testing of the advanced features.

"When large steps can clearly be taken in military capability, will the enemy permit us the luxury of taking a smaller step?" Wells asked.[4]

The committee solicited Allen's comments on two possible courses of action: a reversal of the decision, or twin awards of identical contracts, with both constructing an airplane for a flyoff competition.

"We did not seek this investigation," Allen replied. "Nor do we seek redress in the halls of Congress. As between the two alternatives, however, the second course of action offers the best possibility of meeting the objectives of the committee."[5]

No further action was taken. For the second time in its history, Boeing dropped out of the fighter business.

Juan Trippe, looking for the next step in air transport was eager to take on something new. He was aware of the discussions for a supersonic transport, a project so expensive that only the government could afford to finance it. Daley[6] relates the next series of events, typical of the operating philosophy of Trippe.

"President Kennedy, who had received conflicting advice on the project, was trying to decide whether to back it or not, and he sent a man named Najeeb Halaby to tell Trippe not to buy the foreign supersonic until he had made up his mind. Halaby, as head of the Federal Aviation Administration (FAA), held virtual Cabinet rank.

"Trippe, too, had received conflicting advice. Lindbergh, for one, was strongly against supersonic jets on environmental grounds. Their noise figured to turn airport environs into wastelands, and for all anyone knew, they might destroy the ozone layer above the Earth. Lindbergh was opposed on economic grounds also.

"But to Trippe, even as he approached what ordinary men considered retirement age, nothing was impracticable, and if the SST was to be the next step, then he wanted to be the man who would bring it on. He knew President Kennedy was wavering and might withdraw funding, and so he decided to force the President's hand. When Kennedy promised a decision for the Monday following Memorial Day 1963, Trippe optioned six *Concordes*, and arranged for this news to be made public the day before."

Thus, Kennedy felt pressed to announce that the United States, too, would build a supersonic transport, and called for a joint government-industry program. On August 15, 1963, the FAA invited industry to submit proposals for an airplane "superior to the European *Concorde*." The leap to titanium technology in the manufacture of perhaps the most complex of all machines, was committed.

At the briefing, Douglas, now led by Donald Douglas, Jr., announced that his company would not enter the race. Boeing, Lockheed, and North American were left in the *SST* arena.

NASA had worked out four possible configurations for a supersonic transport, and both Boeing and Lockheed were already under contract to evaluate them. The so-called SCAT-16, for Supersonic Commercial Air Transport, with a variable-sweep wing; and SCAT-17, with a delta wing and a canard up forward, were the two believed to have the most commercial promise.

With years of intensive study and testing behind them, engineers at Boeing were convinced that the variable-sweep, pivoting wing was the best approach. After taking one last, hard look at the delta wing, the variable sweep design promised to save 50,000 pounds. Wells took a look at the figures. "We'll submit the variable," he said.[7]

Supersonic Transport Mock-up—1971

After years of research and development, funds for the construction of two SST prototypes were authorized in 1968.

Lockheed and North American both decided to submit proposals with a delta wing, making the competition one of clear choices in technology.

Maynard Pennell explained the Boeing position in an oral presentation in Washington, D.C., on January 21, 1964.

"The NASA research on the variable-sweep arrow wing, along with our own, has proved that aerodynamic compromise is no longer necessary," he said. "With the variable sweep principle we can achieve superior supersonic performance in terms of payload-range and at the same time, low-speed flying qualities better than present commercial transports."[8]

The FAA began evaluation of the proposals, and it was soon clear that the effects of the sonic boom and the airplane's economics were both very serious problems.

In 1965, the *SST* competition completed Phase II-A, and Boeing again reported to the FAA. The body had been reshaped, the passenger capacity increased, and the aerodynamics improved.

"A 30 percent reduction in seat-mile costs has been achieved and substantiated by wind tunnel test results," Pennell reported. "The airplane will have lower seat-mile costs than subsonic transports on all but the shorter routes."[9]

The development costs were still the big hurdle, and they were mounting steadily. The government had decided to pay 75 percent, and to reimburse the contractor's 25 percent investment in the event of cancellation. Financing for a prototype had yet to be faced.

With a giant new logistics transport design in the competitive phase for the Air Force, a plane known as the C-5A, speculation increased in Washington about the need for a supersonic airplane. Perhaps a 750-seat commercial version of that airplane should be the next step, they reasoned.

With undiminished confidence, the FAA recommended a continuation of the *SST* competition into a Phase II-B. North American was dropped. Boeing and Lockheed remained.

In August 1965, President Lyndon B. Johnson approved the plan to continue—short of a prototype—for a period of eighteen months, with industry still bearing 25 percent of the cost.

In Seattle, confidence never wavered. To give the *SST* the strongest possible emphasis, a supersonic transport branch of the Commercial Airplane Division was formed. T. Wilson, corporate vice-president for operations and planning, was assigned to give overall direction. Heading the program directly as branch manager, and newly appointed as a vice-president, was H. W. "Bob" Withington, an MIT graduate in aeronautical engineering, who had joined Boeing in 1941.

The Soviets were also known to be working on an SST, and Najeeb Halaby, pushing hard for an American go-ahead to the prototype stage, suggested that the Russians might be first.

Defense Secretary McNamara expressed little faith in the ability of the FAA, under Halaby, to manage the program. Feeling that their estimates on developmental cost and purchase price were too conservative, he urged continued studies.

The American *SST* decision quickly became a testing of the wills between two powerful men in the government, Najeeb Halaby and Robert McNamara. Halaby postured the effort in terms of "a life and death struggle, so far as commercial airframe manufacturers were concerned, with the British, French, and Russians. To the winner, the guy who produces the first commercially profitable, safe, and efficient aircraft, goes a $3 billion to $4 billion market."[10] McNamara remained unmoved.

Concerned with the fragmentation of direction, President Johnson replaced Halaby as head of the FAA with Air Force General William F. McKee, instructing him to assume direct control of the *SST* program.

Negative factors continued to pile up when the effects of the sonic boom, heretofore on the periphery of *SST* decision making, moved to center stage.

Subsequent testing resulted in the conclusion that overland supersonic operations would not be publicly acceptable. Thus, the sonic boom was brushed from the table of contention by the simple decision not to fly overland—except at subsonic speeds—worsening the economic equation.

Competition between Boeing and Lockheed tightened. Lockheed, originally viewed as the weaker competitor—with its fixed wing—improved its design. Boeing responded in kind. Its swing-wing design, now with a very large horizontal tail, integrated with the fully sweptback wing, was looking better than ever.

Promotional efforts of the two manufacturers were in sharp contrast. Horwitch had this to say about the approaches of the two competitors: "Boeing was surprisingly subdued, merely trying to relate its *SST* effort to its obvious success in developing commercial jet aircraft. Lockheed's promotional behavior, on the other hand, was flamboyant, public, and aggressive." In August, a two-page Lockheed advertisement appeared in the *New York Times*, claiming that the firm's double delta configuration would be virtually stall-proof and would create a cushion of air under a landing plane.[11]

The manufacturer's proposals were submitted in early September 1966, and technical evaluations began immediately. In December, the Boeing-General Electric design was selected. In Seattle, reaction was restrained—exhaustion and skepticism had taken their toll.

In mid-January 1967, Pan American offered the FAA an important proposal for airline prototype financing—the airlines would deposit $1 million per airplane position, and in return would receive a $3 million credit against the purchase price. By mid-February, ten of the twelve U.S. airlines holding delivery positions, had agreed to participate.

A headcount of United States senators revealed sixty-three were favorable to the SST, twelve leaned toward it, fifteen were uncertain, and ten opposed.

In April 1967, McNamara, the most skeptical of Johnson's advisors, urged a go-ahead, and the president requested fiscal 1968 funding of $198 million. Development phase contracts were awarded to Boeing and General Electric, calling for the construction of two SST prototypes and 100 hours of flight testing at an estimated total cost of $1.44 billion, over a period of about four years.

By June, 113 delivery positions had been allocated to twenty-six airlines; fifty-seven domestic, and fifty-six foreign.

Bill Allen enthusiastically predicted that at its peak, the two SST prototypes would generate 9,000 new jobs in the Company.

In December 1967, the *Concorde* reached its first milestone, when the French-assembled prototype 001 was rolled out of its hangar at Toulouse. Shortly thereafter, at Filton, the British-assembled 002 followed.[12]

The *SST* story had not yet reached its final chapter.

1. Geoffrey Knight, *Concorde, The Real Story*, (New York: Stein and Day, 1978), 23–25.
2. Harold Mansfield, *Vision*, (New York: Popular Library, 1966), 264.
3. Private Communication.
4. Ibid.
5. Ibid.
6. Robert Daley, *An American Saga*, (New York: Random House, 1980), 430–431.
7. Private Communication.
8. Ibid.
9. Ibid.
10. Mel Horwitch, *Clipped Wings*, (Cambridge, Massachusetts, 1982), 40.
11. Ibid., 163.
12. Knight, Concorde, *The Real Story*, 62.

CHAPTER TWENTY-ONE

The Seventeen-inch Decision

Competition with the 707 nearly drove the Douglas Aircraft Company to bankruptcy. The initial advantage of a "paper airplane," allowing promises of improvements in size and range, were more than overcome by subsequent problems. Major retooling was required after the DC-8 was in production, and other deficiencies discovered during flight testing resulted in costly corrective action. Boeing, even with its heavy losses, was nevertheless winning the sales battle.

During the competition with the 727, lack of a Douglas prototype was again painfully evident. New innovations were captives of the wind tunnel; whereas Boeing was free to flight test.

The four-engined DC-9 offered to United, simply a small version of the DC-8, was never able to compete, and Douglas was forced back to the drawing boards.

The short-haul market was opening rapidly, and with speed still the pacing criterion, Douglas opted for a narrower body, with five abreast seating.

In the spring of 1962, Douglas revealed specifications for their Model 2086, a new, short-haul twinjet transport with aft, body-mounted engines, designed to operate economically on route segments of 250 to 300 miles. The airplane was configured to carry fifty-six to seventy-four passengers.[1]

The Model 2086 was the forerunner of the DC-9 series. First the DC-9-10, and following close behind, the -20 and -30. (Once again, to the consternation of historians, the -20 flew about a year after the -30.) The -30, which flew on August 6, 1966, was the first production model—and Douglas moved briskly into the short-haul market.

The public was clamoring to get everywhere faster, and the increased speed, made possible by the reduced drag of the smaller cross section, was an attractive attribute. Soon the DC-9-30, with a nominal capacity of ninety-seven passengers, along with the French *Caravelle* and the newly announced British *BAC 111* twinjets, had captured most of the market for short-haul equipment. By April 1964, of the large U.S. customers, only United and Eastern remained uncommitted to a twinjet machine.

At Boeing, the 727 was absorbing all available resources, but the possibility of the DC-9 growing to threaten its market loomed large, and a study was launched to ascertain whether a twin should be considered.

"'We'd have to start immediately to get ahead of a United Airlines decision on the DC-9.' Steiner told Yeasting in a meeting on April 21, 1964.

"Yeasting was skeptical, but agreed to go to Bill Allen with a proposal. 'I think it would be worth putting up a half million to take a ninety-day look at it,' he recommended. 'I don't believe there is one chance in ten that we can come up with anything that makes sense, but I think we ought to do this to make sure. The DC-9 doesn't have leading edge flaps; we may be able to pick up some other advantages by reason of our later start.' Allen concurred, and the Model 737 program study was begun on May 8, 1964."[2]

With the competition already fixed on five abreast seating, Boeing chose to go to six, providing significant commonality with the 707 and 727 fuselage. Having the same cross section also provided for standardization of cargo containers, including compatibility with the DC-8.

However, in the airplane business, no advantage comes without a price.

The seventeen-inch wider cross section, with its increased drag, resulted in a fifteen-mile-per-hour penalty in cruising speed, compared to the DC-9.

Location of the engines was open to the option of wing or body mounting. Sutter wanted to take another look at the wing mounted design. In theory, the larger engines should not produce the same interference effects with the airflow that forced the 707 to go to pods. Testing proved the concept to be sound, and 1,200 pounds of weight was saved by mounting on the wings.

In Europe, international sales manager Ken Luplow had been discussing a 737 with Lufthansa. The airplane appeared to be ideally suited to serving the multiple major cities in Germany.

With Lufthansa moving favorably toward the 737, Allen was in a dilemma—worse than on the 727. There, he had orders for eighty airplanes in hand with no competitor in the field. On the 737, there was strong competition, and only one potential customer. Allen launched an intensive sales campaign to line up Lufthansa, United and Eastern.

By January 1965, a crisis had developed. Neither Eastern nor United made any commitments. Lufthansa insisted on a Boeing yes or no—ready and willing to buy DC-9s.

In February, the Boeing board was forced to face the problem head-on, with no new movement on the part of the U.S. prospects. Although the market looked bleak, several members argued for a go-ahead, if only because holding off posed a still bigger risk. Fortunately, airline traffic was booming—and so they decided to proceed.

In Germany, at the Lufthansa Board meeting on February 19, 1965, chief executive Gerhard Hoeltje was reluctant—as the only airline customer—to recommend the 737. It would be easy for Boeing to drop the program. With board members already arriving for the meeting, Hoeltje phoned to pin Boeing down. He wanted personal assurance from Bruce Connelly, vice president of the Transport Division.

Ken Luplow made an urgent call to Seattle. It was 10:00 A.M. in Cologne, 1:00 A.M. in Seattle. Rubbing sleep from his eyes, Connelly gave the green light, and the Lufthansa board continued to deliberate. After breaking for a late lunch, they approved an order for twenty-one airplanes.

Within a week, Eastern announced their decision for the DC-9. Success for the 737 was hanging by the United Airlines thread. Production with only Lufthansa as a customer appeared to be financial suicide.

The 737 offered 103 seats, 6 more than the DC-9 sold to Eastern. Douglas featured its greater speed and five abreast seating. Seat-mile cost was becoming the major criterion for equipment selection where traffic was heavy, and the wider body was beginning to look like a good decision.

The competitive battle centered around the perception of market growth and market share; as to whether the airplane with the greatest number of seats, *ceteris paribus*, was the best revenue earner. Nobody wanted to fly empty seats.

With United involved in a major fleet planning program to go all jet by 1970, Boeing concentrated on a long-range program of a 737/727 mix which would meet the airline's combined requirements. The advantage of already having the 727 in the United fleet was significant. To make up for the delay in getting the 737 into service, Boeing offered additional 727 airplanes at attractive terms, with the right to turn back the extra 727s when the 737s became available. The strategy worked.

In April, United announced a gargantuan order: forty 737s, twenty 727 passenger and six 727QC airplanes. They leased an additional twenty-five 727 passenger airplanes, and signed options for thirty more 737s and nine more 727QCs.

On April 9, 1967, Brien S. Wygle took the 737-100 up for its first flight. Wygle, a career test pilot, had many first flights to his credit. Although a native of Seattle, his family moved to Canada, and he enlisted in the Royal Canadian Air Force in 1942. After serving in combat cargo operations in England, India, and Burma, he returned to peacetime ventures in 1946, graduating from the University of British Columbia with a degree in mechanical engineering in 1951. Wygle joined Boeing the same year, as a test pilot for the B-47 bomber program.

The initial delivery to Lufthansa was made on December 28, 1967. Douglas had already delivered 228 DC-9s.

Undaunted, Boeing stretched the body by six feet, accommodating 115 passengers, to meet United's need for a larger airplane. The new derivative was designated the -200. A convertible model, which could be changed from a passenger to a cargo configuration in a few hours, was also offered.

The stubby little airplane, with its wide body cross section, quickly gained the nickname *Fat Albert*. Early sales were encouraging. During the first two years following its initial service with Lufthansa, 223 airplanes were delivered.

737 Operation From Unimproved Airfields

The 737 operated from grass, dirt, gravel, and coral runways—from most any level surface. Here, a 737-200 takes off from a grass field in Hope, B.C., Canada

After the Airline Pilots Association took issue with the two-man crew of the 737, even though it had been certified by the FAA, a labor management arbitration panel ruled that United must operate the 737 with a crew of three; the damper was put on domestic sales. Deliveries dropped precipitously in 1970—to thirty-seven airplanes.

A struggle developed within Boeing to decide the fate of the 737. An objective analysis indicated the airplane would never recover its developmental costs. Airlines could still purchase the DC-9 with a two-man crew, and Douglas' two-year lead seemed insurmountable.

However, foreign carriers were not constrained by the domestic, three-man rule for the 737, giving an argument for those pushing to continue. The optimists eventually won out, and it was decided to offer still more improvements to the airplane and concentrate on the overseas market. The leading edge flap system was redesigned to provide more lift, and more powerful engines were offered, giving the airplane unchallenged superiority for short field operation. For passenger appeal, it was fitted with a new interior—"the wide body look." The improved machine was designated the 737-200 ADVANCED, with first delivery to All Nippon in Japan on May 20, 1971.

Sales almost hit bottom in 1972. Only fourteen airplanes were sold. The production level was barely adequate to operate a profitable line. The program limped along for the next several years, with the specter of phaseout hanging over it.

Boeing redoubled its sales efforts, and hidden in the long period of slow sales was the steady increase in customers buying one or two machines.

The airplane found a home in Africa, where its performance from short, high-altitude fields, even on hot days, was unmatched. To further increase its capability, a kit was designed to allow operation from unimproved runways, and soon it was being utilized on grass, dirt, gravel, or coral.

From a disappointing beginning in 1969, when only two 737s were in service in the entire continent of Africa, the increase was dramatic. By 1978, more than fifty airplanes were flying for airlines blanketing the continent— Air Algerie, Air Madagascar, Air Zaire, Angola, Cameroon, D.E.T.A., Egyptair, Nigeria, Royal Air Maroc, South Africa, Sudan, and Zambia.

Airlines in Asia, Australia, and Latin America also placed a string of orders, with VASP, a Brazilian carrier, purchasing twenty-two, becoming the largest 737 operator outside of the United States.

Fat Albert was dead. Satisfied customers had renamed the versatile plane the *Little Giant*. By 1978, the order total stood at 543 units. Even more significant was the number of operators—which reached seventy—surpassing Douglas.

In 1978, sales took off. A record total of 146 units were ordered, and the production line was accelerated from three to seven airplanes a month, with a further increase to eight and one-half by the end of 1979.

The drive to further improve the 737 intensified. To make the airplane an even better community neighbor, quiet nacelles were introduced in 1975, and a new exhaust gas mixer was developed in 1978 that further reduced the level of low frequency noise. The same year, Boeing provided an improved cockpit, featuring an integrated automatic flight control system, allowing landings during low weather minimum flight conditions. Not long after, British Airways was the first to receive a 737 with a technologically advanced flight deck. The new deck was equipped with digital instruments throughout and featured an automatic engine thrust control system, which achieved substantial fuel savings.

Douglas responded with their own technology improvements, increasing capacity in a series of fuselage stretches in their DC-9-50 and -80 models.

After years of controversy over a three-man versus a two-man cockpit crew, a presidential panel was created to settle the issue. In July 1981, the task force released its findings—allowing a two-man crew.

In late 1980, Boeing offered its customers an even more productive 737; a re-engined, lengthened version, which would accommodate sixteen more passengers. Designated as the -300, its General Electric CFM-56 advanced technology engines were more powerful, more fuel efficient, and significantly quieter.   Orders ballooned. By October 1985, sales of all 737 derivative models totalled 1,418, passing the DC-9 series, which stood at 1,400. Every other working day, a 737 rolled out of the Boeing factory at Renton.

In 1985, the 737-300 led the world in commercial airplane orders, with 252—chosen by twenty-six airlines.

A year later, Piedmont Airlines launched the 737-400, a stretched version of the -300, accommodating up to 169 passengers, with first delivery in September 1988. A month earlier, the 5,000th Boeing commercial jet transport, a 737-300, rolled out of the factory.

The 737 family was now broad and deep, but new attention was directed to the small end. Designated the -500, it was offered in 1987. Southwest Airlines in the U.S., and Braathens in Norway, kicked off the program with combined orders of forty-five planes. About the same size as the old -200, and representing the latest airframe and engine technologies, the -500 consumed 25 percent less fuel,

In February 1990, with sales of all 737 models nearing 2,800 airplanes, number 1,833 off the line—a 737-300—surpassed the record of 1,832 set by the 727. (One 727 was never sold, retained as a test bed for Boeing.)

Somewhere along the way—the exact unit not disclosed by Boeing—the 737 turned the corner into profitability, succeeding the 727 as the company's *cash cow*.[3] Only the "old timers" remembered the days when the airplane was nearly relegated to oblivion.

The continuing improvement in airplane performance, cost of operation, and service in the field were the factors that allowed the 737 to beat the DC-9—in spite of its two-year lead in airline service. However, in the final analysis, one single attribute—the wider body—was the underlying foundation for the competitive difference, providing a seat-mile cost that Douglas could never overcome. The higher speed of the DC-9, reducing flying time by ten to fifteen minutes on close city pairs, was never a factor.

Clearly, a major benchmark in Boeing's climb to world leadership in the commercial jet transport business was the seventeen-inch decision.

1. Crosby Maynard, *Flight Plan for Tomorrow*, Douglas Aircraft Company, 1962.
2. Harold Mansfield, *Vision*, (New York: Popular Library, 1966), 335.
3. Private Communication.

Saturn-Apollo *Moon Rocket*—1967

Producing a thrust of 7.5 million pounds, the 36-story Saturn-Apollo lifts off from Cape Canaveral on its successful first flight of November 9, 1967.

CHAPTER TWENTY-TWO

Going to the Moon

John F. Kennedy's call to his countrymen to go to the moon challenged every American. Never before in the history of nations had such a formidable goal been set before mankind.

Responding to the call, a tide of research and development contracts issued from the NASA centers at Ames, Goddard, Lewis, Langley, and Marshall—later joined by the newly created Manned Space Flight Center at Houston.

The race to space was on. America's cards were on the table. The military had not yet justified a role in space, and civilian efforts under NASA quickly took the lead.

NASA was doing advance planning for a direct lunar flight even before the president's declaration of a timetable. There were two major elements to the program—the *Saturn* launch system consisting of the booster stages to power the flight—and the *Apollo* spacecraft to carry the astronauts.

In a top management meeting, Boeing officials weighed the choices, deciding that the booster system had the best chance of providing business beyond the moon landing.

In the beginning, *Saturn* was being developed by the NASA Marshall Space Flight Center at Huntsville, Alabama. Formerly known as the Redstone Arsenal, where the first American satellite had incubated, the center was headed by Dr. Wernher von Braun. The design, construction, and testing of the prototype *Saturn* was being done there, but industry was invited to compete for the production contracts.

Boeing had been familiarizing itself with the *Saturn* since its inception in 1958, and an office was opened in Huntsville to keep abreast of developments. After several unsuccessful bids on parts of the *Saturn* system, Boeing won a contract to study the merits of solid versus liquid rocket engines in July 1961. The study concluded that liquid propellants would be superior for the large boosters envisioned.

Even before the *Dyna-Soar* was canceled, George Stoner was named to head the *Saturn* proposal, reporting to Lysle Wood, head of the big and growing Aerospace Division. Wood had begun his Boeing career in 1926, after graduating from Montana State College in mechanical engineering.

The government had an empty facility at Michoud, Louisiana, an old ordnance plant from World War II days, which NASA designated as the manufacturing center for the *Saturn* booster stages. The first stage would be 138 feet long and 33 feet in diameter, built entirely of aluminum alloys. No forgings had ever been made approaching the size of those needed for the *Saturn*. The completed boosters, too large for land transport, were scheduled to be barged to the Canaveral launch facility.

Stoner knew how difficult it was to convince personnel to pull up stakes and move, particularly to the Deep South. When the proposal team was formed, he laid down the ground rules.

"You're going to have to move down there to the southland and see that it is done," he said. "If you don't want to make that commitment, tell us now."[1]

The man Stoner picked as his assistant was Richard "Dick" Nelson, an engineering graduate of the University of Minnesota who had been project manager on BOMARC. Nelson took on the task of manufacturing the boosters at Michoud.

Dr. Wernher von Braun, outlining the requirements for the first stage booster, indicated the Advanced *Saturn* should be quoted on the basis of two-rocket engines, but there was a possibility of going to four or more.

Sensing an opportunity to leap ahead, Stoner wanted to go big.

"I think we should recommend the biggest one we can make," he told his proposal team. "The spacecraft people will have a hard enough time getting *Apollo* light enough for a direct launch to the moon. Let's make their job easier."[2]

To posture the size, they checked the heaviest single piece that was being hauled by ship, train, truck, and airplane. Ship compartments were limited to 100,000 pounds, trains about the same, with trucks capable of 70,000. Air transport was also capable of nearly 100,000 pounds, and Stoner decided to aim for launching a payload in that weight range. Studies confirmed that a cluster of five engines, each with 1.5 million pounds of thrust, could lift 240,000 pounds into earth orbit, or 90,000 pounds to escape velocity. The five-engine cluster, with one in the center and four on the corners, made an ideal geometry. Coincidentally, the thirty-three-foot diameter tanks would just clear the roof trusses of the Michoud plant.

In response to the request for bids, the two-engined version was submitted for the *Advanced Saturn*, but the visionary five-engined design was strongly recommended—and submitted as an alternate bid.

Chrysler won the preliminary competition, but the major task was still to be awarded. NASA, confident and with full presidential and congressional backing, moved rapidly.

On December 14, 1961, the Marshall Space Flight Center at Huntsville notified Boeing that they had won the contract to build twenty-four *Advanced Saturn* first stage boosters. A call from von Braun confirmed that NASA was going straight to the alternate proposal—the 7,500,000-pound thrust booster. It would be called *Saturn V*, capable of lifting the equivalent of a Mississippi River steamboat, fully loaded, straight up into orbit of the Earth.

The appetite of NASA was unquenchable, and opportunities abounded for work related to the moon project. With BOMARC winding down, Boeing had engineering expertise that welcomed new horizons. It appeared that photographic preparations for the moon landing was still a fertile field. Perhaps a comprehensive photo-mapping was needed to assure a manned landing success.

Lysle Wood assigned Robert "Bob" Helberg, BOMARC program manager, to look into the possibilities, and make an assessment whether Boeing could win a competition. Helberg had come to Boeing in 1935, starting

Facilities for Space Testing—Kent Space Center—1965

This 50 foot-high, 39 foot-diameter vacuum chamber, largest of the 11 in the Center, is *man-rated*. Here, the Boeing designed Lunar Orbiter is being loaded into the chamber for space simulated testing.

on the YB-17, after graduating from the University of Washington in aeronautical engineering.

Learning that NASA was planning to request proposals for an advanced photographic spacecraft to orbit the moon, and thinking about the expertise that Boeing had gained in managing large systems during *Minuteman*, Helberg went to Wood with a positive recommendation. "If we can bring together the companies that have the specific technologies, I think we can win this," Helberg reported.[3]

Working with Eastman Kodak and RCA, Boeing was well along in planning before the formal request for proposal was released on August 31, 1963. The short-fused request for a lunar orbiter, with a five week turn-around for response, thus worked to Boeing's advantage.

Eastman would design the cameras for a double lens system, taking both wide-angle, and high resolution pictures, the latter capable of distinguishing features the size of a card table. RCA would design the solar panels and batteries for onboard power. A miniature computer was proposed, capable of storing 2,700 bits of information, and serving in place of the camera crew, flight crew, and laboratory crew. The ten-by-ten-by-nine-inch electronic wizard would give commands to the various pieces of equipment. In fourteen days, a minimum of 200 pictures would be taken at close range. The proposal was submitted on October 4, 1963.

Two weeks after the *Dyna-Soar* was canceled, Boeing was notified that they had won the *Lunar Orbiter* contract. The bid price was $80 million dollars. For that sum, on a fixed price incentive basis, Boeing would deliver five spacecraft for flight missions, plus three more for testing purposes.

Space, in spite of previous study contracts, was still a vast unexplored ocean. *Boeing would require hundreds of millions of dollars of specialized facilities and testing equipment, capitalization which had to be committed based on faith in the future.* No less than a completely new facility was demanded. Stoner urged the construction of a single facility to house all the space oriented laboratories separately located around the plant—and to add new ones.

Lysle Wood took the plan to Bill Allen, who agreed that such a facility was an essential step in preparing for space ventures, and more specifically for a *Manned Orbiting Laboratory*, the *MOL*, on which the company was bidding.

Late in 1963, Boeing acquired 320 acres of truck gardening land in the Duwamish valley south of Seattle, on which the Kent Space Center was constructed. The first two major laboratory buildings were only a start for a facility which eventually covered most of the huge site. The main building was devoted to equipment for simulating navigating and maneuvering aspects of space flight as well as housing a space environmental chamber. The space chamber, thirty-nine feet in diameter and fifty feet high, was exceeded in size only by the NASA Goddard facility at Greenbelt, Maryland. The Boeing chamber was capable of an internal vacuum of 10^{-9} mm of mercury, simulating an altitude of 400 miles. The *Lunar Orbiter* spacecraft was placed in the chamber via a giant cover that rolled to one side.

The second building was designed to house the materials and processes staff with its nearly $3 million worth of testing and evaluation equipment, and a new microelectronics research laboratory.

Nate Krisberg, as chief of the technical staff, was given responsibility to activate the new, fully equipped microelectronics laboratory, designed to study and develop integrated semiconductor circuits, progeny of an infant science that proposed to put a complete radio set on a tiny chip of solid matter. Krisberg, a West Point graduate and retired Air Force colonel with a Ph.D. in nuclear physics, had joined Boeing in 1961.

Allen was quick to recognize that an entirely new manufacturing capability was necessary to produce the new devices, and he directed Lysle Wood to go out to the industry and find an expert to head up such a program.

At General Motors, Malcolm T. "Mal" Stamper, a fourteen-year veteran who had worked in its new technology center from its beginning, and was responsible for electronics manufacturing at its AC Spark Plug Division in Milwaukee, was also seeking new horizons. Stamper's name surfaced when Admiral Raborn, in charge of the *Polaris* missile program, mentioned his significant contributions to the new field.

Stamper was invited to Boeing and interviewed directly by Allen and his vice-president of administration and corporate secretary, James E. "Jim" Prince. They decided it was a match, and Stamper was hired in 1962. Stamper recalls that about 5,000 people, split off from several organizations, were put together to form Electronics Operations, a new unit, over which he was named manager.[4]

Graduating from Georgia Tech in 1944, with a degree in electrical engineering, Stamper served as a naval officer during World War II. He was always a team player, harking back to his days as a guard on the Georgia Tech football squad, which played in the Orange Bowl in 1945. Prior to joining General Motors, he studied law at the University of Michigan.

Following his successful development of electronic production, Stamper was named as operations manager for the *MOL* proposal team.

Plant expansion continued to accelerate. During 1965, an additional $165 million was authorized, six times the average level for preceding years. *In the span of scarcely more than two years, plant facilities had doubled.*

In May 1967, NASA selected Boeing as the Technical Integration and Evaluation (TIE) contractor for the *Saturn-Apollo* program. Under TIE, Boeing had the responsibility to certify that the *Apollo* spacecraft and launch vehicles were compatible and ready for flight. The organization consisted of slightly more than 3,000 employees, supplementing NASA and its other contractors. Before NASA pushed the buttons, Boeing was required to provide assurance of the desired result. Thus, prime responsibility for decisions in America's pioneering voyage to the moon was shared between Boeing and NASA.

In August 1966, the Boeing-built spacecraft, NASA's *Lunar Orbiter I*, was hurled into space and placed in orbit around the moon. A talented robot, it obediently photographed the surface, transmitting more than 400 pictures back to earth. The moon had bared its secrets, and the map was in place.

When Neil A. Armstrong and Edwin E. "Buzz" Aldrin, Jr., piloted their *Apollo* lunar module, *Eagle*, to a landing on the moon's Sea of Tranquility, on July 20, 1969, the first major chapter in Boeing's space efforts was rapidly drawing to a close. The moon landing climaxed a program in which the Company had been involved for nearly ten years.

For the technological community, the decade of the sixties had received its baptism for greatness. A glorious page had been turned, and a new decade lay ahead.

1. Private Communication.
2. Ibid.
3. Ibid.
4. Malcolm T. Stamper, interview by Donald S. Schmechel, 1 November, 1986.

Malcolm T. Stamper 1925–
President 1972–1985, Vice Chairman 1985–1988.

CHAPTER TWENTY-THREE

The Jumbos

The Communists were on the move in Southeast Asia. In March 1961, President Kennedy authorized increasing aid to Laos, where rebel forces were attempting to overthrow the government. In neighboring Vietnam, the Viet Cong were killing more South Vietnamese every day in their drive to reunify their divided country as a monolithic Communistic nation. The area was no longer a geographical nonentity. Uneasy details splashed over the front pages of American newspapers.

The domino theory became the prevalent wisdom. One by one, all of the countries of Southeast Asia would fall to the Communists.

The U.S. Department of Defense began thinking about ways to move troops and equipment rapidly to forward areas. The idea of a super-size logistics transport was gaining force.

As director of engineering for the Airplane Division of Boeing in 1961, Maynard Pennell assigned William L. Hamilton, a young engineer and operations analyst, to study the factors involved in the movement of an entire army division by air.

Hamilton had come to Boeing in 1950, after graduating from the University of Washington with a degree in electrical engineering, and later earning a master of science degree in industrial management at MIT, as a Sloan Fellow.

"Bill, I want you to do a comprehensive job of analyzing the airlift requirements for the U.S. Armed Forces over the next couple of decades," Pennell said. Hamilton, a quiet, thoughtful man, only nodded.

"Break it down to the fundamentals," Pennell continued. "We need a rock-solid base to build from."[1]

Hamilton started from scratch, gathering about a dozen other engineers, and went to work building scale models of Army vehicles to load onto the floor plan of an advanced heavy aircraft layout. Boeing had developed a computer program for simulating the loading of aircraft with military cargo. The central consideration became the maximizing of the floor area.

Next, specific concepts were studied by Kenneth F. Holtby and his product development staff. Holtby, a mechanical engineer from CalTech and also a subsequent Sloan Fellow, had joined Boeing in 1947 on the B-47 bomber program. Working with Hamilton's group, in a dramatic departure from convention, they moved the cockpit up and over the body. The resulting configuration not only maximized the floor area on the main deck—the design allowed the entire nose of the airplane to be hinged—opening the giant maw of the fuselage.

The nature of operations—fast loading and unloading at unimproved runways in forward areas by an unarmed plane—further dictated the design parameters.

The final proposed design of over a half million pounds, looked big even in comparison to the eight-jet B-52 bombers, the largest aircraft of any type in service.

By the time the 4,272-page proposal was submitted to the Air Force in September 1964, Boeing engineers had been working on the concept for four years and the investment of Company funds exceeded $10 million.

Originally referred to as the CX heavy logistics transport by the Air Force, it was officially designated the C-5A, and the "big three," eagerly entered the competition.

By 1965, some tough questions faced Bill Allen as to where the priorities should go. In addition to the C-5A, there were two other huge programs in the hopper—both of which the Company was heavily involved in—the *SST* and the *MOL*. Allen directed Harold "Hal" Haynes, vice-president of finance, to review the money problems. Haynes had to keep the Company in a position to move into any one of those programs, and possibly all three.

Haynes, one of Boeing's most respected executives, served under four presidents. Sometimes referred to in awe as the "great white sphinx," in deference to his shock of prematurely snow white hair, Haynes managed the financial world of the Company almost from the day he arrived as assistant to the controller. Before coming to Boeing in 1954, he had been a certified accountant with Touche Ross, Inc.—the Boeing accounting firm—following his graduation from the University of Washington school of finance in 1948.

On August 25, 1965, bad news came on *MOL*, the Manned Orbiting Laboratory—awarded to Douglas. The keen disappointment at Boeing was only partially offset by the expectation that a C-5A decision would favor Boeing.

Word leaked from Washington that Boeing was receiving the highest technical rating on the C-5A, but that Lockheed was low on cost.

An uneasy optimism prevailed. Then, on September 15, 1965, the International Machinists Union called a strike. The old sore—seniority—was opened. Boeing continued to hold that promotions—and layoffs—should be primarily based on the merit system. Mercifully, the strike only lasted eighteen days, settled by an agreement to make a joint study of the Company merit rating system.

Jolting news came during the strike. The Air Force announced the results of the competition for the C-5A. In an emotional message over the public address system, the measured cadence of T. Wilson's voice spelled it out:

"I regret to report that Boeing has lost the C-5A competition. The award was made to Lockheed. It is an understatement to say we are disappointed; however, we are not disappointed in our people. What we learned will be applied to our other business efforts."[2]

In the early sixties, with the "military-industrial complex" under attack, President Kennedy had ordered Robert McNamara to do something about the poor image of the Defense Department for military procurement. McNamara responded by changing the rules.

Termed *Total Package Procurement* (*TPP*), the major innovation of the new philosophy was the requirement for each manufacturer to present a single bid for the entire program. The bid must not only include research and development, but the production phase as well—in short, a total price for the finished hardware.

The bid for 115 planes submitted by Boeing was $2.3 billion. Douglas asked $2 billion, and Lockheed, feeling that renegotiation would be a certain option at a later date, simply presented a bid low enough to be assured of winning. Their bid was $1.9 billion, $400 million less than Boeing, and even $300 million less than the Pentagon's own estimate.

The question of whether the Lockheed bid was realistic, which was McNamara's criterion on the *TFX* competition, did not emerge. *TPP* had become the new darling at the Pentagon.

The C-5A was to be built at the Marietta, Georgia plant. At the time, no one knew exactly how badly the program had been underbid.

There was little doubt that the award to Lockheed was a political decision, steered by Georgia's Senator Richard Russell, then chairman of the Armed Services Committee.[3] For Boeing, fat with commercial orders, the loss could be borne, but for the Georgia Marietta plant, it would be a mortal blow.

At Marietta, shortly after World War II, the C-130 *Hercules* troop transport, was conceived under the tutelage of Daniel "Dan" Jeremiah Haughton. A shrewd man with numbers, Haughton had majored in accounting and business administration at the University of Alabama. Starting as a systems analyst at Lockheed's Burbank headquarters in 1933, he rose rapidly, quickly coming to the attention of the Gross brothers.

By 1949, Haughton was president of two Lockheed subsidiaries. He proved himself a capable salesman, personally covering the entire United States, all the while promising nearly impossible delivery dates and undercutting his competitors on every hand. It was an attribute which endeared him to the hearts of the Gross brothers, and indeed, continued the crystallization of the Lockheed image as a slick operator—playing the promise—and worrying about delivering the goods later.

Within a year, the Haughton-managed subsidiaries were in the black, and Dan Haughton was on his way to the top. In 1952, he was rewarded with the presidency of the Marietta operation.

The *Hercules* was a well designed airplane, admirably suited to the task for which it was intended. After the Korean War was over, the Air Force continued to back the project, even though the prototype had not yet made its first flight.

This happy scenario presented only one problem, and it was major. In order to win contracts, Lockheed had practically patented their tactic of promising impossible delivery dates, with unrealistic costs, a practice referred to as "buying in." Pure Haughton. With his Alabama-inherited, plain-as-hominy-grits manner, he charmed his way to signed contracts, sometimes on not much more than pure personality.

As the *Hercules* cost overrun quicksand began to close around him, Haughton cast his eyes on even bigger prizes to bail out the failing program. With the breakeven point moving into the future, he had to find a formula to sell more and more airplanes. He not only succeeded, but made an estimated $300 million in profit to Lockheed on sales of 1,400 of the C-130s to thirty-seven countries.

What Boulton termed the "Grease Machine,"[4] worked in many modes, but the result was always to get cash into the hands of middlemen who bribed officials, both public and private.

In the case of the F-104 *Starfighter*, an advanced interceptor developed after the Korean War, the much modified, multi-million plane met virtually none of the Air Force's original specifications, and was canceled after the delivery of 170 machines. That left Lockheed with more than 2,300 planes short of its minimum target of 2,500 planes. Modifying the airplane still further, they went after the export market.

Robert Gross was still at the tiller, but close behind was sweet-talking Dan Haughton. Gross picked Japan as the initial target. The Japanese military had already chosen the Grumman F-11A *Super Tiger*, and traditionally, approval by the National Defense Council was no more than a rubber stamp.

Incredibly, Lockheed turned the decision around, and there was no doubt, when the smoke had cleared, that bribe money had subverted the political process in Japan. After Japan, Gross used the same tactics in Europe. The details remained secret until 1975.

In 1961, Dan Haughton was named president of Lockheed, and in 1967, he became chairman.

At Boeing the booming space and missile business of the sixties was being augmented by accelerating sales of the 707 and the 727. Vertol, too, was moving ahead agressively on the *Sea Knight* and *Chinook* helicopters. Nevertheless, with the *MOL* gone, the C-5A loss created a giant spike of anxiety.

As airline traffic continued a steep rise around the world, the Europeans began talking about an airbus, and Boeing began looking into plans to stretch the 707. However, with Douglas already in the market with a stretched DC-8, the idea for a higher capacity 707 was abandoned.

The worldwide need for a larger capacity airplane seemed to be staring the Company in the face.

Joe Sutter, now chief of technology, was bullish. "The happy thing is, we do have something to sell," he reported to engineering director Dick Rouzie.[7]

With the supersonic airplane several years in the future, whatever the new machine was, it would have to come fast.

The giant C-5A aroused the imagination, but its size was intimidating for a commercial version. Not so for Ed Wells, staring in silence at pictures of the 707 in one of the early review meetings.

"If there is one thing we have learned it's that our airplanes are always too small," he said, breaking his silence. "Let's at least double it."[8]

Sutter was certain the elements were there. The most difficult decision was selection of body cross section. Passenger accommodation was not the main consideration, as passengers were expected to flock to the *SST*—very real at the time. The goal was to produce an efficient commercial freight carrier, employing containers. The width of the container was finally chosen as the highway maximum of eight feet, and the airplane was designed for two eight-by-eight containers, side by side.

Extrapolation of historical passenger traffic growth to 1970 set the probable required capacity at about 375, and the 747 was born.

To John Yeasting, vice president of the Commercial Airplane Division, the project was a frightening one. It would take an investment of more than $500 million, dwarfing the investments on the 707, 727, and 737 combined.

Sutter maintained his confident air. "The 747 or something like it has to happen," he said.[9]

Bill Allen, secretly eager in response to the new enthusiasm in the engineering department, turned on Yeasting in his office the morning after the October 1965 board meeting.

"I woke up this morning in a cold sweat. That 747 of yours! Here I've been going all over the country saying how impossible it would be to undertake the supersonic transport without government support. This 747 will cost us at least half of what the *SST* development will cost."[10]

The time for betting the Company—which showed a net worth of $762 million[11]—was again at hand. Allen prepared for the inevitable.

Setting the stage to undertake the 747, the Company tripled its authorized capital stock.

Juan Trippe was among the first to realize that the next step was perhaps not the *SST* after all, but rather a giant jet that would carry at least double the passenger loads of the 707s and DC-8s.

When the C-5A was awarded, Trippe immediately called Gross, attempting to start negotiations for a civilian version. Gross said he had enough problems building the C-5A. Douglas was satisfied with their stretched DC-8, and not interested in a larger airplane. Trippe turned to Boeing.

On December 22, 1965, after a number of conferences among Boeing, Pratt & Whitney, and Pan American; Trippe and Allen signed a statement of their intentions. Boeing would build the 747, and Pan American would buy and operate twenty-five of the giant airplanes.

In spite of its cost—$22 million per copy—more than four times that of a 707-320, the world's airlines rushed to gain delivery positions. Including the Pan Am order, sales to fifteen airlines reached ninety-three within five months after the decision to go ahead was announced, and Boeing had a $1.8 billion commitment to produce. *Both Boeing and Pan American had put their corporate existence on the line.*

Problems abounded. The maximum empty weight of the airframe, pegged at 274,094 pounds in the Pan Am contract, was climbing alarmingly, and after the first year of engineering gestation, stood at 308,924 pounds, threatening a payload reduction of more than 10 percent. The only remedy was to increase the gross takeoff weight, which was raised from 550,000 to 710,000 pounds.

Engine power came into focus. A still more powerful engine was needed, requiring larger nacelles and, indeed, major modifications to the wing.

To produce such a plane in the quantities contemplated—seven airplanes a month at peak production—an assembly building, encompassing 160 million cubic feet would be required, larger in volume than any existing building in the world.

Mal Stamper was moving rapidly in the Company, having been appointed as special assistant to the general manager of the Aerospace Division when Boeing lost the *MOL* opportunity, and his achievements at both General Motors and Boeing were not lost to head hunters. Harold Geenen, chairman of ITT, decided privately that Stamper was a man he wanted. Stamper suggested outrageous terms—which only made Geneen more determined—ultimately offering an annual salary of $100,000, and reporting directly.

Stamper made a quick trip East to accept Geneen's offer. Back at Boeing, President Allen was dismayed but not surprised—Stamper was making $28,000 a year at the time.

After a rapid assessment, Allen offered the choice of five different positions, all at vice-president level.

The offer touched a nerve somewhere in Stamper's complex makeup, and he accepted, sending his regrets to Harold Geneen. His new salary was only $40,000, but the position included stock options. Thus, in June 1965, after only three years with the Company, Mal Stamper became vice-president and general manager of the Boeing Turbine Division.

As Stamper recalls, Allen didn't mince words. "I want you to make our turbine division the best in the world, or get rid of it," he said.

When Stamper reported back, he told President Allen it would cost $75,000,000.

"Sell it." Allen directed.

"Who in corporate will be helping me with the selling details?"

"You're the boss, you sell it."

The board of directors approved the sale and Stamper was out of a job. Allen called him in.

"What would you like to do next?" he inquired.

"How about working on your toughest problem?"

Allen chuckled. He had observed this brilliant, impatient, decisive engineering manager at close range during the gas turbine review period. The gargantuan 747 undertaking was now in sharp focus in his mind, and he knew it would require a giant of a man to make it happen.

After thinking about his options, Allen said, "How would you like to build the world's largest airplane?"

Stamper *smarted off*. "The only airplane I ever built had rubber bands on it."

Not accustomed to nonsense, Allen reared back in his chair. "Do you want to build it or don't you?" he demanded.

Of course, Stamper jumped at the chance.

Allen pointed to an aerial photograph of Paine Field, a former World War II military base near Everett, Washington, which had nothing much to offer except a 9,000-foot, little-used runway.

"We'll need an entirely new plant adjacent to the field, to build the 747," Allen said. "I want you to take responsibility for directing the program from start-up to fleet deliveries. The first airplane has been committed to Pan Am in September 1969."

Stamper stared at the photograph. All he could see was a forest. It was January 1966.

Years later, Stamper told friends, "I haven't seen daylight since."[12]

Beginning with 780 hilly acres of undeveloped and heavily forested land in the early summer of 1966, contractors cleared and leveled 250 acres and laid a two-mile-long railroad spur with a 5.6 percent gradient to serve the factory site.

The first locomotive, pulling outsized rail cars, was moving over the new spur by November. Working around the clock, contractors completed the first increment by January 1967—a low bay manufacturing and mockup building—allowing initial occupancy by Boeing workers. The huge mockup, completed at Plant II, was immediately moved into place.

Only four months later, in May 1967, work was started on the first 747 in the main assembly building—still under construction—and by year end, with the building nearly complete, 5,000 employees were on the job.

The work force, eventually growing to 20,000, became Mal's *Incredibles*. "I remember escorting workers to their cars, telling them to go home, that they'd put in enough hours," he recalls. "But they'd be back in the plant before I was."[13] For himself, he practically lived at Everett, and "probably only had Christmases off over a three-year period."[14]

The Everett 747 facility was essentially an assembly plant, with more than 65 percent of the airplane subcontracted. Only the wing and the thirty-three-foot-long forward body section, enclosing the flight deck, were manufactured in Boeing plants. This commitment to spread the work throughout the United States was maximized on the 747, a continuing Boeing tradition, beginning early in the Company's history. At the time, $2.1 billion in subcontracts were in effect, shared by approximately 20,000 companies residing in all fifty States and several foreign countries.

In spite of major problems on every hand, production moved apace, and the first 747 rolled out of the Everett factory in September 1968, and flew on February 9, 1969.

Bill Allen masked his anxiety in a hearty handshake with test pilot Jack Waddell on that gray day at Paine Field, but his stark words left nothing unsaid: "Jack I hope you know the Boeing Company flies with you today."[15]

Jack Waddell was no ordinary test pilot. Like the legendary Eddie Allen, he was also an aeronautical engineer, obtaining a masters degree from Cornell University in 1952.

Waddell served as a U.S. Navy pilot in the South Pacific during World War II, and was a test pilot for North American before coming to Boeing in 1957.

Astonishing onlookers by its quietness, the plane used only half of the runway for takeoff and flew like the queen of the skies she was to become. At first flight, 196 airplanes had been sold to thirty-one airlines, and Boeing had committed to increase the production rate from seven to eight and one-half airplanes a month.

The situation for Douglas was crucial in 1966 as they attempted to con-figure the correct plane to challenge the 747. With sales of over $1 billion, the company reported a loss in excess of $27 million. On the verge of a financial crisis, they began exploring the possibility of a merger.

North American and General Dynamics were involved in early discus-sions, but the McDonnell Aircraft Company quickly moved to the fore as the most likely candidate. McDonnell, a strongly based manufacturer of military airplanes, had never built a commercial airplane. The merger of the two capabilities seemed ideal.

Talks led to terms, and on a cold, rainy morning in April 1967, the stock-holders gathered at Beverly Hills to vote the Douglas Aircraft Company out of existence. Donald Douglas, Sr., then seventy-five years old, moved to semi-retirement, stepping down from chairman, and becoming a board member of the new company, the McDonnell Douglas Corporation.

The headquarters of the newly merged company was established in St. Louis, with James S. McDonnell, Jr.,"Mr. Mac" as its chairman.

A relative newcomer to the community of aviation pioneers who started their own companies, Mr. Mac had become one of its giants.

Educated at Princeton University with a degree in physics, McDonnell first worked with airplanes at the Army Air Corps Flying School in 1923, where he was a test pilot. After obtaining a masters degree in aeronautical engineering at MIT, he established the McDonnell Aircraft Company in St. Louis on July 6, 1939.

McDonnell expanded quickly, devoting early efforts to subcontracting for larger manufacturers. Before the end of the war, McDonnell designed one of the earliest jet fighters for the Navy, and never looking back, became one of the largest producers of jet fighters in the world. A strongly paternalistic man, he referred to his employees as "teammates" and regularly communicated with them over the loadspeaker system. "This is Mac calling all the team," became commonplace at the St. Louis factory. Invariably, he closed with: "This is old Mac signing off."[16]

At the time of the merger, McDonnell had completed a very successful year, showing a $43 million profit on sales of just over $1 billion.

McDonnell Douglas concentrated on an airplane with three engines, smaller than the 747, believing that U.S. airports would never be ready for the "jumbo" that Boeing had announced. The capacity would be in the 250-to 300-passenger range.

Lockheed, after dropping out of commercial competition when the ill-fated *Electra* ended production—with the C-5A safely in their pocket—was thought to have an advantage in entering the jumbo competition. Haughton, the eternal optimist, saw what appeared to be a new opportunity, and in the fall of 1967, publicly announced that Lockheed was prepared to take orders for the L-1011, also a 250-to 300-passenger capacity trijet, to be known as the *Tristar*. Two months later, McDonnell Douglas followed, taking orders for the DC-10.

With Boeing targeting for the global market and the longer routes, the early cutthroat competition was between McDonnell Douglas and Lockheed. For the trijets, the sale of each plane meant minus one to its competitor.

American Airlines was first to announce. The decision had been agonizingly close. There was hardly a day when there was not either a Lockheed or a McDonnell Douglas man in the head office. At the end of the evaluation, an American Airlines official called Mr. Haughton in to inform him that Lockheed had lost the order. Dan Haughton, as intensely emotional as he was loyal to Lockheed, sat down and cried.

The American Airlines order, made public on February 16, 1968, was for twenty-five airplanes, amounting to a contract price of $382 million, or about $15.3 million per plane. American also took options on twenty-five more airplanes, raising the potential of the order to over $800 million.

With his two-month sales lead having evaporated, Haughton decided to mortgage Lockheed's future a little deeper, slashing the price of each *Tristar* by $1 million.

By the end of March, Lockheed had orders for 118 *Tristars* from Eastern, Delta, and TWA. A fourth order for fifty machines by Air Holdings, Ltd., a hastily conceived consortium launched by Lockheed itself, with Rolls Royce of England as a partner, was achieved. Thus, Haughton had tightened the loyalty of Rolls, the engine manufacturer. They were in the venture together—win or lose.

The score was suddenly 168 to 25, and McDonnell Douglas paused to consider. David Lewis, new president of the Douglas operations, convinced Mr. Mac they had to stay in the race. To show their determination, they chopped one-half million dollars from the price of each DC-10.

On April 25, 1968, United Airlines, the largest United States customer, and last to decide, ordered sixty DC-10s.

To tighten the screws for Lockheed still further, the depth and breadth of the C-5A *(Galaxy)* problems were becoming apparent, threatening to drag down the *Tristar*—and the company—with it. There was no way that Lockheed could build the airplane at the prices quoted. The Pentagon, feeling a shared responsibility, and fearful of a public outcry, quietly agreed to make progress payments before they were due.

Flying the first four airplanes off the line in an integrated plan, Boeing compressed the certification program to ten months—by far the most ambitious in aviation history—and the 747 went into service for Pan Am on January 22, 1970.

The new JT9D series high bypass engines, powerplant for the 747s, ran into serious delays in development.

Early in 1969, twenty-six completed 747s, representing nearly the net worth of the Company, most of them without engines, were parked on the flight line at Everett, Washington, waiting to be delivered.

Nevertheless, confidence prevailed because of the integrity of the airframe, which had sustained a wing loading of 116 percent of its ultimate design load during its structural test to failure. Those results guaranteed a significant improvement in airline performance, translating to either more fuel for extended range, or an increased passenger load.

The arrival of engines in sufficient quantities in late 1969 led to the "year of the 747" in 1970. When the first twelve months of service were completed in January 1971, the operational statistics numbed the mind. Ninety-eight 747s, flying the colors of eighteen airlines, carried seven million passengers a distance of more than 71 million miles. The 30,000 revenue flights represented 15.5 billion passenger-miles, five times that logged by the 707 at an equal point in service.

1. Private Communication.
2. Ibid.
3. Berkeley Rice, *The C-5A Scandal*, (Boston: Houghton Mifflin Co., 1971).
4. David Boulton, *The Grease Machine*, (New York: Harper & Row, 1978).
5. Ibid., 5.
6. Ibid., 44.
7. Private Communication.
8. Ibid.
9. Ibid.
10. Ibid.
11. *Annual Report*, The Boeing Company, 1965, 25.
12. Malcolm T. Stamper interview by Donald S. Schmechel, 17 October, 1986.
13. *Boeing News*, 30 September, 1988, 1.
14. Stamper/Schmechel interview, 1 November 1986.
15. Private Communication.
16. *TIME*, Cover Story, 31 March, 1967.

Thornton A. "T" Wilson 1921–1999
President 1968–1972, Chairman 1972–1988.

CHAPTER TWENTY-FOUR

Disaster Averted

There were no roses for the herculean 747 efforts. In fact, storm clouds swept over the skies of the market. The unprecedented pace of delivery to the 747-hungry airlines of the world in 1969 was a harbinger of trouble ahead.

With the United States in a full blown recession in 1970, 747 airplanes became a glut on the market. Some U.S. airlines sold airplanes, and others left them parked in the hangars.

The heady Boeing sales of $3.3 billion in 1968, an all-time high, faded quickly into history, as the stark realities of 1969 forced the Company to bite the bullet once again—harder than ever before. The bottom line showed an operating loss of $14.3 million, the first in twenty-two years.[1]

The year of 1968 also represented a climax of another sort. On April 29, President William M. Allen moved up to chairman of the board, and T. Wilson—an Allen protege—was appointed to the presidency, signaling the end of the "Allen Era."

The office of chairman had been vacant since 1965, when Claire L. Egtvedt declined reelection. He had served the Company for forty-nine years, nurturing the ethical corporate conscience and integrity of product endowed by William E. Boeing.

As president for twenty-three years, Bill Allen had carried the tradition forward to a degree unmatched in the industry. This formidable task now fell on the shoulders of T. Wilson, at what proved to be a major testing phase in the history of the Company.

Employment had ballooned, averaging 142,400 in 1968, also a record. Some observers accused Boeing of becoming fat and sloppy. *Time*, looking back from a 1980 vantage point reported that "Seattle's nickname for the Company was "The Lazy B.""[2]

The sudden downdraft in the business climate was not limited to commercial airplanes. The last phase of the moon program was being focused in Huntsville, where Boeing was busy designing the *Lunar Rover*. When the decade of the seventies dawned, most of the $25 billion devoted to the manned moon program had been spent. Anticipating the end, NASA announced in January that 50,000 jobs would be cut.

The Lunar Rover *Moon Buggy*—1971–1972

Astronaut preparing to explore the surface of the moon in one of the two Lunar Rovers built by Boeing.

The *SST* was still a going concern, and late in 1969, Congress authorized an appropriation of $85 million for the 1970 fiscal year to continue design and construction of the two prototypes. However, the *SST* was not yet making a significant contribution to the employment picture.

On the national scene, the U.S. economy was sliding into recession. On July 12, 1970, President Nixon signed the first public employment legislation since the WPA in the 1930s, and a year later, in August, imposed a wage and price freeze.

Who knew better than the people at Boeing that change did not just happen—it had to be forced—and welcomed. The Company had always embraced the Heraclitan axiom that neither man nor corporation could step into the same river twice.

Job cutting became the order of the day at Boeing in 1969. Wilson was matter-of-fact, dismissing any other notion than to overhaul the Company from top to bottom. At the time, he remarked: "The logic is simple. If I don't do it, the board will bring in some ice water guy from the outside who will. I decided I might as well be the ice water guy."[3]

Wilson called in his close friend and protege, Tex Boullioun, head of the Commercial Airplane Group. "Tex, we're not getting anywhere. I'm going to get fired in six months if we don't make some kind of a turnaround. I just want you to know there's only one guy that I know of for sure that's going to go before I do, and that's you."[4]

With Boullioun a believer, Wilson embarked on a plan to reduce employees proportionately at every level—from vice-president to floor sweeper. In 1969 alone, 25,576 persons were laid off.[5] Then in 1970, the bloodletting became a river. An additional 41,000 people hit the streets, leveling off at an average employment for the year of 79,100.[6]

The reductions in force were accompanied by reductions in plant capacity, and in 1970 alone, four million square feet were eliminated.

There was more bad news still to come. On March 23, 1971, the U.S. Senate voted to cut off all further funding for the *SST*. The American supersonic airplane was dead, leaving the *Concorde* with no competition outside of the Soviet Union.

During 1971, total employment was again drastically reduced, reaching a low of 56,300. The "Boeing Bust" had consumed the jobs of over 86,000 employees in the span of three years.

When the second *Lunar Rover* landed on December 11, 1972, with the *Apollo* 17 mission, the moon program was completed.

Seattle, and the Puget Sound region—where most of the people were employed—became a disaster area; and statewide, Washington unemployment hit 14 percent, highest in the nation. Someone placed a huge billboard sign adjacent to Interstate Highway 5, with the grim admonition: "Will the last person leaving Seattle, turn out the lights."[7]

Company funded R&D was also slashed. Indeed, the Boeing Scientific Research Laboratory was swept away in the massive layoff campaign.

The year of 1970 had been the harbinger of the role that overseas sales were destined to play in the fortunes of the Company. That year, $716 million in sales of commercial airplanes to foreign carriers were booked, while not a single sale was made in the United States domestic market.

Diversification became the new watchword, with the goal of adding counter-cyclic programs to the product line. The enthusiasm for new ventures reached a crescendo in the operating units of the Company, and Wilson established the Office of Corporate Business Development (OCBD), to aid in focusing these efforts.

The OCBD, a small think tank with a staff of eleven, was headed by vice-president Henry K. "Bud" Hebeler, reporting directly to Wilson. Hebeler had earned a masters degree in aeronautical engineering from MIT, and returned as a Sloan Fellow in business management in 1969.

OCBD had a two-pronged charter. First, to develop a ten-year business plan, updating it annually for presentation to the Executive Council; and second, to make independent assessments of the projects being developed by the operating divisions. Incredibly, this was the first time in the Company's history that such a plan had been formalized.

The diversification wave included light rail transportation, small automated people movers, commercial hydrofoils, energy systems, urban planning, service industries, waste water purification, desalination systems, and even real property development, to name only the most significant projects.

Nevertheless, diversification was more of a wish than a solution, and the Company's heart was never in it. The realization that Boeing's business was building airplanes rapidly took hold.

Thus, in 1972, in what proved to be one of the most significant decisions in the history of the Company, Boeing targeted overseas commercial airplane sales as its top priority. In a major reorganization, the Commercial Airplane

Group became the Commercial Airplane Company, with its own president, super salesman Ernest H. "Tex" Boullioun, reporting to corporate headquarters.

On September 29, 1972, William M. Allen retired after forty-seven years of association with the Company. *In a Company that was known for team efforts, if one were obliged to select the most outstanding leader since William E. Boeing himself, it would have to be Bill Allen.*

T. Wilson was elevated to chairman of the board, and Mal Stamper was elected president.

Early in 1973, with business and financial cooperation appearing to be a certain requirement for international competition, Wilson turned to Hebeler.

"Bud, we need to know more about the capabilities of the rest of the world in aerospace."[8]

The Company had launched a cooperative design study with an Italian firm in 1972, initially looking at a quiet, short-haul machine, and now Wilson wanted to define and broaden the international fraction.

"Our deal with the Italians—how do we know we are teaming up with the best people—the most capable from a competitive standpoint? We need to wring that out."

Hebeler nodded. "I can get two or three guys on it right away."

"One more thing," Wilson emphasized, as Hebeler was turning away. "I want you to boil down the world—to about a dozen countries. Then we need to look more closely at the finalists."[9]

After the task force had reduced the world to twelve country-candidates, Wilson requested that numerical scores be assigned to each. Then, to spread the risk, two were chosen.

It was decided to continue with the Italians as one of the partners, even though they finished seventh in the numerical scoring. Japan came out in the top five—all bunched within four points—and was chosen as the second partner.

During 1973, a memorandum of understanding was signed between Boeing and the Japanese Civil Transport Development Corporation, calling for a one-year exploration of marketing, scheduling, and financial feasibility of a joint development and production program for a new commercial jet airplane. The agreement recognized Boeing's on-going efforts, known as the 7x7, and a proposed Japanese YX jetliner program.

With most of the economy still weak in recession, Boeing began to show signs of new health. Wilson's Draconian actions in setting the Company on a *lean-and-mean* path had pulled it out of its dive. Subsequent performance testified to success. In 1969 it took 25,000 employees to turn out seven 747s per month, and by 1980, 11,000 were able to do the same job.

In May 1970, Boeing Computer Services (BCS) was incorporated as a new subsidiary of the Company, and Boeing committed itself to the marketing of software. Vested with the charter to do the computing for its parent, BCS instantly became one of the three or four largest of all such companies in the United States, with a base of twenty years of experience. The new subsidiary embarked on commercial sales, and in its first seven months, signed contracts with more than 250 customers located in twenty-seven States, the District of Columbia, Canada, and Australia.

Another major objective was achieved in July 1970, when the Air Force announced that Boeing had been chosen as the prime contractor for the Airborne Warning and Control System (AWACS).

Then in January 1971, the Short Range Attack Missile (SRAM), on which Boeing had invested substantial developmental funds, was ordered into production. Eventually, 1,500 SRAMs were built and deployed with the Strategic Air Command's B-52 and FB-111 fleets.

On paper, at least, the Vietnam War was over on January 27, 1973. Long before the war was officially over, the armed services of the United States had been trying mightily to come to grips with the lessons learned in that terrible war. And, of course, Congress was busy second guessing the experts. The Air Force was certain of one thing—in future wars, they must get materiel closer to the front lines—and in a much shorter time.

The aircraft industry got busy studying Short Takeoff and Landing (STOL) aircraft. Shortly, the Air Force kicked off a program called the Advanced Medium STOL Transport (AMST), billed as a replacement for the Lockheed C-130 *Hercules*. What was needed was a short takeoff and landing machine that could carry heavy loads into hastily built, 2,000 foot long, rough runways in forward areas of battle.

Boeing proposed taking advantage of a new concept pioneered by NASA in 1959, called Upper Surface Blowing (USB), by mounting two large engines on top of the wing, to utilize the high velocity exhaust flow over the

YC-14 Short Takeoff and Landing Cargo Plane
First aircraft to incorporate Upper Surface Blowing, the YC-14 competed with the
McDonnell Douglas YC-15, which eventually became the C-17 *Globemaster III*.

upper surfaces for increasing lift. The strange looking bird was called the YC-14. John K. "Jack" Wimpress headed the design team. Wimpress had come to Boeing after earning a bachelor of science degree in aeronautical engineering from Georgia Tech in 1946, and a master of science in aeronautical engineering from Cal Tech in 1948. In 1978, he won the American Institute of Aeronautics and Astronautics Aircraft Design Award for definition of an original concept leading to a significant advancement in aircraft design.

McDonald Douglas entered a more conventional airplane with four smaller engines mounted under the wing, called the YC-15.

In November, 1972, the Air Force awarded contracts to both Boeing and McDonnell Douglas to build two prototypes.

With continued on-again off-again signals from the Air Force, the prototypes were in the early stages of testing when the program was suspended in 1977.

After months of controversy over mission requirements, the Air Force prepared a new request for proposal for a machine to be called the "CX."

They had decided that the real need was for a larger transport that would fly to conventional airfields rather than into battle zones, leaving an airplane like the YC-14 a machine without a mission.

In order to strengthen the Company's stance, the Boeing Military Airplane Company was formed in October, 1979, consolidating development and manufacturing organizations in both Wichita and Seattle, and the CX proposal came out in the spring of 1980.

Boeing's entry was based on the YC-14 design with a third engine mounted in the tail. Lockheed proposed an airplane that looked a lot like the C-141, with a wider fuselage. McDonnell Douglas refined their own YC-15 design.

The award was made on September 3, 1981, with McDonnell Douglas winning the battle. Indecision regarding a production contract continued for ten years, and it was not until September 15, 1991, that the airplane—the C-17—made its first flight.

Luck and timing were on Boeing's side in 1972, when McDonnell Douglas decided to close its DC-8 production line. Mr. Mac—with continuing success in producing fighters for the Air Force—was reluctant to pour excessive resources into his failing commercial airplane operations. He expected the DC-10 to mature to a profitable program on its own after the initial infusion of capital to kick it off.

For McDonnell Douglas, it was a regrettable decision, as demand soon began increasing for a plane to handle the long thin routes that were unprofitable for the jumbos—and the 185 passenger DC-8-62 offered a good capacity match.

Boeing was facing the tough decision of what to do with the 707 production line. With only seven airplanes added to the order books in 1971, the program was not breaking even. Thus, Mr. Mac's decision provided the incentive to keep the line in operation. A production rate of one airplane a month would turn a small profit, and there was a possibility that AWACS, utilizing a modified 707 fuselage, would grow into a sizeable program.

Subsequent events proved the significance of the DC-8/707 decisions in contributing to Boeing's growing dominance of the commercial airplane market. In the years that followed, the Company sold eighty-one additional 707 airplanes. When the final sales tally for the competition was in, the score was 878 for the 707/720 against 556 for the DC-8. Of special significance, was the acquisition of new customers. Noteworthy among those were Tarom of Rumania, the first airline customer in an Eastern Bloc nation; Iraq in Asia; Egypt and Sudan in Africa; and of extraordinary importance—the People's Republic of China, (PRC)—purchasing ten airplanes in 1972.

In addition, 131 modified 707s were sold worldwide as military airplanes (primarily AWACS).

In 1973, with the first of the 707s being delivered to the PRC, a customer-support field office was opened in Beijing—a major milestone in worldwide support, considering the country was tightly closed to the outside world. The office was one of more than sixty such offices that Boeing was maintaining around the world to support its customer airlines. *Indeed, field service had matured to be viewed as one of the linchpins in the Boeing image of product integrity, contributing significantly to airline purchasing decisions.*

With the DC-8-62 out of the competition, Boeing decided in 1973 to produce a 747 derivative known as the SP—for Special Performance—a smaller airplane aimed at the long thin routes. The fuselage was reduced by forty-seven feet, while retaining the identical wing and lift devices. The airplane offered extended range, higher cruising altitude, superior takeoff and landing characteristics, lower noise, and improved fuel economy.

The first SP rolled out of the factory on May 19, 1975, making its maiden flight on July 4. In the autumn of 1975, prior to its delivery to Pan American on March 15, 1976, the airplane was committed to an intensive marketing campaign. The month-long, worldwide sales demonstration tour took the 747SP to eighteen countries, including three dramatic long distance flights: New York to Tokyo, Sydney to Santiago, and Mexico City to Belgrade. Each of the flights covered some 7,000 statute miles.

The 747SP made further history when Pan American, in commemoration of its fiftieth anniversary, flew one of its planes on a record breaking flight around the world over both the North and South poles. The SP covered the 26,383 mile distance in just over fifty-four hours, making only three stops for refueling. Actual flight time was forty-eight hours and three minutes. Although the 747SP was a technical success, it was not a financial success, and only forty machines were sold. The venture demonstrated the questionable economics of shrinking an airplane.

However, overall commercial airplane sales, which hit a low of 97 in 1972—down from a peak of 376 in 1968—rose steadily, reaching 189 in 1974. Then after a slight dip, they grew to a new record in 1978. In that year, 461 new jet transport orders, valued at $11 billion were announced by 85 customers—more than 50 percent of them foreign.

Employment, too, had climbed steadily from the 1971 low, and in 1980, again passed the 100,000 mark, averaging 106,300 for the year.

Ten years had wrought a storybook recovery. In 1970, the Company was teetering on the edge of a precipice, and by 1980 had rocketed to a record sales performance, with a backlog of over $20 billion. The turn-around had been accomplished by tough minded management and dedicated people.

The concentrated drive for excellence paid handsome dividends in other than commercial airplanes. In 1980, the Company won the fly-off competition for the Air Launched Cruise Missile (ALCM), starting a production run for some 3,400 units—the largest single Air Force contract since the Vietnam War.

Also in 1980, AWACS came to maturity worldwide, when Boeing signed contracts for $2.2 billion for eighteen AWACS aircraft for the North Atlantic Treaty Organization (NATO). The B-52 bomber fleet, still a vital force after nearly thirty years in the Strategic Air Command, was equipped with new electronic equipment. More powerful and fuel efficient engines were installed on KC-135s, leading to a complete retrofit of the 732 airplanes in the fleet.

However, commercial airplanes continued to capture the public interest. *Time*, which featured T. Wilson on its April 7, 1980, cover, was expansive in its salute to Boeing, citing only a few of the many praises from pleased customers.

"More than just state-of-art and solid engineering sets Boeing apart in the eyes of its customers, says Derek Davison, managing director of Britannia Airways, a small Luton, England-based charter operator that owns twenty-two Boeing 737s and plans to add three more later this year; 'In the end, a large measure of the thinking in our decision to go ahead with the 737 rested on the confidence we had in the people at Boeing. The most important thing about them is that you can trust them. They take the long view: never try to pull off a deal on information that could lead to misunderstanding. They are better salesmen because they are better professionals.'"

"Explains Donald Jones, American Airlines senior operational vice president: 'Technically, Boeing is very competent, but so are Lockheed and McDonnell Douglas. The major distinction is the excellent sales force. They have salesmen assigned to customers who represent the customer's needs to Boeing as much as sell Boeing planes to the customers. The result is that people develop a great deal of faith that Boeing will do what it says and is leveling with them.'"[10]

T. Wilson was not resting on his laurels. His remark, "I wake up in the middle of the night and do logic problems,"[11] was a measure of his intensity.

1. *Annual Report*, The Boeing Company, 1969, 14.
2. *Time*, 7 April, 1980, 52.
3. Private Communication.
4. *Seattle Times*, 3 June, 1984, Pacific Section, 12.
5. *Annual Report*, The Boeing Company, 1969.
6. *Annual Report*, The Boeing Company, 1970.
7. *Seattle Post-Intelligencer*, 1 January, 1980, D11.
8. Private Communication.
9. Ibid.
10. *Time*, 7 April, 1980, 57.
11. Private Communication.

CHAPTER TWENTY-FIVE

The Corporate Conscience

"As long as Boeing builds the best airplanes, it will be sufficient. The world will recognize the superior product and buy it." Those words, credited to William M. Allen, embodied his corporate business philosophy.

As Allen would not make payments to middlemen, neither would he accept gifts from customers. One day a beautiful handmade fly-fishing rod was delivered to him. It was from C.R. Smith, president of American Airlines. Allen returned it, explaining that a Boeing rule forbade an employee to accept a gift from a company with which Boeing did business. Two weeks later the rod came back—addressed this time to "Miss Nancy Allen," Bill's daughter, with a note from Smith. "This is for Nancy," read the note, "and your damn company rules don't apply to her."[1]

However, in the late fifties, two Englishmen, including one former official of British Overseas Airways (BOAC), now British Airways, were hired as consultants to help sell airplanes to BOAC, and the employ of consultants appeared to be an increasingly necessary practice, particularly for foreign sales.

Early in the 707 program, selling was no more complex than writing up the order, with the airline executive coming to Seattle to sign the final papers.

When the initial wave of market demand was satisfied, it became necessary for the sales force to range farther afield. The intensity of the technological battle demanded a parallel effort on the sales front. New services were offered to the airlines: traffic analyses, route feasibility studies, performance criteria for airports, runway evaluations, economic expectations, and even help in making financial arrangements. Competition increased and model derivatives proliferated.

The same morality that had served the company in the United States seemed outmoded—perhaps even an impediment to overseas sales. Many foreign accounts depended to some extent on the advice and aid of consultants. The conventional wisdom became: *when in doubt, seek help.*

Consultants were retained and paid regular commissions, which were legitimate sales costs. Commissions were paid on a contingency basis. If there was no sale, there was no commission. T. Wilson interceded directly on the issue of consultants, approving each one individually after a rigorous screening program. He demanded compelling reasons for retaining them, often suggesting that "maybe Boeing had too many."[2]

Some Boeing salesmen felt frustrated about the Company's scruples when Boeing would not take the extra step—matching payments that they knew were being made by competitors.

In the summer of 1975, echoes of the "Lockheed Scandal" reverberated through the boardrooms of corporate America. The Securities Exchange Commission (SEC) had disclosed that Lockheed was conducting massive bribery campaigns in overseas markets, and the U.S. Senate Subcommittee on Multinational Operations, under Senator Frank Church, began hearings on their business practices.

Other U.S. firms, including all of the major aerospace companies, came under scrutiny of the Church Subcommittee, the SEC, the Federal trade Commission (FTC), and the Internal Revenue Service (IRS). Many of those companies were eventually investigated by the Justice Department as well.

Responding to the SEC accusations in the summer of 1975, after months of denial, Lockheed acknowledged "that it had made $22 million in payoffs to foreign countries since 1970 to get lucrative aircraft contracts—a practice it termed necessary to meet the competition."[3]

The Lockheed dispute took twenty-one months to resolve, and in May 1977, pursuant to a negotiated court order, a special committee of Lockheed directors filed a report specifying how the company "secretly generated as much as $38 million for questionable foreign marketing practices."[4]

The corporation was attempting to recover from huge losses incurred on the *Tristar* program, clinging to solvency by a slender thread. Only a few years before, they had been rescued from certain bankruptcy by a one-vote margin in the United States Senate, who approved a governmentally guaranteed loan of $250 million to keep the company afloat.

To aid in bringing his company back, Dan Haughton presided over one of the biggest bribing operations of all time. President A. Carl Kotchian acted as top salesman for the company on many occasions, jet-hopping around the world to press the flesh and wave greenbacks before uncommitted airline executives. That story is told in painful detail by David Boulton.[5]

Boulton reports that on one occasion, Kotchian holed up in a Tokyo hotel room for an excruciating seventy days, waiting to see if $3.5 million in bribes would land a crucial sale of twenty-one *Tristars* to All Nippon Airways—who had already taken options on DC-10s. Incredibly, he turned the sale around.

Lockheed's woes did not end with the completion of the SEC probe, they still had the Justice Department to reckon with. In mid-1979, the Lockheed Corporation pleaded guilty to having concealed payments to Japanese government officials, including a $1.8 million payment that allegedly went to the office of Kakuei Tanaka, then prime minister.[6]

Lockheed pleaded guilty to a Justice Department charge of four felony counts of wire fraud, four felony counts of having made false statements to the government, and two misdemeanor violations of customs law.[7]

When the government made its case, Haughton and Kotchian bore the brunt of the responsibility. Both men, forced to resign early in 1976, expressed a mixture of relief and bitterness over the episode that had consumed their careers. In commenting on Lockheed's sales practices, Kotchian remarked: "Some call it gratuities, some call it questionable payments, some call it extortion, and some call it grease. Some call it bribery. I look at these payments as necessary to sell a product."[8]

The Company could not be charged with bribery because Public Law 95-213 (which became known as the Corrupt Practices Act) did not take effect until December 1977. Instead, the Justice Department accused the company of violating criminal laws in attempting to conceal payments from the Export-Import Bank (Ex-Im), a government agency that makes and guarantees loans for overseas sales—and was involved in the All Nippon transactions.

Ex-Im regulations require American firms to sign statements certifying their company has not made any unusual payments, rebates, commissions, or other fees to sell planes.

Interest quickly focused on the practices of Lockheed's main rivals— giant Boeing and its most tenacious competitor, McDonnell Douglas.

At the time, McDonnell Douglas reported that between 1970 and 1975, approximately $2.5 million in foreign fees, commissions, and consultants payments were made to promote sales of commercial aircraft.[9]

Almost three years later, the SEC filed suit in a district court in Washington, D.C., charging the St. Louis-based manufacturer of violating federal securities laws in connection with $15.6 million in payments since 1969, to secure foreign sales. They said the company failed to disclose the payments, made to government officials and airline executives.[10]

In January 1979, the SEC completed its case against McDonnell Douglas. The charge that $15.6 million in improper payments were made in fifteen countries remained. McDonnell Douglas agreed to a negotiated settlement in which it neither admitted nor denied the allegations, but agreed to suspend such payments and to appoint a three-member investigative panel and to issue a report within six months.[11]

The special panel reported on July 20, 1980, that McDonnell Douglas had made $21.57 million in questionable payments to sales agents in eighteen countries between 1969 and 1976. The company justified its action, saying, "Company management became involved in questionable payments because of a motivation to operate the affairs of the corporation in what was perceived to be in the best interests of the shareholders and employees. Management's participation in questionable payments was reluctant and spare and occurred with the conviction the payments comported with local practice and with U.S. law."[12]

In a further action, the Justice Department indicted McDonnell Douglas, as well as four top executives, on criminal charges of mail fraud, conspiracy, and making false statements to a federal agency. This was the first time in the payments investigations that corporate individuals had been charged with illegal practices. Trial was set for January 1981.

In a surprise move, James McDonnell, frail at eighty-one years, but still active as chairman, rejected plea bargaining and demanded a court trial. Mr. Mac, true to his straight-laced, no-nonsense behavior, indicated he would never have condoned the sales practices of the California-based Douglas commercial airplane operations, had he been aware of them. Against the advice of both his lawyers and his doctors, he insisted that the government prosecutors proceed with their case.

"If this company that I have led, is as rotten as you say, then I want to see it in court and all McDonnell Douglas people will have to take the consequences," he told four young prosecutors.[13]

Again, as in the Lockheed case, bribery charges could not be brought, since the alleged actions had preceded the Corrupt Practices Act.

The trial was never held. Following the old man's death the same year, McDonnell Douglas took the plea bargaining path, and in September 1981, the Justice Department agreed to drop criminal charges in return for guilty pleas and payment of fines to settle the civil suit.[14]

The company pleaded guilty to charges related to payments on aircraft sales in Pakistan, Zaire, South Korea, the Phillipines, and Venezuela.

In its 1975 report to the stockholders, Boeing presented its sales practices in regard to consultants:

"The Company has used sales representatives and consultants on a contingent fee basis where such arrangements appeared to be advisable for the conduct of business in the foreign countries involved. A limited number of the sales representatives and consultants held a position with their governments, but management believes none had the authority to purchase or approve the purchase of the Company's products or services. All payments made with respect to foreign business have been clearly identified in the Company's accounting records, and no funds have been diverted, either directly or indirectly, to so-called slush funds."[15]

A year later, after a complete review of consultant practices in foreign business transactions, T. Wilson reported:

"In August 1976, the Board of Directors approved an updated policy statement and implementation instructions relating to sales consultants, political contributions, and financial records, formalizing requirements and procedures designed to assure the Company that in conducting its business it will continue at all times to be in compliance with applicable laws, and that the nature and extent of all payments made by the Company with respect to foreign sales will continue to be accurately recorded in the accounts of the Company."[16]

Top Boeing officials also denied any knowledge of the Lockheed payments at the time the scandal broke. Mr. James E. "Jim" Prince, a quiet, sensitive man, for many years the corporate secretary and personal confidant of both Bill Allen and T. Wilson, always cautioned against illegal action of any kind.

After receiving a law degree from Harvard, Prince had joined the Seattle law firm of Todd, Holman and Sprague, devoting most of his time to the Boeing account. Prince too, had local roots, graduating from the University of Washington in 1930 with a bachelor of arts degree. He joined Boeing full time in 1952 as vice-president for administration.

When Jim Prince was asked to comment on those payments, he shrugged, saying "We may have had some rumors, but nothing at all precise."[17]

As the SEC investigations proceeded, Boeing submitted what it termed to be a complete disclosure in July 1978. In an out-of-court settlement, the Company agreed to provide details of its foreign transactions, without admitting or denying guilt, and to abide by the terms of an injunction barring it from participating in fraudulent activities or filing false reports.

Boeing revealed that it had made payments of $54 million in connection with $943 million worth of airplane sales in at least eighteen countries, which it said, it considered to be legitimate commissions or consulting fees.[18]

Following the settlement with the SEC, a special committee of three outside directors was created by the Boeing Board of Directors to review the Company's procedures for policing questionable payments.

On February 16, 1979, the Boeing review committee of outside directors completed its task, reporting to the SEC that "The Boeing Company has made a complete disclosure of payments to foreign officials, and no further investigations are required."[19]

In spite of those findings, the Justice Department continued to pursue the case.

Although time and sensation had dulled the senses, it was no less startling when it was reported in July 1982, that Boeing had withheld certain facts concerning commissions.

Boeing pleaded guilty to the charge of concealing from the U.S. Ex-Im Bank $7.38 million in irregular commissions, paid to agents in airplane sales in Spain, Honduras, the Dominican Republic, and Lebanon. Payments in Spain and Lebanon accounted for 95 percent of the total.[20]

In spite of a clearly defined corporate policy, a few middle managers in the Boeing sales force had promoted questionable practices. Even though the preponderance of Boeing's total sales commissions were found to be legal business practices, the Company was nevertheless accountable.

Adding columns of figures and citing numbers of countries in which consultants were used, sometimes improperly, does not illuminate nor focus the issue. It is necessary to consider the total fabric of a corporation's history. There is a profound difference between isolated cases of errant judgement on the part of a few individuals on the one hand, and deliberate and enduring corporate policies on the other. Every company develops and follows a corporate conscience according to the personalities and practices of its senior officers—indeed tracing back to the founders.

Easily overlooked when comparing total payments for commissions and consulting fees among the big three of U.S. commercial airplane manufacturers, was Boeing's dominance of the market. In the world car market in the decade of the seventies, General Motors held a 20 to 25 percent share. In the world computer market, IBM had about 30 percent. In the world market for commercial jets, Boeing had 50 to 55 percent.

But history is harsh. Omar Khayyam provides a reminder:

> *The Moving Finger writes; and having writ,*
> *Moves on: nor all thy Piety nor Wit*
> *Shall lure it back to cancel half a Line,*
> *Nor all thy Tears wash out a Word of it.*[21]

Over the centuries, governments have grappled with the problem of bribery and its twin brother, extortion, vainly trying to establish a line where legitimate fees end and illegal payments begin.

In a recent comprehensive work, Professors Jacoby, Nehemkis, and Eells of the Graduate School of Business at Columbia University, conclude that political payments are institutionalized facts of international business. They find that in almost every country in which American businessmen have ventured as investors or traders, they have encountered the phenomenon of the payoff—the practice of bribing government officials as a condition of doing business, of government employees expecting—in fact, demanding—kickbacks on contracts in pursuance of their discretionary power.[22]

In a free enterprise economy such as the United States, where sales commissions are a legal practice—indeed an essential method of stimulating competition—the difficulty arises in transplanting those practices to the overseas environment.

Latin America, Africa, and parts of Asia proved to be areas where bribery was rampant and accepted—if not officially condoned—as a part of normal business practices. It was viewed by the indigenous population as simply dealing among friends. In almost every part of the world, it had a name. In Africa, it was *cumshaw*; in the Middle East, *baksheesh*; in Korea, *chongtok*; in Trinidad, *boobol*; and in Spanish-speaking Latin America, *mordida*.

Boeing salesmen attempted to engage honest men who had legitimate contacts in places of influence, but on the other hand, felt an intense pressure to make sales.

Consultants worked as independent contractors in all respects, with no authority to obligate Boeing in any manner whatsoever. The consultant was also required to assume all expenses and pay all costs in relation to carrying out his duties, receiving no compensation whatsoever until the airplane was sold.

Many consultants worked through two or more years of one-year contracts, spending much of their time, and potentially considerably of their own money, betting on the favorable outcome of a sales campaign, only to find an empty pot at the end of the rainbow. No commissions were offered for the sale of used airplanes, which made up the total fleets of many small operators.

Reports of multimillion-dollar commissions earned by a few legitimate consultants around the world were highly publicized. Nothing was ever said about the dozens of others who never made a penny, and in some cases lost their life's savings on one wrong perception.

Until the time the Lockheed scandal broke into the news, the United States regulatory agencies seemed to stand idly by, with no visible policy, taking little note of the difficult equation that was developing. This inaction gave a sense of security to Lockheed, who had already embodied bribery into its corporate policy, and were forced to further excesses in order to survive as a business entity. Moreover, the lack of government policy encouraged strongly ethically oriented companies to view certain sales activities with their backs turned.

The Watergate revelations in 1972 had introduced a national concern over illegal activities in government, and the climate quickly developed into universal suspicion.

American news media, fresh from their Watergate bonanza, welcomed the revelations, exploiting and sensationalizing each new disclosure. *Time* announced on the cover of its February 23, 1976, issue: "The Big Payoff, Lockheed Scandal, Graft Around the Globe." *Newsweek* printed a special feature story. Many newspapers, including the *Washington Post* and the *New York Times*, embarked on a series of overblown editorial comments which influenced many Americans.

Not until 1977 was a law considered which specifically addressed itself to the problem of bribes. That law was drafted in the unrealistic atmosphere of suspicion that pervaded the times, and thus represented a severe overreaction. On December 19, 1977, President Carter signed into law (Public Law 95-213), the Foreign Corrupt Practices Act of 1977.

The Act was intended to put an end to bribery overseas, imposing heavy fines and/or prison sentences of up to five years on the officers of offending companies. However, the ink was scarcely dry before many responsible people in government began to feel uncomfortable about the Act's long-range effects.

Early in 1977, even the *New York Times* concluded in an editorial that "qualified discretion is preferable to unqualified morality. In a volatile world, the need for flexibility is great."[23]

Nowhere was the effect of the Act more dramatic than in the aerospace industry. In the early seventies, exports of aerospace hardware provided the single highest net fraction to the positive side of the United States balance of payments of any category of manufactured goods, and was second only to agricultural products on an overall basis. United States products not only lost market share as a result of the Act, but more importantly, the precious momentum built up in the decade of the sixties was seriously blunted.

Airbus Industrie, the West European consortium, gained encouragement. Many European governments, already with partial or even total ownership of aircraft production facilities, began more active stimulation of trade through hidden subsidies to enhance their products in the world marketplace.

The European airplane manufacturers had no inhibitions concerning bribes, and their governments seemed unconcerned. The sales campaign in Peru in 1974 provides a graphic example of the realities of some foreign markets.

In spite of intensive sales efforts, including a costly series of demonstration flights of a 737 airplane in Peru, proving its superior performance from short, high elevation airfields, in a hot climate, AeroPeru—the national airline—announced the purchase of Fokker F-28s from the Netherlands.

Later, it was learned that the decision had been "cast in concrete" even before the 737 airplane arrived in Peru, as a result of passing *mordida* of $1.5 million on the $12 million order for three airplanes.[24]

The completion of an airplane sale was the result of a two-to-five year process of incubation; route analyses, economic forecasts, financial studies, and constant technical updating. Many sales campaigns were brought to the very threshold of signing before quietly expiring as a result of a nose dive of the country's economy or a change in key personnel.

Although American airplane manufacturers were still caught in the uneven position of competing with foreign government subsidies in the case of Airbus Industrie, at least the Corrupt Practices Act—in spite of its faults—provided an even field for U.S. companies to compete against one another.

1. *Washington, The Evergreen State Magazine*, November,1988. 17.
2. Private Communication.
3. *Wall Street Journal*, 4 December, 1975, 1.
4. Ibid., 20 February, 1979,13.
5. David Boulton, *The Grease Machine*, (New York: Harper & Row, 1978).
6. *New York Times*, 2 June, 1979, 29.
7. Ibid.
8. *New York Times*, 15 February, 1979, A1.
9. *Aviation Week & Space Technology*, 8 December, 1975, 15.

10. Ibid., 18 December, 1978, 18.
11. Ibid., 8 January, 1979, 25.
12. Ibid. 4 August, 1980, 21.
13. *Wall Street Journal*, 9 October, 1980.
14. *Asian Wall Street Journal*, 11 September, 1981.
15. *Annual Report*, The Boeing Company, 1975, 5.
16. *Annual Report*, The Boeing Company, 1976, 4.
17. *Wall Street Journal*, 7 May, 1976, 1.
18. *New York Times*, 16 February, 1979, D5.
19. Ibid.
20. *Wall Street Journal*, 1 July, 1982, 40.
21. *Rubaiyat of Omar Khayyam*, (London: George G. Harrap, 1940), 42.
22. N.H. Jacoby, P. Nehemkis, and R. Eells, *Bribery and Extortion in World Business*, (New York: MacMillan, 1977).
23. *New York Times*, 23 February, 1977, A22.
24. Private Communication.

CHAPTER TWENTY-SIX

The New Technology Twinjets

By 1978, Boeing was on a roll. Behind was the 1977 strike by the Machinists Union—at forty-five days, the second long-est—but only the third in its history. The year set a new record for commercial airplanes sold, when 461 orders were booked—more than twice that of all other producers combined.

Profits of 5.9 percent of sales were the second highest in history, topping the Fortune 500 companies in total returns, and exceeded only by the 6.3 percent record established in 1941.

There were other positive factors for Boeing. Both Lockheed and McDonnell Douglas were in trouble, with neither the *Tristar* nor the DC-10 making a profit. The 747 booked orders for eighty-three airplanes, having increased from the low of twenty-one in 1975, when the production line was running at a rate less than two airplanes per month. At the end of 1978, the line was humming along at seven—near capacity.

At year end, *Dun's Review* named Boeing as one of the five best managed United States companies, with an expansive prediction:

"It is clear that Boeing will be the only American company producing planes (McDonnell Douglas has almost officially withdrawn from the race, and Lockheed simply does not have the financial resources), and it will compete probably with just one company, the French-English Airbus Industrie."[1]

T. Wilson decided it was time to act. The new technology twinjets had been incubating longer by far than any previous commercial airplane, and no new model had appeared in the industry for ten years. Airline interest had been building for a 180 to 200-passenger airplane to take advantage of the operational economies promised by new engines, and incorporating new technologies all along the line.

Exhaustive efforts to sell derivatives of the 737 and 727 had come up empty when the prime candidate, an additionally stretched version of the 727 failed the market test. Edward Beamish, senior vice-president of planning for United Airlines, after studying the proposed 727-300, told Boeing: "We looked at what it would do for earnings potential and said no, this is not what we want."[2]

Besides economies of operation, there was a wave of airline interest in improving passenger comfort, resulting in an almost universal desire for a twin aisle, wide body interior for a medium-range airplane.

Boeing studies, which included traveling mockups with various seating arrangements—which were evaluated by thousands of potential passengers—finalized on twin aisle, seven abreast seating at 2-3-2. The Model 767, maturation of the 7X7 design studies, was ready for kickoff.

Nevertheless, the new airplane could not cover the total potential medium-range market. It was too large to be considered as a 727 replacement, and with 1,482 of those sold at the end of 1977, it was essential to view that market as a separate opportunity. To replace the 727, Boeing designed the Model 757, a six abreast, single aisle airplane.

When Wilson gave the green light to the twin programs in the summer of 1978, they represented the boldest and most costly commitment in Boeing's history, nearly twice the net worth of the Company.

Forbes, in a complimentary review of some of Boeing's previous ventures, had this to say:

Models 757 & 767—1982

The new technology twins. The wide bodied, seven abreast, double aisle 767 quickly took the lead in early sales, however, the narrow bodied, six abreast, single aisle 757 overtook it in 1988.

"Nothing in the past, though, compares with the multi-billion-dollar gamble the 757 and 767 programs represent."[3]

T. did not consider it a gamble. "I don't agonize over that kind of a decision," he said later in an interview. "We seemed to be ready to take on something new. We had the disciplines and the organization in place that could handle that.... I don't stew and fret too much about the market. That's something over which we don't have any direct control. What I agonize over is whether we're doing a productive job on what we've got, and whether we're meeting our commitments."[4]

The threat of European competition had never been taken seriously by Boeing. Several European airplane models had made a brief entry into the United States, but soon disappeared. The French *Caravelle* and the British *Viscount* were notable examples. The British *BAC-111* held out a while longer. The *Concorde* failed to make any sales.

However, a new energy and a new purpose began to appear in the industry of Western Europe in the early seventies. J.J. Servan-Schreiber, an impetuous Frenchman, first issued the call to arms in 1968. He upbraided his European compatriots for their lack of tenacity and desire in failing to weld together a coherent regional plan to produce equipment which could compete with—and even beat the Americans. Servan-Schreiber worried that by the early eighties, the world's third greatest industrial power—after the U.S. and the Soviets—would not be Western Europe, but United States industry in Western Europe. He correctly perceived the problem not to be a torrent of American riches, but rather a more intelligent use of skills.

Servan-Schreiber challenged his countrymen in the European Economic Community (EEC) to find a way to reverse the trend. He yearned for a concerted, cooperative effort with imaginative goals that could endure. There was no paucity of ideas in the creative minds of the inventive Europeans, it was only their reluctance to turn ideas into practice, which to many was viewed as mundane and unsatisfying. Innovation was left to the ugly Americans—"a nation of tinkerers."[5]

Servan-Schreiber named a number of candidates: space, atomic energy, and supersonic airplanes. The wide acceptance of *The American Challenge*—no book in France since World War II had sold so many copies—testified to a deep-seated frustration felt by many Europeans.

When two of the EEC members, France and Great Britain, undertook the first supersonic commercial transport, they provided a modicum of an answer to the Servan-Schreiber challenge. However, Airbus Industrie, a multinational consortium, was the first venture with a broad base of participating EEC countries. The initial product, the A300 Airbus, proved to be technically as good as planned, however, its impact as a world market contender was still viewed with skepticism by U.S. producers. In 1973, the round-the-world appearances, which included a fly-in at the First International Air Show in Brazil, were written off as last gasp efforts to bolster a sagging program. *At Boeing, perhaps the strongest engineering enterprise in the world, Airbus Industrie efforts were viewed with arrogant disregard, even put aside as laughable.* Only eleven firm orders were in hand at the end of 1974.

Realistically, there was widespread concern about the cohesiveness and after-sales support of an aerospace facility that straddled several national frontiers, as Singapore Airlines assessed the A300 as late as May 1976, buying the Boeing 727 instead.

Airbus kept trying. They offered attractive financial terms. Low interest rates and no principal payments for the first year were not uncommon. The terms were backed by the host governments of the manufacturers. An industry-tested manager was hired from American Airlines to oversee the marketing campaign in the U.S. The consortium turned itself inside out to prove it was in business to stay.

The fortunes of Airbus changed abruptly in 1977 when Eastern Airlines accepted an offer too good to refuse—the lease of several A300B machines at a cost far below market. As a sweetener, free maintenance support was provided for a six-month trial period. After the trial period was over, Frank Borman, President of Eastern, was convinced. In mid-1978, he bought twenty-three of the airplanes and took options on nine more.

In actual fact, Airbus Industrie provided a concession in the $778 million order—a load factor guarantee which amounted to $168 million. In effect, Eastern was compensated by Airbus for the difference in the cost of operating the 240-seat A300B and its smaller U.S. competitor. Airbus Industrie then recovered those costs in full through a government subsidy.

Orders for the Airbus jumped to sixty-nine planes in 1978, and took off with ninety-eight in the first five months of 1979. The Eastern decision not only wedged the door open to the American market, it served notice to the rest of the world that Airbus had arrived. *The camel's head was under the tent.*

When Airbus Industrie announced a directly competitive airplane to the new technology Boeing 767 in mid-1978, the 224 passenger A310, the last of the doubters still had not disappeared, arguing that it was simply a shortened A300.

The family concept, so successfully employed by United States producers, was also offered by Airbus. The new intensity succeeded in winning over the airlines of Western Europe—previously almost exclusively American turf. By April 1979, Lufthansa, KLM, Swissair, and Air France had ordered or taken options on a total of 151 airplanes of the two models, with twenty-five other airlines in Europe and Asia ordering or taking options on an additional 210 airplanes. Notable among the latter was Singapore Airlines, who announced an order for six A300B transports with options for six more—a 180-degree reversal of its stand taken two years earlier.

The world's airlines now viewed the European technology as equivalent to the Americans, and there was no match in the financial arena. *Airbus made its next great break into the U.S. market when Robert Crandall of American Airlines purchased thirty-five stretched A300s. Air Canada followed, then Federal Express, America West, and TWA. In 1991, Delta placed an or-*

der for nine A310s. As an inducement to Delta, the contract included generous provisions which permitted the carrier to cancel its order in twelve to eighteen months with no financial penalty. Finance had become the final arbiter in the competitive battle with Airbus, with government subsidies providing the advantage in both global and U.S. markets. The U.S. Commerce Department indicated that Airbus Industrie received more than $16 billion in subsidies since its formation in 1969—to cover consistent losses. According to one source, "The estimated $500 million loss at Airbus (1989) would represent the 21st annual deficit in its 21-year history.[6]

Finally, after six years of talks, U.S. and European negotiators, in April 1992, announced a tentative agreement that would cap direct European government subsidies at 33% of new developmental costs and limit direct benefits—such as new technology developed for the military that can be applied to commercial aircraft—to 4 to 5% of those outlays. Thus, the subsidy controversy appeared to be over.

In the final analysis, industry experts agree that had it not been for subsidies, there would never have been an Airbus company. No group of private banks would have come up with the billions needed to launch a new aircraft industry and sustain it through its early years.

Nevertheless, Boeing still excelled in a third area—equally as crucial for a successful airline as technology and finance—customer support.

Boeing guaranteed to put critical spare parts on board an airplane within four hours after the airline request, to be flown anywhere in the world, and even borrowed from the production line if the customer's airplane was *AOG* (Airplane on Ground). In addition, the pro forma purchase agreement provided for a fulltime engineering representative, located at the airline's main base prior to delivery of the first airplane, and to remain for twelve months after the last airplane was delivered, maintaining uninterrupted technical support. In many instances, the engineering representative remained at the airline several years longer, and for large operators, the Boeing office became permanent. Many of the offices had more than one representative and included Boeing mechanics, usually with licenses in aircraft and engine maintenance.

The men in the field were charged with twin objectives: first, to assist customers to the greatest possible extent; and second, to send operating information back to Boeing.

In 1976, customer support was elevated to division status, reporting directly to the executive vice president. George D. Nible, previously manager of the 747 division, was named to head it. Nible was a self-made man like "Bud" Hurst and Charlie Thompson—rare in a company dominated by engineers—having joined Boeing as a mechanic in 1941.

By 1978, 124 representatives were located in the field, manning 75 bases on 6 continents. When Customer Support celebrated its fiftieth anniversary in September 1986, the organization had nearly 2,800 people, mostly involved in spare parts.

On July 14, 1978, United Airlines committed $1.2 billion for thirty 767s, still a "paper airplane," and a week later, T. Wilson ordered it into production. In November, American and Delta ordered the 767, bringing total orders to eighty, and TWA followed with ten a month later. The airplane sold faster than any previous model, with 135 orders on the books within a year; the three largest Canadian trunk carriers, and All Nippon adding to the four U. S. carriers.

Orders for the 757 were slow, with British Airways and Eastern Airlines contracting for a total of eighty-two firm orders and options.

When Mr. Mac passed away in 1980, McDonnell Douglas entered a phase of uncertainty, unmatched since the earliest years of the Douglas Aircraft Company. The investigations into questionable payments resulted in a committee of directors recommending that a majority of the board be non-management people, and the company accepted the recommendations, ending the dominance of the board by insiders.

Although the company's fighter plane business was very strong, a new commercial airplane had not been launched for ten years. The DC-10, still a long way from break-even, seemed to be a jinxed airplane. A near fatal blow came in May 1979, when an American Airlines plane lost an engine during takeoff in Chicago, killing all 273 passengers on board. The FAA promptly issued a grounding order. This was the third fatal crash involving a DC-10 in the nine years it had been production.[7]

Most damaging of all was the crash of the Turkish Airlines DC-10 near Paris, in March 1974, which was traced to a faulty design of the rear cargo door mechanism. A series of service bulletins had been released to solve the problem, which affected 135 DC-10s, flown by twenty-three carriers.[8]

The FAA had decided to ground the DC-10 fleet until modiications were completed—however, McDonnell Douglas, concerned over the loss of image and the affect on sales—persuaded the FAA to treat the modifications as routine.

Investigation revealed that the modifications had not been made to the door of the crashed Turkish airplane. More serious still was the claim by McDonnell Douglas, early in the investigation of the crash, that the modifications had been incorporated.[9] When the remains of the door were retrieved from the Paris woods, it was obvious they had not.

Accidents are no respecter of logo or origin. Indeed, the worst accident in commercial airline history was the Japan Air Lines, Boeing 747 crash on August 12, 1985, which claimed 520 lives. However, in the rare instance that workmanship or part quality was contributory, Boeing was quick to accept the responsibility. In the Japan Air Lines 747 crash, even while the investigation was continuing, Boeing agreed to share the compensation to survivors and families on a fifty-fifty basis with the airline. Boeing concurred that an incomplete repair made in error by Boeing technicians seven years earlier may have been a factor.

After the Chicago crash, DC-10 sales slowed to trickle and never again recovered. The program fell far short of breaking even. With a total of 446 airplanes sold, the last DC-10 rolled out of the Long Beach plant in November 1988.

McDonnell Douglas won the competition against a Boeing 747 tanker design for the Air Force with their KC-10, which helped to bridge the production line gap until a new, larger version of the DC-10, known as the MD-11, was ready. A total of sixty KC-10s were sold.

The DC-9 breathed new life as the DC-9-80—a stretched airplane with more powerful engines—heralded a series of derivatives. After twenty DC-9-80s were leased by American Airlines in a bold new financial initiative, McDonnell Douglas leased or sold 190 units in a little more than a year. Dun's 1978 prediction of the company's demise was suddenly obsolete. In April 1983, the DC-9 designation receded into history—renamed the MD-80 series—with additional improvements.

Lockheed had taken some big blows. Long the largest defense contractor in the U.S., its image had been diminished by massive cost overruns on the C-5A program and a resulting $200 million write-off in 1971. Al-

Engine Size

The jet engine size grew dramatically as the airplane size increased. Here a covey of stewardesses fits into the nose cowl of a 767 engine.

most simultaneously, the bankruptcy of Rolls Royce caused the company to go to Washington for a $250 million bailout loan. At the same time the investigations into illegal payments were burdening the company. By 1976, Lockheed had lost the lead in defense contracting to General Dynamics, with McDonnell Douglas second, and Boeing moving to fourth from its 1970 twelfth place. By 1981, Lockheed had fallen to sixth.

On December 7, 1981, with an outlook for a continuing $150 million-a-year loss on the *Tristar*, the directors voted unanimously to kill the program. Lockheed's initial break-even prediction of 300 units had soared to 500—and only 244 sales were actually realized.

Taking a $400 million write-off on a plane that had lost $2.5 billion in its thirteen years of existence, *Lockheed again dropped out of commercial airplane competition.*[10]

Four years, one month, and five days after placing the order, United Airlines took delivery of its first 767. "It's about the most exciting day I've had the opportunity to participate in," said Richard Ferris, chief executive officer of the airline.

"Boeing promised us an airplane that would do certain things," Ferris said. "This airplane not only is on schedule, in fact, it's one day ahead of schedule, but it also has performance that exceeds the expectations of, I believe, the Boeing Company, and I know, of United Airlines."[11]

Mal Stamper, after the delivery ceremonies at which he officiated, confirmed the 767's dramatic actual performance above the design goals. "We've come up with an airplane that is better in takeoff performance, better in landing performance, has more range by some 800 miles, and has 4,600 pounds more capability in terms of carrying load, and it does it with about 8 to 10 percent more fuel efficiency."[11]

"Getting it into service, getting it under our original cost estimates and one day early—I don't know how you can improve on that. And that's due to the great team at Boeing," Stamper said.[11]

Indeed, there were many firsts, not the least of which were the twin contracts with the Italians and the Japanese. Aeritalia produced 12.5% of the total value of the 767, and Japanese factories produced 15%—all thousands of miles from the assembly line in Everett, Washington.

When fatigue testing of a complete 767 airframe—first off the line—was finished, it had been put through 100,000 simulated one-hour flights. In three and one-half minutes, all segments of a typical trip were simulated: taxi out, take-off, climb, cabin pressurization, cruise, descent, depressurization, landing and taxi in. The 100,000 flights simulated forty years of airline service.

Significantly, the equivalent of ten years of service had been completed prior to the initial revenue flight by United Airlines.

Sales of the new technology Boeing twins, after the large early orders, turned sluggish. In 1982, American Airlines canceled its order for fifteen 757s, citing lower earning expectations. In 1984, the 767 booked only twenty-four sales, even dropping below the 757, which captured thirty-seven. The following year, sales for both planes sat in the doldrums; the 767 line producing only two planes a month, and the 757 outlook even bleaker, booking sales of two planes for the entire year. Break-even was nowhere in sight.

History was again proving the volatility and riskiness of the commercial airplane business. The heady predictions of 1,200 or more of each model filling the skies of the early nineties seemed very remote.

"In the aviation industry," said Wolfgang Demisch, Managing Director of Wasserstein, Perella Securities Inc. in New York, "you make these decisions every ten years, give or take a few. You then have to live with the consequences for the next fifty."[12]

Indeed, some industry wags were beginning to call the venture a bad decision.

1. *Dun's Review*, December, 1978, 36.
2. *Fortune*, 25 September, 1978, 46.
3. *Forbes*, 26 November, 1979, 42.
4. Private Communication.
5. J.J. Servan-Schreiber, *The American Challenge*, (New York: Atheneum, 1968), 29.
6. *Business Week*, 18 December, 1989, 47.
7. *Seattle Times*, 27 May, 1979, A7.
8. John Godson, *The Rise and Fall of the DC-10*, (New York: David McKay, 1975), 174.
9. Ibid., 237.
10. *International Herald Tribune*, 21 December, 1981, 7.
11. Private Communication.
12. *International Herald Tribune*, 12 September 1985, 20.

China Takes Off

An invisible "technology curtain" separated the ancient from the modern in February 1980 when this photo was taken, after delivery of the People's Republic of China's first 747SP. Photo by E. E. Bauer, from his book, *China Takes Off*, University of Washington Press, 1986.

CHAPTER TWENTY-SEVEN

China Takes Off

When Mao Tse-Tung declared the People's Republic of China (PRC), on October 1, 1949, Americans—almost in their entirety—were expelled from the country. A few secured employment with the new government as translators, economic advisors, teachers, doctors and social workers. These were joined by a handful of prisoners of war who chose to remain with their Chinese captors rather than return home. In short, from 1950 to 1971, less than fifty Americans resided on the Chinese mainland.[1]

At the time, Mao was not only Chairman of the Communist Party, but of the new Republic itself. Nine years later, he initiated the *Great Leap Forward*, hoping for an overnight industrialization of China. He had not reckoned with his vast unskilled homeland and its threadbare infrastructure. By 1965, the skeletons of the hundreds of thousands of backyard iron-smelting furnaces were stark monuments to its dismal failure.

Indeed Mao had been replaced as Chairman of the Republic by Liu Shaoqi. Worse, he had been openly criticized by the Politburo. Viewing the situation as would a battlefield commander, six months later Mao launched the *Great Proletarian Revolution*, a last ditch attempt to recover the idealism, drive, and religious fervor with which the early revolutionaries maintained their thrust on the *Long March*.

In the decade that followed, the intellectuals were purged, and China lost the education of nearly an entire generation—the very generation that it so sorely needed to carry the burden of modernization programs.

Having nowhere to turn, Mao began to depend more closely on his advisors, chief of which was Premier Chou En Lai, the only intellectual whom he trusted.

China was in its fourth five-year economic plan, and for the first time, Mao listened when Premier Chou emphasized the need for purchasing Western equipment. Thus, in April 1971, stirrings toward change were beginning to be felt in the PRC, and tentative steps were taken on both sides toward a more open relationship. The first Americans to arrive in China since the PRC was declared were members of a table tennis team, anxious to try their skills against the proverbial powerhouse of the sport.

The team arrived on April 19, 1971, followed by three U.S. newsmen the next day, and a few days later, President Nixon eased a twenty year-old embargo on trade with China. In November, when the flag of the PRC was hoisted at the United Nations, and the flag of Taiwan was brought down, the PRC was recognized as the official China, marking the beginning of a new relationship between the two countries.

At Boeing, sales and marketing had been elevated to vice presidential status, when Clarence "Clancy" Wilde, an aeronautical engineer who had left Northwest Airlines as its superintendent of maintenance, was appointed to the new post, reporting to president "Tex" Boullioun. With sales of commercial airplanes overseas then the highest business priority for the Company, the sales staff was organized with about thirty regional directors to cover the world. These salesmen spent more than half of the time on the road, conducting business out of their briefcases. Sometimes referred to as the "*Wilde Bunch*," no country was too small, no regime too recalcitrant, no revolution too intimidating, no climate too harsh, no schedule too severe.

President Nixon met with Chairman Mao in Peking (now Beijing), on the 22nd of February 1972, and the door was opened. The Boeing Asian sales team, having heard through third parties that the Chinese were interested in

Boeing aircraft, immediately applied for an export license. The accepted route for salesmen to the internal Chinese bureaucracy was via the annual Canton (now Guangzhou) Trade Fair, however, the two sides met initially in Hong Kong, and later were invited to Peking. In the best of all worlds, luck was on their side. Unbeknown to the sales team, the Chinese had already made up their minds. Sometimes a name can exert a magic influence on the course of history. The Chinese, attentive to glowing reports about the 707 airplanes, were ready to work out the details of the purchase.

They were unwilling to listen to McDonnell Douglas' overtures, and the 707 became more of a buy than a sale. *It was the reputation of the Boeing Company and its products that sold the airplane.* To the Chinese, the DC-8 was just the latest in a series of DC airplanes, whereas the 707 had implanted something special in their minds. When the export license was granted by the U.S. Department of Commerce in July 1972, the agreement was all but finalized, and on September 12, Boeing announced that the PRC had purchased ten 707-320 *Intercontinental* airplanes. The total sales price for the ten aircraft was approximately $125 million, which represented the largest single purchase ever by the Chinese of aviation equipment. The contract was between Machimpex, the machine building arm of Foreign Trade, responsible for buying airplanes, and Boeing, but the airplanes were to be operated by the Civil Aviation Administration of China (CAAC)—a monolithic government organization—and sole airline in the third largest country in the world. Four of the airplanes were passenger versions and six were convertibles.

The China of 1972 was woefully unprepared for modern commercial operations. The airports were under strict military control, there was a severe shortage of pilots and trained maintenance personnel, and passengers had to get permission from the government to travel. Further, the majority of airplanes in the CAAC fleet were old.

The first 707 airplane was delivered in the fall of 1973, and the last in the spring of 1974. Shortly before the delivery of the first airplane, Boeing dispatched David "Dave" Cockerill to Peking as part of the pro forma to provide twelve months of field service support to the Chinese. Trained in England in engineering, Dave was enthusiastic about this new adventure. He and his wife were billeted in the Peking Hotel, most modern in China, but a third class hotel by Western standards. In 1973, China was still very tightly closed, and foreigners were only allowed to travel fifty kilometers from Peking without a special pass from the security administration—sufficient to visit the Great Wall and the Ming Tombs.

Dave tells of one of his memorable experiences. "It will not be necessary for you to come to the airport every day, Mr. Cockerill, we will call you if we need you," the CAAC official, Mr. Xu Zengle said, smiling.

"I wanted to be as agreeable as possible, so I consented," Dave recalls.

"But due to their penchant for secrecy, they hardly ever called. I remember one incident in particular, which demonstrated how intensely they felt on this issue. One day while jacking the airplane, they dropped it on the tail jack, which penetrated the fuselage at the stabilizer main frame. Embarrassed, they built a plywood wall around the airplane, and proceeded to make repairs. When it was all finished, they came to the hotel and invited me to come out to the airport. Escorting me to the repaired airplane, they pointed to it proudly. 'What do you think?'

"After careful examination, and a review of the drawings, I said, 'Oh you have done a fine job—congratulations!'

"I was relieved, at least my approval increased their confidence."[2]

It was a difficult assignment for the Cockerills, but expected for Boeing field service personnel, who had to agree in advance that they would accept an assignment anywhere in the world on short notice. Further, the wives had to agree also.

At the end of the pro forma period, the PRC office was put in moth balls, and support was provided by periodic visits from the Boeing office in Japan.

On January 31, 1979, President Carter and Deng Xiao Ping, Deputy Minister of the PRC, signed an agreement to normalize the relations between the two countries. Leonard Woodcock was named as the first U.S. ambassador.

The original purchase of the ten airplanes included an enormous quantity of spare parts, including forty new engines, four times the recommended number for normal operations. The Chinese were simply not sure how well the normalization would hold up, and didn't want to be caught short.

Unannounced to the world, the Chinese had decided to develop a commercial airplane manufacturing capability, to be located in Shanghai, and they parked one of the 707s in the factory there to use as a guide for building a modern jet airplane of their own, known as the Y-10. The airplane, reported to have been begun two years before the first 707 arrived, finally flew in September 1980. By their own admission, the Y-10 was overweight, and not a very good airplane. Reliable sources indicate that the Chinese spent about $300 million(U.S.) on the program over a period of eight years. Two airplanes were completed and a third partially constructed, before the production concept was abandoned, and the Chinese decided to continue to buy Western products.[3]

In December 1978, the CAAC announced the purchase of three 747SP airplanes, the first to be delivered in February 1980. The normalization became real to mainstream Americans when it was learned that Coca Cola had contracted to build a bottling plant in Beijing.

In January 1980, thirty days prior to the arrival of the first airplane, Eugene "Gene" Bauer was sent to Beijing to reestablish the Boeing office. Bauer had earned bachelors and masters degrees in metallurgical engineering, and an MBA in international business from the University of Washington—first coming to Boeing in 1941. Bauer and his wife were billeted in the Peking Hotel, which had been blessed with a new wing—built by the Chinese in 1976—the most modern in the entire country, but still equivalent to a second class U.S. hotel.

By the time they reached China, somewhat less than a year after Deng Xiao Ping and President Carter had declared a normalization of relations between the two countries, the immediate objective of Deng's policies—improvement in the standard of living—was already being felt.

Without realizing it, they found themselves at the hinge of history in China, at the eye of the hurricane, its calm belying the currents of change that surged around them.

At the time, the 164 airplane CAAC fleet, in addition to the ten 707s, consisted of thirty-six British *Tridents*, and six *Viscounts*, with Russian planes making up the remainder, including three Il-62s.

In his book, *China Takes Off*, Bauer relates the story of that first meeting in Beijing.[4]

"The day after my arrival, Mr. Yu, the interpreter, picked me up at the hotel and took me to the old office near the airport. Around a large rectangular table, five officials of the CAAC took their places on one side and Mr. Yu sat with me on the other side. The purpose of the meeting was to lay out the rules of operation. Everyone was all smiles, and Mr. Xu, in perfect English, began.

"It will not be necessary for you to come to the office every day, Mr.

Bauer. You can stay at the hotel and we will call you if we need you."

Forewarned, I responded quickly. "But Mr. Xu, if this is the case, you don't need me here at all. I might as well go back to the United States."

There was a stunned silence. The Chinese seemed to go into a state of shock.

"It's like asking a doctor to give advice for a patient that he cannot see," I continued—"no, I must come to the office every day, talk with the flight crews and maintenance personnel and make routine visits to the airplanes."

The Chinese recovered quickly and began a lively discussion among themselves. Finally, Mr. Xu announced, "Yes, Mr. Bauer is right, the office hours will be from 8:00 until 5:00, six days a week." Then he added, a little apologetically, "But it will not be possible to go on the field unless you are escorted by a CAAC official."

However, the very next day, Mr Yu came into the office and said. "Mr. Bauer, we want your photograph."

When I inquired as to the reason, Mr. Yu answered, "We're going to issue you a pass to go on the field."

The reluctance of the CAAC officials was understandable. The airport was under military control, and access was assigned to central security, not a part of the CAAC organization.

The utilization of the 707 airplanes was only four hours a day, when most Western airlines were exceeding seven, with some as high as nine, and this was of major concern to Boeing. From the beginning, the CAAC officials had complained about the "hydraulic problem." Bauer was told in no uncertain terms by his bosses, "to get to the bottom of this."

It took several agonizing months, but the cause was determined to be a combination of a severe environment, poor maintenance, and a Chinese penchant for pinching pennies. In an all-saving society, filters in the hydraulic system were routinely washed out with gasoline and reused—a forbidden practice—and inferior materials were used for gaskets, O-rings and seals. Further, the spare butyl rubber hoses—though new—had overaged after eight years on the shelf, and had become brittle.

It took months to convince the Chinese that a $30 filter was a crucial component in protecting the $8,000 hydraulic pumps, and that the butyl hoses should be discarded.

After instituting a filter replacement schedule in accordance with the maintenance manual, and using approved materials elsewhere in the system, delays and canceled flights due to hydraulic pump failures were reduced dramatically, and airplane utilization climbed to a respectable level. After that, Bauer could do no wrong, and he became like a father to the airline, remaining as manager of the Boeing office for five years.[5]

The 747SP order was one of the first steps taken by Deng in the modernization campaign to bring China into world commerce. The vast nation had been ravaged by Chairman Mao's ten year Cultural Revolution which did not end until his death in 1976.

The significance of the Boeing decision in 1972 to keep the 707 production line open was reinforced by the 747SP purchase.

The 707 airplanes proved to be the best ambassadors imaginable in welding the Chinese into the Boeing family. They simply would not consider anything but Boeing planes.

McDonnell Douglas intensified their efforts, offering to initiate a coproduction facility in Shanghai to produce the DC-9-80, and later the MD-80 series. They argued that CAAC would be able to leap straight to production.

Boeing took a different approach, offering to have the Chinese manufacture parts for both the 737 and the 747 in their Xian Aircraft Factory. The Chinese accepted this philosophy of learning to "crawl before you walk, walk before you run, and run before you fly," concept.

Realistically, the Chinese were in no position to start manufacturing airplanes to Western standards. Their materials of construction could not pass Western specifications. Thus, Boeing shipped aluminum forgings, sheet, plate and extrusions to the Xian Aircraft Factory, and they simply machined the parts. Boeing sent inspectors to pass on the finished product.

Competition between the 737 and the DC-9 became more intense, and the Chinese requested that Boeing bring a 737 to China for a demonstration flight on the Chengdu–Lhasa route, and on a number of short, unimproved airfields. (At the time, the Lhasa airport, at 11,800 feet, was the second highest commercial airport in the world, exceeded only by LaPaz in Bolivia).

The chosen bird, *Chief Detudamo*, was leased from Air Nauru, one of the airlines's *Little Giants*, a six-year-old thoroughbred 737-200C, with 14,000 flight hours. It was a convertible model, which could be used as all passenger, partial cargo, or all cargo, and was also equipped with a rough field kit. Between September 16 and 21, 1981, the airplane visited seven cities in six days and made twenty-five flights from short, hot, high, and rough fields without a pause.

The Chinese viewed flying to Lhasa as a nearly impossible feat for a twinjet. The 808 mile route from Chengdu presents an unbroken chain of jagged peaks with a mean altitude of some 14,000 feet, where a few hundred miles to the south, the Himalayas stand as silent sentinels, warning the flier not to stray too far from the air corridor. With no fuel at Lhasa, the plane was required to carry round trip fuel.

Even after the successful demo, the Chinese were slow to indicate any progress toward a decision, and a parade of Boeing officials came to Beijing during 1982, and ultimately, Tex Boullioun himself made a final offer for a ten 737 airplane sale—one he was prepared to turn his back to. They had not budged an inch from their position of a year earlier on what they were willing to pay, claiming that "since we are the poorest of all your customers, we should get the lowest price," while Boeing had continued to improve its terms throughout the year.[6]

Boeing sent Richard W. Welch, V.P. of finance and contracts, second in command to Tex himself, to deliver the proposal. He brought Frank Shrontz along, who was then vice president of sales.

At the final meeting, the Chinese director of finance likened the negotiations to a 1,000 meter race. "Boeing has already run the first 900 meters, and now has only to run the final 100 meters in order to close the deal," he announced with a broad smile. He could not believe that Boeing had delivered its rock-bottom offer.

Welch, squirming in his seat, seemed ready to cave in, when Shrontz, seeking a quick end to the impasse, stood up and said, "I think the race is over," and turned as if to go.[7]

The Chinese capitulated, and on November 6, 1982, fourteen months after the demo, the purchase agreement for ten 737-200 airplanes was signed. Later in November, contracts were signed for a fourth 747SP, and a 747-200 Combi. There is no doubt that this one defiant stand by Frank Shrontz significantly aided all future negotiations with the Chinese.

In response to the Chinese interest in building up their own manufacturing capability, Boeing contracted with the Xian Aircraft Factory to build vertical tail fins for the 737.

The Xian Aircraft Factory is the largest in China, employing 20,000 people, of which 2,000 are engineers. Their product line includes several models of Chinese military aircraft.

McDonnell Douglas finally broke into the win column when, in December, the Chinese took delivery of two MD-82 airplanes, but China seemed to remain firmly in the Boeing camp. The effort to bring production to China followed a torturous path, eventually becoming known as the "MD-90 Trunkliner" program.

In the end, twenty aircraft were built in Long Beach, Calif., which China Aviation Supply Corporation (CASC) agreed to sell, and twenty were supposed to be built in China. Only three of those were actually completed. The program finally died in 1998. Production in China simply proved to be too expensive.[8]

In 1985, CAAC, the monolithic, government owned company began to assume a regulatory role, and state owned, and even private airlines began to spring up. However, the military continued to wield a heavy hand in operations, and it was not until 1995 that China's Air Force began transfering control to the civilian authorities.

In a further move to adopt international standards, the CAAC announced that domestic tickets would be the same price for Chinese as for foreign passengers. Previously, Chinese passengers paid about half that charged to foreigners.

By January 1990, the old fleet of 164 airplanes had been largely replaced by newer airplanes and reached a total of 170, predominantly Boeing—flying 300 domestic and 50 international routes. The following June, they ordered 36 additional Boeing planes—valued at $4 billion—including 747-400s.

Then, in October 1997, China purchased eight Model 777s as part of a $3 billion order for fifty planes, and for three years in a row, every 10th airplane (all models) off the line was destined for China.

Nevertheless, competition had begun to become spirited with Airbus Industrie. In 1996, the CAAC concluded a $1.5 billion order for thirty A320 transports. This order had political overtones—since tensions had increased between the U.S. and China involving Taiwan and trade. Seven out of ten airplanes flying in China were Boeings, but with the annual harangue in the U.S. over "most favored nation" trade status for China, that figure was expected to change.

In a bid to strengthen its market dominance in China, Boeing signed a contract in August 1994, with the Xian Aircraft Factory to produce the 737 horizontal stabilizers as well as the vertical fins. By May, 1999 they had delivered the 599th fin, completing the contract, and had almost completed the contracted stabilizers. Parts were also being manufactured for the 747; for example, trailing edge wing ribs.

The Xian operation is a model of efficiency. For Boeing the manufacturing process is overseen by a small staff of five, headed by engineer Steve Morse. Engineering liaison, procurement, and quality assurance are all handled by Morse and his team. The assemblies are not reinspected upon arrival in the Boeing Renton plant.

On a previous contract, for the manufacture of the 737 forward access door, 1,680 units were shipped with zero rejections.

In the late nineties, the Xian factory was awarded a contract for 1,500 shipsets of vertical fins for the *Next-Generation 737*, and the stabilizer contract went to Shanghai. By 1999—in addition to Xian and Shanghai—parts and assemblies for Boeing airplanes were being manufactured in Shenyang, Chengdu, and Chongqing.

When asked about quality, Larry Dickenson, Senior Vice President, Asia Pacific, was quick to respond. "The quality of parts coming out of China is better than that coming out of our Wichita plant."[9]

After a career in sales at McDonnell Douglas, Dickenson moved to Texas Air Corporation, parent company for Continental and Eastern Airlines in 1983, coming to Boeing in 1986. He holds a bachelor's degree in business administration from California State University, and attended the Advanced Management Policy Institute at the University of California.

In 1994 Boeing established a permanent office in Beijing with its own president, Michael Zimmerman. To further emphasize Boeing's commitment to China, in 1996 the Company sent the entire board to China for a meeting. Zimmerman retired in 1997 and Ray Bracy became the new president. Bracy came with an impressive background—degrees in mathematics and engineering from the U.S. Naval Academy and an MBA from Harvard. The permanent staff grew to forty, but Bracy was quick to admit that the size of the office had no relation to production. "This office must be treated as an investment resource," he said. "Although some may view us as merely a figurehead, our strength is in government affairs, public relations, and training," he continued.[10]

Boeing also agreed to invest $100 million over two years in building a 2,900 square meter headquarters in Beijing, and an overseas spares center at Beijing's Capitol Airport, replacing the original consignment center. The new facility was designed to be on par with operations in London and Singapore and be able to offer next-day shipment from among 35,000 spare parts.

Further, Boeing positioned two simulators—one a full motion—in the country, to help CAAC improve air safety.

Then, in still another move to help in the support arena, Boeing purchased a 9.1 percent share in the Taikoo Aircraft Engineering Co. in Xiamen, China, which will be able to conduct heavy maintenance, including 747 passenger-to-freighter conversions.

To be certain that no stone was left unturned, Boeing increased its field service bases in China to seventeen, from six in early 1993.

As the century drew to a close, the number of airlines in China had ballooned to over 30, some with branches, flying 322 Boeing airplanes of a total fleet of 477—a 68 percent share. Airbus Industrie had 64. The remainder were Russian.

Boeing predicted that China would purchase 1,800 commercial airplanes over the next two decades, valued at $125 billion. This is probably a conservative figure. If one considers that China is the third largest country in the world, and in 1999 had some 30 airlines, and the U.S.—the fourth largest—had more than 90 airlines or operators flying some 7,000 airplanes, there will be a time in the future when China will rival the U.S. One need only to go back to the early eighties to note the naysayers such as Fox Butterfield, in his *China, Alive in the Bitter Sea,* who predicted nothing but chaos and misery—but were proven wrong by the great visionary Deng Xiao Ping. Deng cited the example of Japan's Meiji Reform which began in the late 1860's, transforming the country into a modern industrial society. "If they succeeded then, we proletariats should be able to do better now." [11]

China has the largest railroad system in the world, but no national system of highways, with motor vehicles mostly relegated to the cities, and bicycles predominating in the countryside. A mountainous country, China will likely never develop a national highway system, instead, taking a quantum leap from the railroad and bicycle to the airplane. For those who say China is too poor a country, it is only necessary to note that merely one-fourth of the population need participate in air travel to equal the U.S. in total numbers.

Indeed, the naysayers had been too intent on observing the waves, and had failed to notice the ocean.

In spite of China's historical preference for Boeing airplanes, the intense efforts of Airbus Industrie began to take their toll in the nineties. Doubly frustrating for Boeing was the increasing influence of political factors on business decisions. With "China bashing" on the increase in the United States, Airbus Industrie was able to gain that all important edge at the highest levels.

Further, having already made a significant penetration of the Chinese market with the A320—a very competitive airplane against Boeing's 737 family—Airbus could be expected to win more and more orders. The A318 and the A319, derivatives of the A320, claim almost complete commonality.

1. E.E. Bauer, *China Takes Off,* (Seattle: University of Washington Press, 1986), viii.
2. Private Communication.
3. Bauer, *China Takes Off,* 85, 86.
4. Ibid., 19, 20, 21, 46.
5. Ibid., 31, 32.
6. Private Communication.
7. Ibid.
8. *Aviation Week & Space Technology,* 10 August, 1998, 17.
9. Larry Dickenson interview by E. E. Bauer, 19 January, 1999.
10. Ray Bracy interview by E. E. Bauer, 3 May, 1999.
11. Bauer, *China Takes Off,* 206.

Frank A. Shrontz 1931–
President 1985–1988, Chairman 1988–1996.

CHAPTER TWENTY-EIGHT

Challenges and Change

The cards began to fall in a new high stakes game in the spring of 1982, when Airbus Industrie bid for the lead in medium-range airplane sales. Announcing the Model A320, an all-new 150-passenger twinjet, they promised deliveries in 1988.

McDonnell Douglas, having opted to pass in 1978, was also studying a new twin—known as the Model D-3301.

Boeing had been studying a 150-passenger airplane, but the list of *unk-unks* (unknown-unknowns) was longer than ever, and the Company paused to digest them. Then in March 1984—an agonizingly long wait for airline fleet planners—Boeing signed an agreement with Japan to develop a brand new competitor to the A320. However, no announcement was forthcoming for a kickoff nor for a timetable. Boeing was playing close to the vest.

At the time, Tex Boullioun stated flatly, "The A320 is absolutely impossible economically. It's going to be tough for anybody to come up with a new, small airplane that makes any money."[1]

Setting the tone for delaying decisions by the world's airlines, Joe Sutter told the 1983 Paris Air Show attendees:

"We're just sounding a note of caution for people looking at airplanes like the A320, because time marches on and technology marches on. Structures, aerodynamics, systems, and engines are constantly improving."[2]

Although T. Wilson's first love was new airplanes, he paid increasing attention to derivatives. One of the chief spokesmen for wringing out all the potential of the 737 was F.A. "Frank" Shrontz.

On February 25, 1985—the year that the 737-300 booked its incredible sales total of 252 units—Frank Shrontz was named as president, Mal Stamper moved up to vice chairman—a new post created by the board of directors—and Dean Thornton was named president of the Boeing Commercial Airplane Company.

Shrontz was the eighth president, but only the second lawyer in the history of the Company. All the others were engineers. A graduate of the University of Idaho College of Law in 1954, with an MBA from Harvard in 1958, he came to Boeing the same year—as a contracts coordinator. By 1967 he was assistant to the vice-president for contracts and marketing.

In 1973, Shrontz left Boeing to become Assistant Secretary of the Air Force, followed by Assistant Secretary of Defense, returning to Boeing in 1977. Those posts prepared him well for the military side of the Company, which was in a rebuilding phase when he returned.

The appointment of Dean Thornton to follow Shrontz in heading up commercial airplanes was an excellent decision. Thornton had a strong background in finance. He joined Boeing as assistant treasurer in 1963, after graduating from the University of Idaho with a BS degree in business. By 1968, he had risen to director of finance for commercial airplanes. In 1978, he became the vice president and general manager of the 767 Division, and in 1984, a senior vice president of the Boeing Company. Throughout his career he had a close working relationship with Harold Haynes, the peerless financial genius who was Chief Financial Officer (CFO) of the corporation.

As president, one of the major decisions facing Shrontz was to define the nature of Boeing's business mix in a period of decreasing military sales—

accompanied by stiff new research and development requirements prior to contract award.

In the Boeing Aerospace Company in 1985, President Mark Miller drew up a list of five "must-win" projects: SRAM II, follow-on of the highly successful short-range air launched missile; updated avionics for the anti-submarine P-3 plane; a hard mobile launcher for small ICBMs; a remote control launching system for the ICBMs; and modules for the proposed NASA space station. By the end of 1987 all five had been won.

Miller came to his new responsibilities with an impressive background. A mechanical engineering graduate from Oregon State University in 1948, he had been director of engineering on the *Saturn V*, and manager of TIE *Apollo*.

In 1983, Boeing won a production contract for six Inertial Upper Stages (*IUS*), an unmanned space tug used to move satellites from the space shuttle to their final positions in orbit.

On the military side, Boeing made a strong bid to reenter the fighter airplane field. An industry team led by Lockheed, with Boeing and General Dynamics as major subcontractors, designed and built two YF-22 prototype fighters. Boeing furnished the wings and aft fuselage section, as well as developing the overall avionics software. The Company had not built a fighter plane since the experimental XF8B-1 in 1944. The YF-22 made its first flight on September 29, 1990.

The successful development of the avionics for the B-1 bomber led to a major subcontract from North American for the production airplanes, and the AWACS surveillance plane continued its success in sales to Saudi Arabia and the NATO countries.

In late 1985, the Boeing High Technology Center was created as a long range, basic research facility. When the facility opened the following year, five technologies had been identified as key elements: radio frequency, microelectronics, information processing, photonics, and materials and devices—aimed at keeping Boeing on the leading edge of technical excellence. Heading the new laboratory complex was Dr. Edith W. Martin, first woman to become a Boeing vice president. Dr. Martin had a doctorate in information and computer science from the Georgia Institute of Technology, among other credits, including graduate studies in mathematics at the Universtat Karlsruhe, Germany.

An exciting new development—the marriage of a helicopter and a turboprop—became a reality in a teaming effort with Bell when the tilt-

Advanced Tactical Fighter—YF-22

Boeing teams with old rivals, General Dynamics and Lockheed, to design an advanced fighter for the 21st century.

rotor, all-composite construction, V-22 *Osprey* was rolled out in May 1988. Designed to take off like a helicopter, but offering the speed and range of a turboprop, the V-22 was conceived to serve the needs of all four U.S. armed services. The team won the Collier Trophy for 1990.

In spite of new technology firsts on military and space frontiers, major focus remained on commercial airplanes. However, the next genera-

Tilt-Rotor V-22 *Osprey*
The Bell-Boeing vertical takeoff airplane, showing both modes of flight.

tion promised to be facing a more severe gestation period than ever before.

Scarcely three months after the Boeing-Japanese agreement was announced, Pan American ordered twenty-eight Airbus planes, including the new A320s, for more than one billion dollars. It appeared that Airbus would run away with the future medium-range market, as Boeing continued to study the options.

In 1985, Boeing announced its market strategy—essentially to battle Airbus for the early market opportunities with derivatives of the 737, while taking several giant strides in technology for a future machine. With nearly 2,000 737 airplanes flying the world's skies, *commonality* became the leading criterion for future derivatives.

Boeing visualized major technology developments in aerodynamics, flight systems, structural materials, and propulsion, the latter promising a 60 percent improvement in efficiency over the existing engines. The new darling was called the UDF, or UnDucted Fan, a design with aft facing engines, and multiple, counterrotating blades.

The question of whether derivatives could stop the A320 challenge began to be answered in 1986. It seemed to be no. In September, Northwest Airlines, long an exclusive customer of Boeing, surprised the commercial airplane community—signing an agreement to purchase up to 100 A320s. That decision was taken in the face of Boeing's offer of the 737-400, with comparable capacity.

To round out its stable of commercial airplanes, in January 1986, Boeing purchased de Havilland Aircraft of Canada, Ltd., from the government of Canada. Of its major products, the DHC-6 Twin Otter, the DHC-7 short takeoff and landing aircraft, and the DHC-8—a thirty-six passenger commuter airplane—the DHC-8 offered the most potential for commercial sales.

Ronald B."Ron" Woodard, who was most recently the director of program management for the 707/727/737 Division, and previously had been director of international commercial airplane sales, was appointed as president in early 1987. With his strong background in sales, Woodard was expected to jump start the flagging Canadian operation.

Woodard came to Boeing in 1966, assigned to the engineering team in 707 structures, after graduating from the University of Puget Sound with a degree in chemistry, and an M.S. in systems management from the University of California.

The arrangement with Japan went far beyond the subcontracting mode of the 767, involving an equity share and participation in all phases. The airplane was designated the Model 7J7 in recognition of the new partnership. A separate division in the Company was formed, headed by James "Jim" Johnson, a 1965 graduate from Iowa State with a masters degree in aeronautical engineering. Selected for the Sloan Fellowship program, he received an MBA from MIT in 1977, and was appointed to vice-president in 1987.

There were major problems to solve in the development of the UDF engine, however unbridled enthusiasm prevailed on all fronts.

The General Electric GE36 aft-mounted engine was chosen, and rigorously tested on a 727. First flight was scheduled for 1991, with certification to be completed in January 1992.

However, with key airlines unable to agree on passenger capacity, and engine growth requiring additional development, Boeing announced in mid-1987 that there would be a fifteen-month delay. Abruptly, at year end the costly program had moved back into the "new project development" category.

When Jim Johnson summarized the operational factors which drove the 7J7 decision, he emphasized three major items: fuel costs, capital costs, and maintenance costs.

Fuel costs—30 to 35 percent of total direct costs in 1978—had fallen to 18 percent by 1987, voiding the engine efficiency advantage. Capital costs per pound of thrust had gone up by 15 percent. Maintenance costs doubled during the nine-year period, representing almost one-third of the total direct costs in 1987.[3]

On December 31, 1987, T. Wilson retired, and Frank Shrontz succeeded him as chairman of the board. Mal Stamper remained as vice chairman, but had not been passed over for lack of confidence. He was simply the victim of *Father Time*, having reached the invisible barrier of 62 years of age. As vice chairman, he did not go on the shelf—contributing mightily to the new challenges of change.

Looking back from 1987, the banner year of 1978 paled in comparison. Sales were over $15 billion, triple that of 1978, and the backlog stood at $33 billion. The Company was sitting on $3.4 billion in cash and short term investments, the 747 joined the 737 as a *cash cow*, and Boeing was designing still another derivative, the 747-400.

In naming Boeing as the country's third most admired corporation in 1987, *Fortune* editor, Kenneth Labich, wrote:

"Boeing has always been known as a company where all the employees, no matter the color of their collar, take a serious interest and genuine pride in their work. In many ways, the loyalty and dedication of the Boeing work force has been instrumental in building the company's legendary excellence. Most people at the company with some gray in their hair turn out to have been Boeing employees for at least 30 years."[4]

Shrontz inherited a Company that was the most prosperous in history. Nevertheless, earnings on sales had fallen to a worrisome 3.1 percent, down from the 1980 high of 6.4 percent. Employment had ballooned again—to 136,000 at the end of 1987.

The signs of a self-satisfied complacency were all too obvious to top management: increased absenteeism, customer complaints on quality, defective parts, missed deadlines, and a general laissez-faire feeling that prosperity was finally guaranteed. It was the kind of climate that was more difficult to address than bona fide adversity.

"You look at companies that have disappeared," said Philip M. "Phil" Condit, executive vice president of the Commercial Airplane Company. "What they did, they did well, but they failed to change."[5] Condit, a new star in the Company, graduated from the University of California with a B.S. in mechanical engineering, and received an M.S. in aeronautical engineering from Princeton. He was an MIT Sloan fellow in 1974.

In 1988, sales exploded. Completing a fourth consecutive record year, announced orders were made for 636 commercial jet transports and 54 commuter aircraft, worth $30.1 billion. At year end, the commercial backlog stood at $46.7 billion.

There seemed to be no end to the sales tide as it rolled on into 1989. In February, All Nippon Airways placed a $3.15 billion order for twenty 747-400s—the largest order for the new queen of the air—which logged sales of 192 planes to twenty-two customers less than two months after completion of certification.

In March, the 757/767 twins began to confound the naysayers about the viability of those programs, with American Airlines announcing a $2 billion order.

As 1989 drew to a close, the decade of the nineties appeared to be already on the books for Boeing. The factory was producing twenty-eight airplanes a month and airlines were placing orders as far in the future as 2001. The rate was increased to thirty-four in 1990 and plans were in place to increase it again—to thirty-eight planes a month by mid-1991—the company's seventy-fifth anniversary year. Projections of the future market indicated that the 1990–2005 period would demand 9,935 jetliners worth $626 billion. Historically, Boeing had enjoyed a 54 percent share.

Yet in an increasingly volatile world, it would be corporate suicide to consider coasting into the future. In times of economic downdrafts, options disappear overnight, and firm orders are often canceled—generating only modest penalties. During the recession of 1982, American Airlines terminated an order for fifteen 757 twinjets valued at $600 million, because of "inadequate profits and a discouraging outlook."[6]

In one of the most dramatic events of this century, on the 10th of November 1989—as the Eastern Bloc began to shed the shackles of Communism—the entire face of Europe was changed in a single day. Three months later, in stark testimony to the unpredictability of the aerospace industry, Aeroflot, the Soviet Union's airline giant, announced the purchase of the Airbus Industrie A310 twinjet.

At home, action quickly crystallized toward major reductions in defense spending. Scarcely six months had passed since Boeing completely restructured its noncommercial organization—and it was already obsolete. It was conceivable, indeed probable, that defense-oriented work could be cut in half from the 30 percent achieved in the late eighties.

Turning a profit on defense work was becoming increasingly difficult throughout the industry. In 1989, Boeing reported an operating loss of nearly a half-billion dollars on defense work—due to "technical, cost, and schedule problems."[7]

The *Stealth*(B-2) bomber, a highly classified Air Force project—under wraps for almost ten years—came to light in August, 1989, when Boeing revealed the Company had been operating as a major subcontractor to the Northrop Corporation. Boeing was building more than half of the parts for the B-2, including the wings, rear part of the fuselage, fuel system, bomb bay, and landing gear. The project was under almost constant attack in Congress. The original Air Force request for 132 planes was cut to 75 by Defense Secretary Dick Cheney, and in 1992, the U.S. Senate capped the program at twenty aircraft. At its peak, nearly 11,000 Boeing people were working on *Stealth*.

Even the most promising new military airplane, the V-22 *Osprey*, was riding a rocky course, following a recommendation by the Secretary of Defense for cancellation.

During 1990, the military was still striving to rationalize its posture in the face of a radically changing environment, when in August, Iraq's Saddam Hussein invaded Kuwait. The ensuing Persian Gulf war, which broke out the following January, complicated the military force equation by yet another order of magnitude.

The bottom line for Boeing's defense and space business improved in 1990—but still showed depressive red ink—with an operating loss of $418 million.[8]

Comanche RAH-66 Reconnaissance Helicopter—1999

A Boeing-Sikorsky team is developing the 21st century, armed reconnaissance helicopter.

Nevertheless, there was good news for Boeing in 1990 when the YF-22 won the fly-off competition with the YF-23, developed by McDonnell Douglas and Northrop, and in April 1991, the team was awarded the prime contract—with a potential value of $60 billion.

Following that win, in April 1991, the U.S. Army chose Boeing-Sikorsky over McDonnell Douglas-Bell Textron to develop the LHX Helicopter, under a $2.7 billion contract. The first machine, the RAH-66 *Comanche*, flew on January 4, 1996. The Army hoped to replace its aging fleet of 3,000 Vietnam-era gunships.

The V-22 *Osprey* kept hanging on, in spite of recurring pessimism in the halls of Congress, and by 1996 had entered a $1.38 billion low-rate production phase, with first deliveries scheduled to the U.S. Marine Corps in 1999.

On the commercial airplane side, competition intensified. McDonnell Douglas, nearly written off as a producer of commercial airplanes in 1978, breathed new life. In February, 1989, American Airlines placed what was the largest single order in history—estimated at $7 billion for up to 150 airplanes, including eight firm orders and forty-two options for its MD-11, newest challenger to the 747.

Airbus landed a $3.6 billion order in March for the A320. Significantly, the order was from a U.S. carrier, Trans World Airlines.

When the GPA Group, Ltd., of Shannon, an Irish leasing firm, placed orders for 308 planes worth $17 billion in April, 59 percent—182 planes—were Boeing models. McDonnell Douglas was second with 72, and Airbus captured 54.

Only eight days after the Irish leasing order, United Airlines blasted all previous Boeing sales records into the dustbin with a $15.7 billion order for 370 airplanes, including options.

Success was compounded with problems. Quality began to suffer as thousands of employees worked extensive overtime.

Billed as a derivative, the 747-400 was in many ways a new airplane, challenging Boeing and its subcontractors all along the line. Most troublesome was the electronics system. In the face of working out the "bugs," the delivery schedule that Boeing had set for itself proved to be unrealistic. By mid-year 1989, deliveries were lagging almost three months, and the preponderance of the year's planned total were still ahead. *Boeing became the target of unabashed and angry criticism. The uphill battle continued to worsen.*

In 1989, too, fallout accelerated from an April 1988 Aloha Airlines accident wherein the upper half of a forward fuselage section departed from a 737 airplane in flight. The subject of aging airplanes was brought dramatically to the front pages of the world's newspapers. After that accident, members of the press, who appointed themselves as instant experts, began decrying the safety of airplane structures.

With more than 5,000 Boeing jets crisscrossing the world's skies—making a landing or takeoff about a million times a month, exposure was intense. The media began trumpeting findings regarding even the smallest cracks.

Reporting reached the height of triviality in a September 1989 account of the finding by Alaska Airlines of a small crack in a door frame of a 727.[9] The principal result of the eight-inch column on the front page of the business section was to needlessly frighten the traveling public. In fact, such fatigue cracks are expected as airplanes age, and can be found by routine inspection, allowing early repair.

The Aloha accident was studied in great detail by the National Transportation Safety Board (NTSB). Thirteen months later, in May 1989, the board concluded that the accident's "probable cause" was the failure of Aloha's maintenance workers to detect the presence of significant disbonding and fatigue damage along the aluminum alloy skin of the nineteen-year-old airplane. The FAA was criticized for insufficient rigor in the enforcement of the emergency "alert" service bulletin which Boeing directed to all operators several months before.

In the face of press criticism, Boeing's market share—rather than falling—increased. Customers appreciated the integrity which Boeing consistently built into its airplanes.

The maverick year of 1989 held other surprises. An increasingly restive labor force, eyeing the billions cascading into Boeing's coffers, could scarcely wait until October 3, when their contract would expire.

In commercial airplanes, by far the largest product volume, work had become compartmentalized and routine. The "*Outplant Crew*" of Minuteman days, and the "*Incredibles*" of the early 747 program were history. Those larger-than-life challenges had been replaced by the humdrum of the production line. Wages and fringe benefits had become the focus.

Hardly bothering to read—much less understand the Company's new contract offer—more than 40,000 machinists gathered at Seattle's Kingdome, where by an 85 percent majority, they gleefully voted to strike. The holiday atmosphere was described as "controlled hysteria" in the local press.[10] At midnight, 57,000 employees, represented by Lodge 751 of the IAM, hit the bricks.

The work stoppage was the first since October 1977, and only the fourth in the history of the Company. Where the 1977 strike had heavy undertones of the desire for a union shop—lost in the 1948 walkout—the 1989 strike was solely about money and mandatory overtime.

The strike was also a showdown for organized labor in Washington State, where Boeing was the largest private employer, setting the pace for other union contracts.

Boeing was caught by surprise at the new militance of the IAM, believing their offer of wage increases plus improved medical and retirement benefits would be handily approved.

Frank Shrontz was firm. "We're not going to pay more money," was his blunt reaction.[11] The lines were drawn for a protracted strike. Boeing supervisors and non-strikers—it was estimated that only about five percent crossed the picket lines—took on the task of completing and delivering airplanes as best they could. However, delays that were attributable to the strike carried no penalties.

The union did not reveal its bottom line. Tom Baker, union president, would only say it had to be more.

Both sides settled down for a long wait. On November 4, Boeing improved its offer—which union officials promptly rejected—declining to submit it to a vote by the membership.

Shrontz indicated the strike had already caused irreparable losses to the Company, after it was only three weeks old. Nevertheless, customers maintained their trust in the Company and its products. On November 15, with no end in sight to the strike, Delta Airlines placed an order for 100 737-300 airplanes valued at up to $4 billion.

By mid-November, as the last of the dry leaves skittered past the pickets' feet, anxieties began to mount. Bills were piling up, and the $100 per week from the union's strike fund, which began in the third week, did not go far.

After earlier unsuccessful attempts to bring an agreement, federal mediator Doug Hammond called the parties together again on November 13. A few hours later, sensing no movement on either side, he took the unusual step of laying his own proposal on the table. After a marathon fifteen-hour session, his compromise became the basis for agreement.

On November 21, the membership voted by a 81 percent majority to go back to work, and the forty-eight-day strike, longest since 1948, came to an end.

On December 18, 1989, the day of reckoning for the SPEEA negotiations arrived, when the engineers responded with an emphatic *No!* to the Company's offer for a new three-year contract. At the same time they declined to vote to strike.

In reality, not even the hungriest SPEEA engineer expected a strike vote. Engineers by nature find the idea of a union repugnant. Moreover, SPEEA, a voluntary union, had never achieved more than a 60 percent membership level. Further, in spite of cries of low pay, they were well off, averaging $40,000 a year. Most of the problem seemed to be personal pride. With starting salaries rising in a never ending spiral, a three-year Boeing engineer would be making about the same as a new hire.

Two months after the December *no*, the membership voted *yes* to a new contract which included larger bonuses.

The Company had been built by engineers—and management was laced with graduates. Thus, although SPEEA represented some 15,000 engineers and scientists in the 28,000 bargaining unit, the Company total of *degreed* engineers stood at over 19,000 in late 1989, about 12 percent of the labor force.

In a thorny year, there seemed to be no respite for Boeing officials. On November 13, lawyers for the Company entered a guilty plea in Federal Court in Arlington, Virginia, to two counts of conveying government property without authority. The plea bargain marked the end of a three-year federal probe into Boeing's role in what prosecutors described as widespread security violations to obtain secret Pentagon and National Security Council spending plans. Boeing agreed to pay $4 million restitution, $1 million for the cost of the investigation, and $20,000 in fines. The government property covered by the plea consisted of two documents—a Department of Defense Five-Year Defense Program Summary and Program Element Detail, and a Program Decision Memorandum.

The documents, which were used to plan funding and priority of defense programs, were brought into the Boeing Rosslyn, Virginia, office by Richard L. Fowler. Fowler was a Boeing employee from 1978 to 1986, previously a career civilian budget official for the Air Force.

In acknowledging that the practice was widespread, the prosecution appeared to have targeted giant Boeing to focus industry attention.

As in the mid-seventies case of illegal payments for commercial airplane sales overseas, the document activities were the province of a few less thoughtful men in middle management—in complete violation of corporate policies and practices.

When asked about the episode, Vice Chairman Mal Stamper, in charge of the Company's ethics committee, had a ready reply:

"What happened here is quite simple. We have 160,000 employees. We hired one fellow a number of years back, from the Air Force, and when he came, he kept his connection with the Air Force and brought documents with him, that he said everybody does. They were secret documents, of value to him, and he thought they would be of value to the Company. It was, of course, illegal, immoral, and unethical. When we found out he was doing it, we fired him."[12]

Stamper, noting that about 30 percent of Boeing's revenues came from defense business, summed the Company's approach to that business:

"As one of the nation's leading aerospace contractors, we have an obligation—a moral imperative—to be above reproach. We can neither hide behind statistics nor make excuses about only a few untrustworthy people out of tens of thousands of good employees—or isolated breaches of trust out of countless legitimate actions. Our goal is to be without fault. If that takes forever, then we will work at it forever."[13]

At the end of 1990, Boeing's backlog stood at a record $97 billion. Of that total, 94% was represented by orders for more than 1,800 commercial airplanes—yet to be built.

The flood of orders during the eighties masked the progress of the competition. Tex Boullioun's prediction back in 1984 that "the A320 is absolutely impossible economically," had created a false sense of security and a certain continued complacency in regard to Airbus.

There was more—with a historian's advantage of hindsight— an event of profound significance was clearly apparent. In April 1990, Harold Haynes retired after thirty-six years with the Company. More importantly, he had been the CFO since 1975. The torch was passed to Boyd Givan, who had been second in command to Haynes, but cut from vastly different cloth. Haynes had taken an active part in every financial decision since 1975. Not a single commercial airplane was sold without his scrutiny as "financial gatekeeper."

Boeing had excellent salesmen who charged ahead with a glint in their eyes and an intensity of purpose. There is nothing wrong with that—it's what they were paid to do—in fact their bonuses were based on sales. However, while salesmen had their hand on the throttle, nobody had their foot on the brakes. Boyd Givan should have been that man. In fact, he was simply a "number cruncher," reporting results rather than sharing responsibility for creating them. The total equation tilted far too heavily toward the selling end. *Market share increased, while profits dwindled. The process was destined to continue unobserved and unchecked until it nearly derailed the Company.*

The first all-new model since the A300, the A320 entered commercial service in the spring of 1988. It claimed more extensive use of composites in the structure, a new generation of quiet engines, and most significant, fly-by-wire controls, replacing electro-mechanical flight controls with electronic signals—all aimed at lower empty weight, and subsequent lower fuel burn. The A320 also introduced "stress alleviation" of its wings, with computer controlled ailerons and spoilers to automatically deflect sudden wind gusts, thus reducing wing bending moments with an increase in passenger comfort. Airbus even "stole a page" from Boeing in its attention to the passenger compartment, making the body 7.5 inches wider than the 707/727/737/757 airplanes, allowing slightly wider seats or a wider aisle. A seemingly small advantage—but highly appreciated by passengers—who find it possible to pass the serving carts in the aisle. *Perhaps it will become known as the 7.5 inch decision.*

The 737-400—best of the 737 derivatives—had lost competitions to the A320 with Pan American, Northwest Airlines, and TransWorld Airlines.

Lo! The camel was inside the tent!

To make matters worse, the 7J7 was the wrong airplane for the time, and its abandonment after more than three years of effort—consuming thousands of engineering hours—proved to be a major blow to Boeing's dominance of the medium range market.

1. *Seattle Times*, 20 March, 1984, Section D.
2. *Boeing News*, 9 June, 1983, 1.
3. Private Communication.
4. *Fortune*, 28 September, 1987, 64.
5. Private Communication.
6. *International Herald Tribune*, 27–28 February, 1982.
7. *Annual Report*, The Boeing Company, 1989, 2.
8. Ibid., 1990, 14.
9. *Seattle Times*, 2 September, 1989, B8.
10. Ibid., 4 October, 1989, A8.
11. Ibid., 24 October, 1989, 1.
12. M.T. Stamper interview by E. E. Bauer, 13 November, 1989.
13. M.T. Stamper, *If We Are Smart*, Speech before the National Contract Management Assn., Los Angeles, 22 July, 1988.

CHAPTER TWENTY-NINE

Boeing Reinvents Itself

Mal Stamper, who had missed the opportunity to win the post of chairman because of age, was not sitting on his hands. As early as 1985, when heir-apparent Frank Shrontz was named president and Stamper was appointed to the new post of vice chairman—to get the adrenalin flowing again—he hatched a new program named Operation Eagle. Its goal was no less than to change the culture of the Company from the more authoritative top-down type to a more participative type.

Thus, even while enjoying the most prosperous period in its history, Boeing was developing a blueprint for massive change.

A Company-wide program to more fully inform employees as to the Company's standards of business conduct was formalized in 1985 when government contracts were subjected to intense criticism by the media and some members of Congress. Allegations of mischarging and overcharging produced legislation which increased the complexity of defense procurement.

Central to those standards was the Company's basic ethics creed: "All Boeing employees are expected to conduct their business with the highest ethical standards and treat with fairness and integrity all employees, customers, suppliers, and associates to earn and maintain their trust."[1]

As the new president, Frank Shrontz embraced Operation Eagle, and after one year of operation, in December 1986, Stamper and Shrontz reported to all employees in *Boeing News*.

"Operation Eagle was conceived as an awareness program. It seeks to communicate that as employees we can personally make a difference in our future, our Company's future, and our country's future.

"The basic elements of Operation Eagle boil down to three ways in which each of us can really help:

"First, and foremost, is simply doing our job right the first time. Avoiding mistakes improves the product in a dramatic way....

"Second, each of us can work with special enthusiasm and dedication....

"Third, each of us can approach our work with an inquiring mind, looking for innovative and creative ways to enhance quality and increase the efficiency of all that we do. It is in creating change that we succeed in making progress. We must outthink our competitors, as well as outperform them, and outwork them if we are to succeed."[2]

When Stamper retired in April 1990, Shrontz not only pursued the measures that had been adopted but intensified them. Soon Boeing had introduced a program called Continuous Quality Improvement, which they instituted in the Commercial Airplane Group. Formal training programs were set up, which all managers were required to complete.

In a further effort to shake up its employees, Boeing filmed a fake newscast in 1990 as an apocalyptic warning of what the future would be like if the Company failed to change. The newscast showed an empty airplane factory with workers filing out, heads down, surrendering their badges to a security guard. The newscaster, in baleful tones, announced, "It's the end of an era today, as the aerospace Company shuts its last plant."[3]

Reinventing the Company would be difficult enough in bad times, when there was an obvious need, but now—in good times—employees were being asked to work even harder toward a goal with a central thrust of reducing jobs. Grumbling was widespread, and naysayers abounded. Nevertheless, management moved aggressively on all fronts.

Next, and most significant, Shrontz initiated a series of study missions to Japanese "world class" companies, including Toyota, NEC, Nippon Steel, and Komatsu. He sent 100 top executives to Japan, but before leaving they were asked to digest eighteen fat books on Japanese quality. Initially skeptical, they returned with a feeling of awe. Then Boeing designed a four-day course which they dubbed "Managing for World-Class Competitiveness," to train the next level of managers. The course was designed to encourage efficiency from top to bottom, from accounts receivable to metal fabrication in the factory. Each manager was directed to train his immediate subordinate, in what became known as "cascade training." Boeing pushed the program to the lowest level of employees, eventually training everyone on the factory floor.

Tightening up on its operations, Boeing began taking a harder look at de Havilland. The Company had been beset by labor problems almost from the beginning, and despite heavy infusions of cash for research and development, as well as new facilities, profitability was never achieved. Paul Nisbet, aerospace analyst with Prudential Securities of New York, estimated de Havilland lost about $50 million for the year of 1990 alone.[4] As early as 1989, Boeing had begun to seek a buyer, and after talks broke down with Aerospatiale of France and Alenia of Italy—in January 1992—Boeing announced the sale of de Havilland to Bombardier Inc. of Montreal and the Province of Ontario.[5] With the sale, the smallest airplane in the Boeing commercial line became the 737-500, a machine in the 100-passenger class.

Curiously, Woodard's failure as president of de Havilland did nothing to slow his career—upon his return to Seattle, he was promoted to vice president of the Renton Division.

As Boeing reached its 75th birthday on July 15, 1991, the Company paused to look back and review some of its major accomplishments since World War II:

- *The B-52* would soon complete its fourth decade as the backbone of the nation's strategic bomber force—a primary instrument of both peace and war.
- *The 707*, with Pan American making its inaugural commercial flight in October 1958—after delivering 878 commercial airplanes, and later as the airframe for AWACS—the line was shut down after nearly 30 years.

- *The KC-135 tanker,* the other offshoot of the original 367-80 jet prototype, saw extensive service in the Gulf War, refueling both the AWACS and the B-52s in flight.
- *The C-46 Sea Knight and the C-47 Chinook* helicopters, originally operational in the early sixties were key performers in the Gulf War. The *Chinook* began a factory modernization program extending into the mid-nineties.
- *The Minuteman,* from contract award in 1958, until the last missile was produced in 1978, consistently beat schedule and cost targets, providing the nation with one of the best managed, mission-capable strategic systems in its history.
- *The 727 trijet,* kicked off in 1960—with a production run of 1,832 units over a span of twenty-four years—was expected to still be in service in the twenty-first century.
- *The Lunar Orbiter*—an obedient robot, contracted to take 200 photographs of the moon—promptly sent back 400.
- *The Saturn V*—after Chrysler had won the preliminary contract—NASA utilized Boeing's 7,500,000-pound-thrust first stage, which launched the Apollo astronauts to the moon.
- *The Lunar Rover*—the Boeing designed moon buggy—was deposited on the surface of the moon on December 19, 1972, closing man's first chapter in exploring its surface.
- *The 737*—with a single customer, Lufthansa, for only twenty-one planes—grew into a family. On the anniversary, Boeing had sold nearly 3,000 machines.
- *The 747*—undisputed queen of the world's skies for more than twenty years—was Boeing's resolute response to McNamara's award of the C-5 transport to Lockheed. It would not be presumptious to expect its derivatives to be in service at Boeing's 100th anniversary in 2016.
- *The 757/767 twins* were beginning to establish a strong position in the medium-range market in the face of extensive government subsidies for its Airbus Industrie competitor.

But the past was prologue. Now there were new crises to face. The early sales strength of the McDonnell Douglas MD-11 was a harbinger of another round of fierce competition, which had become the hallmark of the

United States commercial airplane business. In 1990, the three major engine producers: General Electric, Pratt & Whitney, and Rolls Royce, offered new "super engines" with ten-foot diameter by-pass fans, capable of producing 70,000 to 95,000 pounds of thrust—a giant leap from the 45,000 to 55,000 pound thrust levels of the seventies. With these new engines, a window was opened for a twin-engined plane with superior range and capacity to the three-engined MD-11.

With a newly minted president—William Clinton—taking office in 1992, the winds of change were blowing strongly across the entire country. In his State-of-the-Union message, he proposed a *largest in history* economic package of new taxes and spending cuts which called for sacrifice from every American. Facing a national debt of $4 trillion, and an annual budget deficit of $330 billion, the time had come to face the cruel issues.

Nevertheless, a fresh optimism pervaded the thinking of people in all walks of life. Young, intelligent, and dedicated, Clinton represented the baby boom generation, largest single consumer group in the history of the nation. People everywhere were willing to accept bold experiment, to risk more greatly, perhaps for the first time in two decades. The majority was no longer ominously silent. Fresh ideas and new initiatives were springing up. However, the recession of 1990-1992 proved to be more stubborn than any since the Great Depression. Unemployment was stuck at 7%, and the topic of the day was jobs.

Many major American corporations were downsizing to improve efficiency and productivity. Sears announced a major realignment, sweeping with it the venerable catalogue which had been the "wish book" for many generations of Americans. IBM, the blue ribbon giant for a half century, set in motion a complete reorganization—and fired its CEO. General Motors reported a loss of $4.5 billion for 1991—worst ever.

Airlines worldwide had been flying into headwinds, reporting the largest losses in history. Eastern Airlines and Pan American, two of the original giants, had long since gone out of business, and their planes disappeared from the skies. Continental and TWA were operating under Chapter 11 of bankruptcy. Northwest and US Air were struggling—seeking mergers with foreign companies. Even the strongest U.S. carriers; American, Delta, and United were suffering losses—and cutting personnel.

The next indication that the Boeing dominance of the medium range market might be in jeopardy came in 1992, when, in one of the most hotly contested sales campaigns in Boeing's history, United Airlines announced an order for up to 100 Airbus A320 planes. Boeing had offered its 737-400, a repeat of the Northwest scenario in 1986. After fourteen years of ordering only Boeing planes, United, largest U.S. airline, was sending the Company a message.

Boeing went back to the drawing boards. The result was the *Next-Generation 737*. As it had a number of times in the past, the *Little Giant* would be reborn. The -300,-400, and-500 would be replaced by a 737-X series of airplanes. The design of the new planes was market-driven and would include newer engines, a larger wing, greater range, increased speed, reduced noise, and fewer emissions, while maintaining the 737's simplicity, reliability, family commonality, and low operating costs. Boeing worked extensively with thirty airlines to come up with a product that would be competitive well into the next century.

In fact, Boeing introduced every innovation possible, while still staying within the "derivative" rules. Widening of the fuselage, or introducing fly-by-wire would have forced the design into the "new" airplane category, with attendant costs of hundreds of millions of dollars for recertification. Further, *commonality*—the greatest attribute of the 737—would have been highly compromised.

Gordon Bethune, vice president and general manager of the Renton Division of the Commercial Airplane Group, said, "Our customers were quite clear about what they wanted—and didn't want—in the 737-X. They asked us to change as little as possible, unless it related to range, noise, speed, or seating capacity."[6]

Bethune came to Boeing in 1988 as a vice president—in charge of Airline Logistics Support. Prior to coming to Boeing, he held a number of management positions in commercial airlines. He earned his bachelor of science degree from Abilene Christian University at Dallas, Texas, and graduated from Harvard Business school's advanced management program. In 1994, Continental Airlines, operating under Chapter 11, lured him away to be chief executive, where he brought them back to profitability.

As the reinvention revolution proceeded apace at Boeing, the triennial labor contracts were up for renegotiation in October, 1992. For the machinists, the process was a smooth one, and a new three-year contract was signed.

For SPEEA, it was different, yet another time for soul searching. Recollections of 1989 events loomed large in the thinking of SPEEA negotiators. Who could forget that the forty-eight day strike—second longest in the history of the Company—had produced positive results for the union.

The view from the catbird seat in 1989 strongly suggested that the wave of orders for commercial jets would wash over the entire decade of the '90s. Thus, SPEEA, emboldened—and unmindful of the storm clouds over the commercial airlines of the world, surprised most observers by rejecting the Company's offer, and giving strike authorization to its negotiating team. Ghosts of the "hungry hundred" of the 1950s—a time when SPEEA went through the most militant phase in its history—began reappearing.

The Company—counting on the weak resolve the union had shown in the past—promptly refused to improve its offer, cut off negotiations, and on December 15, 1992, unilaterally put the monetary offer in effect.

If the Company was bluffing, there was now only one way to find out, and that was to implement the strike option. Moving cautiously, the SPEEA negotiators decided to call for a one-day, protest strike.

The unusually bright skies of early January 1993, normally the year's wettest month—brought high spirits, and 70 percent of the 28,305 workers represented signed up for the strike. However, on the appointed day, Tuesday January 19, 1993, the weather reverted to its normal pattern. Torrents of rain brought reality and time to think for the thousands of pickets carrying their soggy signs.

As year-end 1992 profit results poured in, it was apparent that the world's airlines would sustain a staggering loss of $9 billion for the three years beginning with 1989—a figure greater than all the profits made in the preceding forty-four years.

SPEEA paused. Telephone calls revealed that less than half would support a lengthy strike. New ballots were sent out. Even before they were counted, Boeing announced a thirty percent cut in its production rate—to be phased in over the next eighteen months.

The SPEEA membership caved in, with sixty-two percent of those voting responding with a "yes."

The High Technology Center, formed in 1986 with much fanfare, came under scrutiny. The center, under Dr. Edith Martin, had embarked on an ambitious program of basic research.

With operating groups seeking additional resources for applied research, the laboratory failed to win continued support and was abandoned in 1992. Dr. Martin resigned and left the Company.

In August, 1992, Phil Condit was named as president of the Boeing Company, and in December 1993, Ron Woodard was named as president of the Commercial Airplane Group, succeeding Dean Thornton, who retired in early 1994. Supersalesman Woodard set his sights on increasing market share.

In the two years of 1993 and 1994, Boeing slashed employment by 29,000.[7] Factory costs were reduced dramatically, reflected in the price of airplanes, and an increased competitiveness.

But there was more to be done. Boeing was still saddled with an outmoded production system dating back to World War II days. Getting from the initial order by the customer to the delivered article was a costly, complex system. In 1994, the Company began a major initiative, scheduled for completion in 1998, aimed at simplifying and streamlining the complex process of engineering each airplane order to exact customer specifications. Further, the new system would simplify the processes used to schedule and order parts—including outsourcing—and manage inventory. The improved system, combined with a switch to more efficient, "lean" manufacturing techniques, was expected to significantly reduce both the time and cost required to produce commercial airplanes.

Growing by stages, the old system of "effectivity" callouts on the engineering drawings of the B-29 days had evolved into about 400 separate computer systems.

The new system, designed to replace all the others, had a mind boggling acronym—DCAC/MRM—pronounced *Deekak-emram*, for Define and Control Airplane Configuration/Manufacturing Resource Management. Without going into detail—which would occupy an entire chapter—the system consisted essentially of three Tailored Business Streams (TBS). TBS 1 would include all components common to all airplanes of a major model, i.e., 737, 747, which would include wing and body structure, empennage, landing gear, and many other parts. TBS 2 would include all components common to a sub-model, i.e., 737-500, 747-400, which had already been designed, manufactured, and certified for a previous customer. TBS 3 would include customer driven, newly defined components not previously designed, manufactured, or certified.

According to James "Jim" Jamieson, Executive Vice President, who explained DCAC/MRM in layman's terms, this data would then drive the system from the "as defined" configuration entirely through the manufacturing cycle, identifying all parts and processes, and end with an "as built" configuration.[8]

Jamieson came to Boeing in 1973, after earning two degrees in science and engineering from MIT. After numerous assignments in engineering on the commercial airplane side of Boeing, he was appointed as chief project engineer on the Model 757. Rising rapidly, he reached his current position in 1998.

The drastic cuts in employment and increased turbulence on the factory floor began to take a toll. Slowly, but inexorably, a price was being exacted. When the contract with the machinists union (IAM) came up for renewal on October 5, 1995, it was defeated by a 78% vote. In a second vote immediately following, the membership opted to strike. Some who had voted to accept the contract joined the strikers' ranks to show solidarity.

The next morning, pickets appeared at eighty-four locations in the Puget Sound area.

Boeing officials defended the proposed contract, saying the Company needed to lower its production costs to survive in an increasingly competitive marketplace.

Industry observers regarded the Company offer as being in line with labor cost trends around the country.

The union was not buying. Particularly rankling was a first time effort to ask employees to share a part of the rising medical costs. Top executives were also sharply criticized for their million dollar salaries and bonuses. With Boeing stock posting a healthy rising trend, announcements of stock bonuses were in the news. Frank Shrontz took more than a fair share of the heat. No one remembered that he had declined a raise in salary, offered in 1993. Job security was also up front in union demands. Subcontracting overseas was particularly criticized—and demands were made to share in those decisions.

The average employee in the factory had no appreciation of the pressures in dealing with foreign customers, who insist on in-country assembly contracts as a condition to purchase airplanes—viewing the practice as giving away jobs.

There was a darker aspect to the mood of the striking workers. After several years of intense building them up as the "Company's Most Valued Asset," they now felt as pawns in a game in which they had no voice.

Time ran, and an impasse set in. A few crossed the picket lines, however reluctantly. The October rains were heavier and colder than usual. A strike fund provided only $100 a week, and the burdens of bills falling due increased. The union put out feelers to open bargaining talks. The Company lent a deaf ear, announcing that the offer was final. With airlines suffering financially, no one was in a hurry to take deliveries, and late deliveries would not be penalized for reasons of a strike.

As Thanksgiving approached, Boeing agreed to reopen the talks, and on November 19, offered a modified proposal which improved the medical deduction picture, pension benefits, and subcontracting language. Union management recommended that the rank and file accept the proposal and called for a new vote.

With the strike now in its 47th day, it threatened to become the second longest strike in Boeing's history, exceeded only by 48 days in 1989 and 140 days in 1948.

In an angry mood, the membership turned their backs on their leader's recommendation and voted 61% in favor of continuing the strike. Boeing was stunned.

Perhaps, Boeing hadn't completely digested the fact that a watershed change had taken place in America in the last thirty years. Tens of thousands of workers hired in the fifties and sixties had been born in the Depression, were veterans of World War II and Korea, and were dedicated to their jobs. Universities churned out two and a half million graduates on the G.I. Bill, many of them engineers. For those people, the job was the center of their lives—even at the expense of their families. In his book, *The Greatest Generation*, Tom Brokaw heaps praise and adoration on this once in a century generation of dedicated men and women.[9] Their children were the baby boomers.

In the latter decades of the century, it was this baby boomer generation who made up most of the work force throughout the United States. For them the quality of life was far more important than the job, and self esteem was the new watchword. In many ways, the "new" Boeing was welcomed with open arms. Indeed, where the "old" Boeing was rigid, demanding, and even arrogant, the "new" Boeing was supportive, patient, and yielding. Suddenly, Frank Shrontz and his management team realized they had contributed to letting this new genie out of the bottle. Perhaps they had no choice—the events simply represented the flow of history.

The turndown of the latest Boeing offer left no room for an easy solution, and many predicted it would not be settled by yearend.

The rains of November turned to a week of bitter cold in early December, followed by high winds, but the strikers seemed more determined than ever.

With production beginning to be seriously hurt, Boeing agreed to come back to the table, and after nearly six days of tough bargaining, made a new offer. On December 13, the membership voted for accceptance—ending the 69 day strike. The final offer called for wages and lump-sum payments that union negotiators said were worth about $20,000 to the average production worker over the life of the four-year contract.

On Thursday morning, December 14, more than 84,000 western Washington homes were without power due to raging winds, but a degree of calm had settled in over Puget Sound, with Boeing, the regions largest industrial employer, back at work.

SPEEA signed what by any measure was a lucrative four-year contract. In sum, the average engineer's salary at Boeing will reach $64,000 per year in 1999, up from $46,000 in 1992.[10]

In a move to take some of the pressure off expected layoffs in 1995, Boeing offered a one-time quasi-golden parachute, early retirement incentive plan. The plan covered all employees over 55 years, who had been with the Company for at least 10 years. Of the 13,000 eligible employees, approximately 7,000 accepted the plan, which cost the Company $600 million in a one time charge to pre-tax earnings.[11]

The reinvention program was unique in that it was implemented when the commercial airplane business was booming, and the results helped greatly during the business downturn of the early nineties. It was during this time that Boeing had to step up to the costs of launching the 777 jetliner and the *Next-Generation 737* series.

Nevertheless, the jury was still out on the long term effects of the reinvention, which in the final analysis had caused the Company to give up so much of its famed discipline.

The new militance of the work force, as demonstrated by the two long, costly strikes of 1989 and 1995, suggested a new outlook, the history of which is still to be written.

Phil Condit, president, was not appointed to CEO until April of 1996, and had yet to face his baptism in the arena of labor strife. It would be his turn in 1999.

1. *Annual Report*, The Boeing Company, 1985, 3.
2. *Boeing News*, Eagle Progress Report, December, 1986.
3. *Business Week*, 1 March, 1993, 60.
4. *Seattle Times*, April 11, 1991, B2.
5. *Annual Report*, The Boeing Company, 1991, 2.
6. *Boeing News,* 2 July, 1993, 1.
7. *Annual Report,* The Boeing Company, 1995, 56.
8. Jim Jamieson interview by E.E. Bauer, 11 January, 1999.
9. Tom Brokaw, *The Greatest Generation*, (New York: Random House, 1998).
10. *Aviation Week & Space Technology*, 15 January, 1996, 37.
11. *Annual Report*, The Boeing Company, 1995, 40.

Alan R. Mulally 1945–
Senior Vice President 1997–

CHAPTER THIRTY

The Twenty-two
Inch Decision

It had been ten years—the summer of 1978—since T. Wilson pulled the trigger, launching Boeing on its development and marketing of the new technology twins, the Models 757 and 767.

Forbes had called it a multi-billion dollar gamble that shaded all new model decisions of the past.

Perhaps it was time to consider a new airplane incorporating all the advances in technology that had occurred over that period. However, in an industry where there are no riskless decisions, a consistent winner simply had to be right almost all of the time. The 7J7 experience was a constant reminder.

Boeing felt there may be a niche in the market between the 767 and the 747, and began studying derivatives of the 767. In October 1988, the Company was reviewing results of an intensive study of the possibilities.

John Roundhill, chief engineer of preliminary design, had just finished a marathon, five-hour presentation covering seven different 767-X scenarios, while Boeing senior executives listened. When Roundhill put his pointer aside and asked for questions, there was only one—and it was major—and unanimous.

"Why haven't you looked at a new airplane?"[1] Frank Shrontz asked. It was perhaps the most obvious question to be posed. A new airplane would fit the niche much better than a derivative. The big difference would be cost. To launch a new airplane would constitute yet another huge gamble.

Roundhill, an alumnus of the University of Washington with a master's degree in mechanical engineering, was a 1967 honor student who continued with graduate work at both Cal Tech and the University of Washington, joining Boeing in 1968.

Taken by surprise, Roundhill recovered quickly. "We haven't done it," was his matter-of-fact reply—"we need to do our homework."

The next question came immediately. "When can we see some data?"

Roundhill dredged up a last ounce of courage. "The day before the Christmas holidays," he said, laughing.

After the meeting he went back to his unit of about 200 engineers. "Let's start working on a new airplane," he directed.[1]

The customers agreed with Boeing on the need for an airplane smaller than the 747-400 and larger than the 767-300, but none of the configurations offered met their requirements. Designing a new wing would not do it—stretching it to its limit would not do it—larger engines would not do it—neither would double decking. Boeing even looked at a partial double deck, with the top deck above the aft half of the fuselage. This monster picked up a nickname—the *Humpback of Mukilteo*—after a small town near the main assembly plant at Everett, Washington.

Thus, the Model 777 was conceived, and Alan Mulally was named vice president and general manager of a new 777 Division. He immediately focused the task. "For the first time in history, the airlines have a choice," he announced. "Airbus has a match for every Boeing plane, except for the 747," he added.[2]

Mulally was one of the brightest of the crop of engineers who joined the Company in the sixties. With bachelor of science and master of science degrees in aeronautical and astronautical engineering from the University of Kansas, and a masters in management from MIT, he joined Boeing in 1969, and spent most of his career in commercial airplanes.

Boeing was the third entrant in this market niche. The McDonnell Douglas MD-11, a stretched version of the DC-10 and the Airbus Industrie Models A330/A340, had already announced. The MD-11 was scheduled to be available to the airlines in 1990, and the Airbus machines in 1993.

It was this keen competition that forced Boeing to enter the race at all. Without competition, a new, high capacity twin would only draw sales away from the 747 and the 767.

Indeed, it was already very late, and the clock was running. However, Frank Shrontz remained unruffled and candid about priorities. Concerned about the deliveries of the 747-400, which were running behind schedule, he was adamant concerning Boeing's policy.

"What I don't want is to have management attention and resources we need to get the 747-400 job done diverted to a new airplane. If that means postponing the 777, so be it."[3]

"When it happens, we want the 777 to be a little bigger, a little faster, and better than the competition in every respect,"[4] said then vice president Phil Condit, emphasizing the company's deep-seated dedication to the continuity of Bill Boeing's entrepreneurial spirt. Having decided to enter the competition, the strategy was to beat the three-engine MD-11 and the four-engine A340 with a lower operating cost twin-engined airplane, leaving the A330 twin as the main competition.

When choosing body width, Boeing's initial focus was on the L-1011's and DC-10's flying the world's airlines. With 690 of the two models sold, most of which were still flying, they would be the first logical target for replacement. Thus the inside body width was chosen to be slightly wider than those airplanes, providing improved passenger comfort. Mulally suggested it might be called the *five inch decision*.[5]

In a competitive study in 1990, Boeing found the 777 would have the same operating cost as the A330. However, the width of the 777 was 22 inches greater than the A330, providing for ten abreast seating, and guaranteeing an unmatchable seat-mile cost advantage. Thus, Boeing was able to take advantage of its late start by offering a more competitive airplane. *Perhaps it would be more appropriate to call it the twenty-two inch decision.*

McDonnell Douglas had not launched an all-new plane since the two companies merged in 1967. The MD-80 and MD-90 series were simply derivatives of the DC-9, and the MD-11 was a stretched version of the DC-10.

John S. McDonnell, son of Mr. Mac, the legendary James McDonnell, who founded the company in 1939, and ran it until his death at 81 in 1980, took over as CEO when his cousin Sanford retired in 1988. Despite success in the military markets, John McDonald took on an uphill battle.

Early in the 1980s, the company had seriously considered getting out of the commercial airplane business. However, in 1983, James Worsham, a super salesman who headed the Douglas division, persuaded American Airlines to lease twenty MD-80s on a trial basis. American liked the planes, and especially the bargain basement lease terms. The following year, American bought sixty-seven more MD-80s. The deal brought the company back to a position of respectability. By 1989, McDonnell Douglas had 401 firm orders on the books for the MD-80, and another 518 options. They also logged 95 firm orders and 220 options for the MD-11. Abruptly, they predicted that revenues would balloon from $4.9 billion in 1988 to $10 billion in 1991. The backlog stood at an impressive $18 billion.

After its long famine, McDonnell Douglas went on a hiring spree, more than doubling the work force to 44,000. Overnight, things got out of control. With thousands of inexperienced workers, quality slipped badly, requiring costly and time consuming rework. The factory problems got so out of hand, that the company lost money building the ten-year-old MD-80 in the first half of 1989.[6]

Chairman John McDonnell decided to change the way they did things, appointing Robert Hood—a manufacturing expert—to replace Worsham, who retired. Then the company introduced a sweeping reorganization plan. Every one of the 5,000 managerial and supervisory posts were eliminated, and 2,800 new posts were created. Then all 5,000 were asked to apply for one of the new posts, with the 2,200 losers to be stripped of their managerial responsibilities.

"They created chaos," observed Richard Shevell, a former senior engineer at the company, who moved to the position of professor emeritus in aeronautics at Stanford University.[7]

By 1992, orders for the MD-11 had slowed to a trickle, and McDonnell Douglas began to study options. They looked at a major stretch called an MD-12, with a new wing and new engines, targeting first flight for early in 1995. With a near agreement on a memorandum of understanding with the engine manufacturers, and evaluation of proposals from nine communities around the U.S. for location of a final assembly plant nearly completed, the company suddenly announced new design concepts for the MD-12. The new version would use four engines and have a double decked cabin for the full length.

The discussion of a totally new aircraft after several years of refinement of a trijet derivative, took the industry by surprise. One well placed observer said, "It blew our socks off."[8] *In retrospect, with Boeing fully committed to the 777 twin, if McDonnell Douglas had been able to pull this one off, they could have competed for the top of the sky that had been the sole province of the 747 since 1970.*

However, with all of the mixed signals concerning commercial airplanes, and wing problems on the C-17 military transport program, Wall Street reduced the company's stock to speculative grade. In response, McDonnell Douglas launched a major reorganization in the summer and fall of 1992, and in 1993 astonished many industry observers with a turnaround, reporting a net income of $396 million versus a year earlier loss of $781 million.[9]

Nevertheless, the double decked MD-12 would have been a huge program, and the company negotiated a memorandum of understanding with Taiwan Aerospace Company (TAC) to purchase up to a 40 percent share of a new company formed around McDonnell Douglas' operations in the U.S.

Although Taiwan regarded such a venture as an opportunity, there was deep concern over the financial health and staying power of McDonnell Douglas over the long term.

With Airbus Industrie claiming an increasing share of the market, mainly at the expense of McDonnell Douglas, industry analysts turned negative.

"A partnership with TAC would be negative for the whole commercial aerospace industry, creating additional capacity in an industry that already has excess capacity," Salomon Brothers analyst George D. Shapiro said.[10]

In the final analysis, there was no sound basis to go forward.

At Boeing, the airplane that emerged from the design studies was a giant twin with a capacity of up to 420 passengers.

By any measure, the 777 was a huge machine. The engines for the baseline airplane produced 70,000 pounds of thrust. As the airplane grew in subsequent derivatives, the engine power went up to 90,000 pounds, the limit offered by the engine manufacturers. Those large engines had a diameter equal to the width of a 737 fuselage. The horizontal tail of the 777 was the same span as the 737 wing.

After rigorous testing on a 757, fly-by-wire was introduced, a first for a Boeing commercial airplane. Considerable attention was paid to new materials. Composites constituted about 9% of the empty weight of the aircraft and for the first time were used in primary structure. The main areas of use were the floor beams and the horizontal stabilizer. Use of composites as primary structure was proven earlier, when five horizontal stabilizers were flown on service 737 airplanes. Several new aluminum alloys were utilized, primarily alloys with higher specific tensile and compressive strength, with equivalent fracture toughness and corrosion resistance. Titanium was also used quite extensively. However, the lightweight champion, aluminum-lithium, although it passed all the tests, was abandoned for primary structure because of concerns over long term durability.

Perhaps the most unusual feature was the optional folding wing. Folding the outboard twenty-one feet of the wing reduced the span from a 747 to that of a 767, allowing utilization of the same airport gates as the DC-10s and L-1011s. Customers were offered this option at a weight penalty of about 3,000 pounds—equivalent to about fifteen passengers (no airline exercised this option).

The baseline airplane had a takeoff weight of 515,000 pounds. A growth version, the 777-300, would have a takeoff weight of 590,000 pounds, with a wing loading of 140 pounds per square foot. (Wing design had come a long way from the B-29 which had a wing loading of 69 pounds per square foot).

With the airplane configured, all that was needed was a launch customer. Consultation and feedback from the airlines had been continuous during the preliminary design and configuration phase, so the initiative was up to the airlines. The most desired launch customer was United Airlines, Boeing's oldest, having purchased nearly 1,000 of its planes since the beginning of commercial aviation.

In all, United had to evaluate thirty-three airplane/engine combinations. They were behind schedule and in a hurry, inviting all three competing airframe customers, and all three engine companies to come to their headquaters in Chicago on the weekend of October 13-14, 1990, and not to leave until a deal was hammered out. Phil Condit had made plans to visit his daughter at Colgate University. Should he cancel? With the de-

Model 777—The Jumbo Twin

Boeing's response to the challenge of the McDonnell Douglas MD-11 and the Airbus A330.

sign and performance parameters already cast in concrete, all that remained was the financing and legalese of the final contract, an area outside his responsibility. Condit decided to go.

But he was uneasy, and time dragged. Mostly, he sat staring at the phone—which never rang. Unable to stand the suspense any longer, late Sunday afternoon Condit grabbed an airplane to Chicago, only a short flight from Hamilton, New York. He joined the Boeing people in the waiting room and worked on a crossword puzzle.

Eventually, the United spokesman came in and said, "You've got the deal." Jim Guyette, executive vice president of United apparently had already decided he wanted the 777 but was afraid that the chairman might be leaning toward Airbus based on financial considerations, so he penciled a note on a single sheet of paper at 2:15 A.M. Monday morning that gave a general statement of how the companies would work together to produce the best service-ready airplane. It was entitled "B-777 Objective," and it said simply:

"In order to launch on time a truly great airplane we have a responsibility to work together to design, produce and introduce an airplane that exceeds the

expectations of flight crews, cabin crews, maintenance and support teams and
ultimately our passengers and shippers.

> *"From day one:*
> * *Best dispatch reliability in the industry;*
> * *Greatest customer appeal in the industry;*
> * *User friendly and everything works."*[11]

It was dated October 15, 1990, and signed by Guyette, who asked Dick Albrecht and Phil Condit to sign also.

United signed a contract for thirty-four airplanes with options for an additional thirty-four.

Back at the plant, Mulally gathered his people together, and said simply, "Let's build an airplane."[12]

The effort involved 10,000 people, working for a period of five years, and expending five billion dollars. At its peak, more than half were engineers. The original 747 plant at Everett, Washington, equivalent to forty-five football fields, was almost doubled—at a cost of nearly $1.5 billion.

Fortunately, the Company's existence was not at stake. Boeing was cash rich, as a result of the profitability of other models. Nevertheless the exposure was great—the 11th airplane was in the production line when the first 777 flew.

Boeing was still in the process of reinventing itself, and in a bold gamble, had decided to eliminate the engineering drawing system, the Company's heart from its beginning.

To replace the engineering drawings, Boeing designed the airplane entirely on computers. The program, which was called CATIA, (for computer-aided, three dimensional, interactive, application)—came from Dassault Aviacion in France, where it was used to help the French build fighter planes.

Neil Standal, the 777 vice president, assistant general manager, explained the magnitude of those changes, pointing out that Boeing was concurrently "designing the system by which we are designing the aircraft."[13]

Standal was one of those rare Boeing executives who were self-made men. He began his Boeing career in 1956 as a mechanic while attending Pacific Lutheran University, where he graduated in 1960. A microcosm of the company itself, he kept changing with the times, bringing new expertise to the job.

Some 2,200 computer terminals utilizing the CATIA three-dimensional design system provided the backbone of the 777 project, feeding data to the largest cluster of mainframe computers in the world; eight IBM 3090-600Js.

In a nutshell, use of the computer to configure the airplane and simulate all the parts and assemblies before any metal was actually cut promised a tremendous cost advantage. In the old method, engineering drawings were released to the factory, followed by production engineering drawings, and finally tooling drawings. Feedback to the engineers for interference and other problems, was a tortuous, time consuming activity.

The old system was replaced by use of "design build teams" (DBT's) made up of all facets of the design-production-flight process. The number of DBTs grew as the program progessed—exceeding 235 at its peak.

Using an add-on program called EPIC, developed by the Boeing computing staff, engineering mockups were also eliminated.

The system even had its own digital mechanic, CATIA-man, a visual robot that could crawl into a computer's image to see if a real mechanic could get to hard-to-reach parts.

In August 1992, when Phil Condit was named President of the Company and a member of the board, the primary responsibility for bringing the 777 to fruition fell on the shoulders of Alan Mulally.

Almost sixty international suppliers fabricated parts for the 777. Japan provided about 20% of the fuselage structure as well as other components. Other parts came from Australia, Brazil, Canada, France, Ireland, Italy, Korea, and Singapore.

It would be inaccurate to say there were no problems in the long design, production, and flight testing period. However, in each case, the responsible DBT focused on the problem until a solution was achieved. An example was the rudder, fabricated by a small company in Australia called ASTA (Aerospace Technologies of Australia). The rudder was made of graphite fiber, woven into cloth and laid up in multiple layers over a Nomex honeycomb core, and cured in an autoclave. After fabrication was begun, engineering found through model testing that a flutter condition could develop with the existing design and a major modification was required. Later, two additional modifications were required before the problem was solved. It was only through superhuman efforts that ASTA was able to deliver the rudder on time.

Another example was the engine testing.[14] John Cashman, chief pilot, had argued for a flying test bed for the new Pratt & Whitney engine. Even though thorough testing had been completed on the ground, Cashman was nervous. He had lots of opposition. Even Ron Ostrowski, chief engineer, felt the flying test bed could be dispensed with. It was up to Alan Mulally to make the final decision, and he supported Cashman. Old Number One, RA 001, the first 747 to be built, was borrowed from the Museum of Flight, brought back to flight condition, and the new engine installed at the left inboard position.

In November of 1993, on the third flight of the test bed engine, Cashman's fears were realized when the engine surged, equivalent to a stall, which could be serious during takeoff in service. For Mulally the surge was a gift—good news—because it provided a critical piece of data. It was determined that the clearance between the blade tips and the fan case was excessive, allowing passage of too much air. For production engines, the problem was easily fixed.

When the first 777 rolled out on April 9, 1994, Boeing had logged 147 firm orders and 108 options.[15] Sales of the MD-11, which had been flying passengers since 1991—and by early 1992 stood at 136 firm orders and 157 options—had stalled.

On June 12, 1994, Chief pilot John Cashman made a "near perfect" first flight of three hours and forty-eight minutes over Washington and Puget Sound.

Cashman joined Boeing in 1966, after graduating from the University of Michigan with a bachelor's degree in aerospace engineering. He also did post graduate work at the University of Washington's Master of Business Administration program. He had flown all of the Boeing models beginning with the 707, and became chief pilot for the commercial airplane group in 1990.

The *Next-Generation* 737s were ready to roll. In November, 1993, Southwest Airlines announced its intention to be the launch customer for the 737-700, and in January, 1994 signed a contract for sixty-three of these new airplanes. The following September, Hapag-Lloyd of Germany kicked off the -800, and in March 1995, Scandinavian Airlines ordered the -600s. Then, in November, 1997, Alaska Airlines launched the -900, last and largest of the new series.

In July, 1996, in a joint venture between Boeing and General Electric, a brand new business jet was offered. Derived from the 737-700, the plane embodied unique features for corporate travel, offering more flexibility than any other business jet. The plane quickly developed market acceptance, and in October, 1999, Boeing announced the sale of a larger version, the BBJ2—based on the 737-800—which is twenty feet longer than the original. The new model, scheduled for delivery in late 2000, offers 25 percent more floor space, and twice the luggage capacity. With the announcement of the new machine, Boeing had booked orders for fifty-six airplanes.

The remaining ambitious goal for the 777 program was Boeing's determination to have approval of ETOPS by the time the first airplane entered commercial service. ETOPS, the acronym for Extended-range Twin-engine Operations, allowed 180 minutes of flight over water with one engine out. Normally, FAA certification of ETOPS would not be considered until the airplane had proven itself in service for a two year period.

Thus, four years earlier, Boeing and United had developed a test plan that would demonstrate the 777's capability to perform ETOPS flights. It was agreed that the 777 would fly 1,000 flights—equivalent to a year of normal operations—in temperatures ranging from less than minus 20 degrees F., to more than 100 degrees F., at thrust ratings of 84,000 and 77,000 pounds, and simulating various flight scenarios.

At any given time, half of the flight test engineers flew day and night across the United States, while the other half worked on the ground. The airplane flew on United Airline's routes, flight attendants provided meal service, and mechanics fully serviced the airplane and prepared it for its next flight. The team started on schedule and ended on schedule—which was the nature of the entire 777 effort.

The first Model 777 was delivered on time and service ready on May 15, 1995, fulfilling the commitment made when the program was launched in October, 1990. Also, in May 1995, the FAA approved ETOPS for the Model 777, thus paving the way for United's inaugural flight from London to Washington, D.C. on June 7.

Boeing's stock stood at about $56 per share, up about 30 percent from its 62-week low of $42.50. Many analysts predicted the price would climb to $70 within the next eighteen months.[16]

The Boeing Company and the 777 team were awarded the Collier Trophy for 1995—for the "world's most technologically advanced transport."

In February 1997, Phil Condit was elevated to Chairman of the Board, and Frank Shrontz moved to Chairman Emeritus.

By any measure the creation of the 777 was a phenomenal example of 10,000 people working together. *Working Together* had been the slogan from the beginning and it was the name of the first airplane delivered to United Airlines. The slogan was painted on banners that went up throughout the factory, on posters, baseball caps, badges, and T-shirts. It was repeated as a mantra in speeches and discussions between Boeing and its customers and contractors. John Cashman, who was an unbeliever in the beginning, had this to say.

"My view, early on, being somewhat of a cynical pilot, I didn't think it would work, I just thought it was another program with a lot of words...but I came to understand the vision of Alan and Phil as to what it really was. The key element was getting the right people...but it's hard to get political enemies to work together...and after they got people that would do that, I still didn't think it would work. Then, as we went along in many marathon meetings, everybody got to know everybody else's problems and successes. As the rapport built up, the mass of people that were traditionally moving in forty directions, started moving in one direction."[14]

In spite of the euphoria, the war with Airbus was far from won. At the time of delivery, Airbus claimed firm orders for 260 of its A330/A340 planes.[16]

1. Karl Sabbagh, *21st Century Jet*, (New York: Scribner, 1996), 28.
2. Private Communication.
3. *Fortune*, 17 July, 1989, 44.
4. *Boeing News*, 22 March, 1991, 7.
5. Alan Mulally interview by E. E. Bauer, 27 January, 1999.
6. *Fortune*, 28 August, 1989, 80.
7. Ibid.
8. *Aviation Week & Space Technology*, 16 March, 1992, 14.
9. Ibid., 7 March, 1994, 54.
10. Ibid., 4 May, 1992, 25.
11. *The Boeing Archives*

12. KCTS Productions, *21st Century Jet, The Building of the 777.*, (Seattle Washington and London England) 1995/1996.
13. *Aviation Week & Space Technology*, 3 June, 1991, 34.
14. John Cashman, interview by E.E. Bauer, 12 January, 1999.
15. *Aviation Week & Space Technology*, 11 April, 1994, 36.
16. *The Seattle Post Intelligencer*, 7 May, 1995, F3.

International Space Station

A National Aeronautics and Space Administration (NASA) artist's conception of *Freedom*, the International Space Station. Boeing is the prime contractor for the sixteen nation project, due to be completed in 2005.

CHAPTER THIRTY-ONE

Space Revisited

Time has dimmed the memory of mighty *Saturn*, the awesome booster that shook the farthest reaches of Brevard County at Cape Canaveral—lifting the *Apollo* spacecraft up to man's rendezvous with the moon on July 20, 1969. Close behind was *Rover*, the wheeled vehicle that traversed the moon's surface. It was the stuff of fantasy and legend.

Generations born after 1969 could scarcely visualize that such an undertaking had actually happened, and even to those living then it seemed unreal.

Perhaps man had visited the moon for both the first and last time—or so it seemed in the early seventies. Major funding for NASA was sharply reduced as a reluctant Congress began to view manned space as too costly an adventure, the fruits of which could be achieved more cheaply with unmanned vehicles. However, there seemed to be a consensus that a reusable vehicle capable of placing payloads in near-Earth orbit should receive the major emphasis, and the term "space shuttle" was coined.

In mid-1970, under an eleven-month contract from NASA, a Grumman/Boeing team began a study of alternate space shuttle concepts. The goal was to build a vehicle that could make as many as 100 trips to and from Earth orbit, carrying men and materials at significantly lower costs.

During 1970, twenty-nine different shuttle concepts were evaluated. The most economic and technically feasible concept was selected, and the team focused on one single design for the remainder of the contract.

Associated with the Boeing/Grumman team in this work was a broad range of companies, including General Electric, Eastern Airlines, Northrop, Avions Marcel Dassault of France, Avco, Dornier of the Federal Republic of Germany, and Aerojet General.

Thus, Boeing had high hopes of winning the prime contract for the space shuttle, and it came as a major shock when NASA announced on July 26, 1972 that North American Rockwell had won.

With the loss of the shuttle, confidence waned in the prospect of any substantial new business. In 1973, Boeing noted:

"A shift in national priorities has tended to deemphasize the nation's space program, and the prospect of immediate additional major business in that field cannot be viewed as bright."[1]

Nevertheless, Boeing continued to search for new opportunities in space technology, and in 1973, the Company made a significant contribution to space exploration when *Mariner 10* began its 640-million-mile journey to Venus and Mercury. The spacecraft, designed and built at the Boeing Space Center, was delivered to the Jet Propulsion Laboratory for NASA on schedule and within the budget proposed by NASA in 1969.

A decade before their merger in 1967, McDonnell and Douglas were moving toward cooperation in space systems. Out of its experience with missiles in the 1950s, Douglas was developing launch vehicles. Meanwhile, McDonnell was designing hardware for space exploration. In the late 1950s, even before the launch of the Soviet *Sputnik* in 1957, when NASA began seeking someone to build a manned spacecraft, McDonnell did not have to assemble a team. They had a team in place, working at company expense.

On January 12, 1959, McDonnell was selected by NASA to build America's first manned spaceship. The contract, issued on February 13, 1959, called for the construction of twelve one-crew-member space capsules (the total was later increased to twenty). The result was *Mercury*, which on May 5, 1961, carried the first American, Navy Commander, Alan B. Shepard, Jr., 115 miles above the Earth in a fifteen minute suborbital flight—landing in the Atlantic Ocean. He was followed quickly by Air Force Captain Virgil I. "Gus" Grissom on July 21. On February 20, 1962, Air Force Lt. Col. John H. Glenn, Jr., became the first American to orbit the Earth, aboard a *Mercury* spacecraft.

Mercury was soon followed by *Gemini*—a two man craft—and after several unmanned flights, astronauts Charles Conrad and Gordon Cooper spent eight days in space, splashing down in the Atlantic on August 29, 1965 in a *Gemini* spacecraft, also built by McDonnell. The *Gemini* program put twenty astronauts into space in twenty months, and brought them back safely.

When the giant *Saturn V*, used for the moon shots, came along in the late sixties, it was an effort by many in the industry. A three stage rocket, the first stage was built by Boeing, the second by North American, and the third by Douglas.

The next significant near space venture after the moon landing and *Lunar Rover,* was *Skylab*, the Manned Orbiting Laboratory (*MOL*), built by McDonnell Douglas, and launched into orbit by the *Saturn V* booster on May 14, 1973. *Skylab* survived until July 1979, housing three astronauts for eighty-four days during its stay in orbit.

It was the last of the *Saturn* series, with a perfect record of thirteen successful launches in thirteen attempts.

Americans were notably absent from space for nearly a decade, while the Soviets continued to pile up records for duration in orbit. A month after *Skylab* ended, the Soviets announced a record of 175 days aboard their *Salyut 6* space station. Then a year later, they achieved 184 days, twenty hours and twelve minutes, and in October 1984, with *Salyut 7*, 236 days, twenty-two hours and fifty minutes.

On February 19, 1986, the Soviets launched a new space station, *Mir* (Peace)—on which they established still another record for time in space—over 438 days.

September 17, 1976 will be recorded in history as the raising of the curtain on the next major phase of NASA's manned space efforts. On that day, the first Shuttle Orbiter, officially known as *Orbiter 101*, and bearing the name *Enterprise*, rolled out of its birthplace at Rockwell International in Palmdale, California.

With NASA pinpointing the space shuttle as its number one priority, loss of the prime contract simply increased Boeing's determination. The Company initiated three key programs to support those operations. The first was the design and fabrication of the support systems module for the 2.4 meter space telescope, an instrument intended to carry astronomy above the distortions of the Earth's atmosphere. In 1975, Boeing won this contract.

The second was the adaptation of a 747 airplane to carry the shuttle piggyback in conducting earthbound landing tests, as well as to return future shuttles to the Cape after landing in California. This project was completed in 1977.

The third shuttle-related program was the design and development of the *IUS*, an outgrowth of a successful Air Force program known as *Burner II*. The contract was won by Boeing in 1976, which led to a production award in 1983.

Boeing Services International (BSI), a wholly owned subsidiary of Boeing was formed in 1977 to support and refurbish base operations at a number of Air Force and Army installations, as well as for NASA, particularly at the Kennedy Space Center.

On Sunday, April 12, 1981, the space shuttle *Columbia* rose off Pad 39A at the Kennedy Space Center, Cape Canaveral a few seconds past 7 A.M., and Americans returned to space. BSI was there to support the operation.

Reactions at Kennedy were reported by Donna Mikov with Boeing public relations.[2] "Go baby go!" cried BSI test conductor, Fred Leidner as he slapped the computer console in front of him. At one point in the countdown, just before the end of a nine-minute hold, George Page, NASA launch director read a message from President Reagan to the crew. "Talk about emotion. I couldn't have read that message. I would have been choked up and crying," reported Mikov.

The shuttle was in orbit for more than fifty-four hours. Astronauts John W. Young and Robert L. Crippen, after performing a number of checkout activities to test the orbiter's systems in space for the first time, glided in to a picture-perfect landing at Edwards Air Force Base, California.

In 1984, the Company bid on the NASA proposal for design of the common modules for the *Freedom* space station. The common modules were intended to serve for crew living and working quarters, for manufacturing, technology, and life sciences work, and for logistics resupply.

At Huntsville Alabama, Boeing's nerve center for space operations since an office building was opened in 1958, ground was broken for the first new building on a 110 acre site at Jetplex Industrial Park, near the airport. The 170,000 square foot building was used to consolidate 500 of the 750 Huntsville employees who had been housed in leased facilities. Boeing had taken an option on an additional 500 acres ajoining the property. In 1990, a half-million square foot facility was completed, employing 4,000 people.

The Huntsville Division was headed by vice president and general manager, Robert "Bob" Hager, a thirty-six year-plus employee, who graduated from the University of Washington with a master's degree in civil engineering. Hager started in structures and dynamics—strongly oriented to missiles and space—directing the Minuteman program from 1973 to 1976, and managing the *IUS* development.

The space station program entailed many peripheral efforts. By 1985, Boeing had won twenty advanced development contracts involving technologies related to the main station, including studies concerning microgravity and materials processing.

The shuttle program was proceeding well, when on January 28, 1986, disaster struck. Space shuttle *Challenger*, the second of the three orbiters contracted for, exploded in a ball of fire ninety seconds after liftoff—the first in-air disaster since Alan B. Shepard, Jr., took a fifteen minute ride fifty-six missions earlier. The 1967 explosion resulting in the death of three astronauts, occurred on the launch pad.

On board the *Challenger* were six crew members and Christa McAuliffe, a thirty-seven year old New Hampshire scool teacher, selected as America's first ordinary citizen to travel on a space shuttle. Her students were among the millions watching the event on television.

The launch of *Challenger*, which was to have been the twenty-fifth shuttle mission, had been delayed for three days because of bad weather. Liftoff, scheduled for 9:38 A.M., was delayed for two more hours because unusually low temperatures caused ice to form on the shuttle and its support structure.

Challenger lifted off flawlessly at 11:38 A.M. and rose for seventy-four seconds. Then, at an altitude of ten miles, just as its main engines were to be pushed to full power, it erupted in a ball of fire. The last words from the shuttle were, "Roger, go to full power," spoken to mission control by Francis R. Scobee, mission commander.

By 1989, Boeing had completed a series of structural tests of the full scale prototype of the space station common modules, which provided data crucial to the assurance of a thirty-year lifetime in the hostile environment of space.

Production of the *IUS* heralded a continuing future for Boeing in transspace propulsion, and in October 1989, an *IUS*, orbiting aboard the shuttle *Atlantis*, gave the Galileo probe its start on a six-year journey to Jupiter.

The Company was in a continual process of reorganization as part of its reinvention. Thus, in 1990, all activities involved in defense and space were amalgamated into a new Defense and Space Group. The new organization, which was formed to improve overall performance in this business area, was given the responsibility to operate as a single profit and loss center.

Due to budget constraints, the U.S. Congress directed NASA to replan the international space station, *Freedom*, on a different time scale. Nevertheless, in December 1991, NASA pushed the button for Boeing to proceed with final hardware design.

The space station was beginning to look like a career-spanning activity. With the program in its eighth year from conception, John Winch—newly named program manager—suggested that when the orbiting space lab's been in orbit for thirty years, Boeing employees will look back on 1992 as the onset of the program's "good ol'days."

John Winch had been *Lunar Rover* program executive in 1970. He came to Boeing in 1966 after six years with NASA at Huntsville, after graduating from the University of Alabama in 1959 with a bachelor's and a master's degree in physics.

"If you don't enjoy this part of the program, you don't belong in this business," he said, noting that 1992 would be marked by building and testing hardware, putting the design to bed once and for all, and doing "everything necessary to prepare for flight."[3]

Moving into hardware established more realism to the program. People recognized it was no longer just a paper study.

In August 1993, the dedicated effort on the space station was rewarded when NASA named Boeing as the prime contractor on the nation's $10.5 billion project. The visionary undertaking involved sixteen countries and was scheduled to be completed in 2005. Boeing had designated the program as a "must win" in the early eighties.

The Company, which beat out Grumman Aerospace Corp., McDonnell Douglas, and Rockwell International's Rocketdyne division to get the prime contract, also provided engineering and spare parts for a year after the launch of each package. The three losing companies became subcontractors to Boeing.

Boeing's efforts in space will not be totally revealed, for at any given time significant and large scale intelligence spacecraft of a top secret nature were being produced for the National Reconnaissance Office. For example, one satellite, launched in 1997, was valued at $750 million, equivalent to about six 777 airplanes.

A truly Paul Bunyan/Captain Nemo adventure was kicked off in August 1996, when the Sea Launch Company, a joint venture of Boeing, Norwegian, Russian, and Ukranian companies, broke ground at Long Beach, California, for a fifteen acre home port for sea-based satellite launching. The site was on a man-made peninsula formerly occupied by the U.S. Navy. After upgrading existing buildings, and improving a 1,100 by 60 foot pier for docking two space-launch vehicles, the facility was ready for its first launch.

The launch platform itself was a twenty story high, converted North Sea drilling platform called the Odyssey. Odyssey made the journey from a Russian shipyard, via the Suez Canal and across the Pacific Ocean to Long Beach, arriving there on October 4, 1998.

Boeing Commercial Space Company owned 40 percent of Sea Launch. Co-owners are Kvaerner a.s. of Norway, RSC Energia, of Russia, and NPO-Yuzhnoye of Ukraine.

In addition to the Odyssey, the project included the Sea Commander, a 660 foot, specially designed rocket assembly and mission control ship that carried up to 250 technicians.

Kvaerner was responsible for preparing the launch platform and constructing the command ship, which was built in Glasgow, Scotland.

The Ukranian-built rocket, *Zenit* was chosen to launch U.S. satellites

Sea Launch

The Zenith-3SL Rocket launching a dummy payload to the 23,000 mile Earth orbit to demonstrate the maturing of the Sea Launch system on March 27, 1999.

into an equatorial orbit. The graphite composite shroud for the payload was built by Boeing at its Seattle area facilities.

For each launch, the Odyssey makes a ten-day trip from Long Beach to the launch site, about 1,000 miles south of Hawaii. The site was picked because it is on the Equator, where the Earth's surface races eastward at better than 1,000 miles per hour. A rocket fired there needs less fuel to reach the 17,500 mph velocity necessary to establish a stable orbit. Less fuel means more payload, which translates to significantly less cost per pound to orbit.

Announced in August, 1996, and completed in December, was the acquisition of Rockwell International's space and defense business by Boeing.

The acquisition involved five Rockwell divisions, a service company, a "think tank," and a joint venture, forming a new wholly owned Boeing subsidiary. The deal involved about 21,000 employees, mostly in the Los Angeles area. The acquired Rockwell units had sales of $3.2 billion in fiscal 1995, compared with $5.6 billion for the Boeing Defense & Space Group.

Boeing paid for the acquisition by issuing $860 million of new Boeing common stock to Rockwell shareholders and assuming $2.16 billion of Rockwell debt. The acquired components of North American Rockwell were named simply Boeing North American.

Boeing gained Rockwell's work on the space shuttle and the international space station; and capabilities in launch systems, rocket engines, missiles, satellites, military airplanes, and guidance and navigation systems. The nerve center for space was transferred from Huntsville, Alabama to Seal Beach, California.

In announcing the acquisition, Phil Condit remarked, "The assets and capabilities we are acquiring are an extremely good strategic fit with our long term objective of creating shareholder value. This merger accelerates us on our way to achieving our twenty-year vision, which calls for Boeing to be a fully integrated aerospace Company, designing, producing, and supporting commercial airplanes, defense systems and defense and civil space systems."[4] Indeed, one had only to take a backward glance at the *Apollo* program to recognize that very powerful capabilities—previously in competition—had been brought together.

Rockwell had a long history in the aerospace community. Formed in 1928, as North American Aviation, an eastern seaboard holding company, they moved to Los Angeles California, seven years later. Headed by James "Dutch" Kindelberger and chief engineer Lee Atwood, they prospered during World War II, ascending to national prominence, building some of the world's most famous aircraft. The company produced more than 15,000 P-51 *Mustang* fighters and 10,000 B-25 *Mitchell* bombers.

In the Korean War, the company provided the F-86 *Sabrejet*—the country's first fully sweptwing aircraft which dominated enemy *MiG* fighters, and shortly thereafter the F-100 *Supersabre*, the first production airplane to fly supersonic in level flight.

In 1957, North American won the contract for Weapons Systems 110A—which evolved as the B-70. Although only two units were built and the program was canceled before the airplane flew, this heritage carried into the '80s, with the production of the B-1 bomber. One hundred of these supersonic bombers were built, with Boeing as a major subcontractor.

In 1961, North American's Space Systems Division won contracts to build the *Apollo* Command and Service Modules, and the second stage of the *Saturn V* rocket, as well as the Launch Escape System and the Lunar Module Adapter. Their Rocketdyne Division was selected to build the engines for all the *Saturn V* stages, including the Boeing-built first stage, which employed the most powerful rocket engines ever built.

In 1967, Rockwell Standard and North American Aviation merged to form North American Rockwell.

In the early seventies, the Space and Rocketdyne Divisions won contracts for the space shuttle orbiters as well as their main engines. With the loss of the *Challenger*, four shuttles remain: *Columbia, Discovery, Atlantis,* and *Endeavor.*

George Torres[5], Director of Communications for the Boeing Space Group, predicts that these refurbishable vehicles will easily reach their design goal of 100 missions—sufficient to complete the *Freedom* station—and still be flying beyond the year 2010.

North Americans' history also extends below the sea. In 1958, the *USS Nautilus*, guided by an Autonetics Division *Navigator*, made the first Arctic transpolar crossing under the ice cap.

In sum, the history of North American has been intertwined with that of Boeing for half a century.

On March 27, 1999 Boeing's *Sea Launch* was validated as an operational system, when a successful demonstration launch was completed from its floating platform in the Pacific Ocean, 1,400 miles south of Hawaii. Designed specifically to put up commercial communications satellites, the

Zenit-3SL rocket carried a dummy payload to the 23,000 mile orbit.

Then on October 9, 1999, the first live satellite was successfully launched. The telecommunications market is exploding—potentially a trillion-dollar business.

Sea Launch demonstrates the best attribute of the Company—constantly reaching for that elusive edge in technology.

1. *Annual Report*, The Boeing Company, 1973, 11.
2. *Boeing News*, 16 April, 1981, 1.
3. John Winch Interview, by E. E. Bauer, 2 December, 1998.
4. *Boeing News*, 2 August, 1996, 1.
5. George Torres interview by E. E. Bauer, 10 November, 1998.

Philip M. "Phil" Condit 1941–
President 1992–1997, Chairman 1997–

CHAPTER THIRTY-TWO

The Ultimate Challenge

With the announcement of the acquisition of the Rockwell aerospace and defense business less than five months old, Boeing took on not only its ultimate challenge, but also its ultimate opportunity.

On December 15, 1996, Boeing and McDonnell Douglas exploded a bombshell heard around the world, when they jointly announced that they had signed a definitive agreement to merge.

Boeing CEO Phil Condit's *Vision of Boeing in 2016*, first elucidated in a speech at the March 4, 1996 manager's meeting took a giant step forward.

In that speech, Condit outlined the Company's business path for the long term to become an integrated aerospace Company and a global enterprise. He laid out four fundamental principles:

F15 Air Superiority Fighter

The F-15 ruled the skys for more than two decades, and will be succeeded by the F-22 Raptor.

Integrity, Customer Satisfaction, Shareholder Value, and People Working Together.

Condit also identified the three core competencies which he believed to be essential to success:

Detailed Customer Knowledge and Focus, Large Scale Complex System Integration, and Lean, Efficient Design and Production Systems.[1]

Under terms of the merger, which became official on August 1, 1997, the cost to Boeing was an estimated $13.3 billion, with the awarding of 1.3 shares of Boeing stock for each share of McDonnell Douglas stock. From the time of the merger declaration and its finalization, the two companies continued to operate separately.

At the time of the merger with Boeing, two-thirds of McDonnell Douglas' revenues and nearly all of its earnings were from defense products, while defense spending was shrinking.

More than two decades prior to the merger of the McDonnell Aircraft Company and the Douglas Aircraft Company in 1967, McDonnell had begun the process of establishing itself as the predominant producers of fighter aircraft for both the Navy and the Air Force. On New Year's Eve in 1942, when jet powered aircraft was still in its infancy, a U.S. admiral placed a call to Mr. Mac in St. Louis.

"Would you like to build the first jet powered naval fighter," the admiral asked. "You bet!" was the instant reply.[2] The next day Mr. Mac, the CEO of the three-year old company, flew to Washington, D.C., and within a week a design proposal and a contract followed. The result was the sleek looking FH-1 (originally the FD-1) *Phantom*, which brought the aircraft carrier into the jet age. The *Phantom* was followed immediately after World War II by the F2H *Banshee*, the first jet fighter to be produced in quantity. The *Banshee* achieved fame in the Korean War, immortalized in James Michener's book *The Bridges at Toko-Ri*. The *Banshee* rang the million dollar bell for McDonnell Douglas aircraft and the F4 *Phantom II* rang the billion dollar bell. For two decades it played a central role in defending the peace. More than 5,000 *Phantoms* were produced. Then in 1972, McDonnell gained a big win with the F-15 *Eagle*, the newest air superiority fighter, and still the unmatched operational machine in the nineties.

In 1986, the Navy's Blue Angels, having flown McDonnell Douglas airplanes since switching from Grummans in 1968, took delivery of F/A-18s. In 1995, the F/A-18E/F *Super Hornet* strike fighter emerged from major modifications to the F/A-18 which first became operational in the late seventies.

But there was no resting on past laurels. Now the trend was more than cyclical. There weren't many big defense programs out there. Lockheed, with Boeing as a major partner, had won the contract for the next air superiority fighter, the F-22 *Raptor*, against McDonnell Douglas and Northrup. Worse still, the Defense Department had chosen Boeing and Lockheed Martin as finalists to compete for the Joint Strike Fighter—not McDonnell Douglas.

The commercial airplane market was robust and expanding, but McDonnell Douglas continued to lose market share to Boeing and Airbus Industrie.

John McDonnell, Chairman, needed to do something drastic—and fast. Surprising industry pundits who expected an internal promotion, he reached outside the company, hiring Harry Stonecipher from Sundstrand Corpo-

YF-18A Hornet Strike Fighter

The *Hornet* series is continuing as the F/A-18E/F, *Super Hornet*, the nation's newest fighter and attack aircraft, promising to be in production for many years.

JSF—Joint Strike Fighter

In competition with Lockheed-Martin, Boeing has a contract to build two concept demonstrator variants of the Joint Strike Fighter. Contract award is expected early in the 21st century.

ration in 1994, immediately naming him as Chief Executive Officer.

Stonecipher had earned a stellar reputation in the industry. Graduating from Tennessee Technological University with a degree in physics in 1956, he joined General Motors as a senior lab technician. In 1960 he moved to General Electric's engine operations as an evaluation engineer, worked up through the ranks, and was named vice president and general manager of the division's commercial and military transport operations in 1979. He headed the entire division from 1984 to 1987. Showing a flair for financial matters, Stonecipher served on the board of directors of General Electric's Financial Services.

In 1987, Stonecipher left General Electric to become corporate executive vice president of Sundstrand, and in a short time advanced to president and chief operating officer, and a member of the board. In 1989, he was named CEO and in 1991, chairman of the board.

During his career at McDonnell Douglas, Stonecipher was credited with turning around the C-17 *Globemaster III* airlifter program, which became a model procurement and won the 1994 Collier Trophy. Then in 1998, the program won the Malcolm Baldridge National Quality Award, the nation's highest honor for excellence in the workplace. The Air Force ordered 120 C-17s, 80 of which were part of one of the largest multi-year procurements in history. Boeing could also thank McDonnell Douglas for the *Delta* series of expendable launch vehicles, and in particular, Harry Stonecipher, who made the decision to go to *Delta III* while still the CEO. On the commercial side, McDonnell Douglas, under Stonecipher's leadership, launched the 100-seat MD-95 twinjet with ValuJet Airlines, after a hotly contested competition.

McDonnell Douglas financial performance soared under Stonecipher, with the stock increasing from $18.48 just prior to his arrival to more than $70 just before the consumation of the merger.

The last great hope for McDonnell Douglas to recoup market share, and challenge the 747's monopoly at the top of the market, was the proposed four engined, doubled decked, 600 passenger MD-12. In October, 1996, Stonecipher went to Long Beach for a summit meeting to decide whether to go ahead. He had to answer two questions—where is Douglas going with its commercial business, and what will it cost to get there?

The investment could easily reach $15 billion over the following decade,

C-17 *Globemaster III*
The Air Force's premium airlifter won the Collier Trophy in 1994 and the Malcolm Baldridge National Quality Award in 1998.

and the airlines had shown only mild interest. Douglas' president, Michael Sears, who earlier in the year had been sent out to Long Beach to take over the failing Douglas commercial operations, had been an ardent champion of the jumbo program.

Sears was a wunderkind with two degrees in electrical engineering from Purdue University and a master's degree in engineering management from the University of Missouri, who joined the St. Louis operations in avionics in 1969.

Now, he readily agreed that the risk was too great. "I would love to do this airplane," he told Stonecipher. "Our people would love to do this airplane. But fundamentally it is probably not the best thing for the shareholders of this company."[3]

That realization led Stonecipher to ask an even larger question—does McDonnell Douglas have a future in commercial airplanes?

At the end of the two-day meeting, he came to the sobering realization that the answer was no. Stonecipher reached a painful conclusion— McDonnell Douglas had no future. It was either buy or be bought.

He knew that Texas Instruments(TI) and General Motors were both anxious to sell their defense electronic operations. But from the beginning, Stonecipher felt that a merger with Boeing would be the best deal for the future.

There had been secret talks over the previous three years, all failing when it got down to price, but suddenly events began moving at jet speed.

Condit had called Stonecipher on Friday, December 6th. The Boeing board, he said would be meeting in a regular session on Monday. "We're going to have serious discussions about the possibility of doing something with McDonnell Douglas," Condit said.[4] Stonecipher reported that their board also had a meeting scheduled for the same day in St. Louis, where they would be discussing other possible deals.

Stonecipher offered to fly to Seattle and meet with Condit on Tuesday morning. They met in the private Boeing suite at the Four Seasons hotel in downtown Seattle. It was a cold, cloudy morning similar to that rainy day in April 1967 when the Douglas Aircraft Company merged with the McDonnell Aircraft Company.

Inside, the atmosphere was cozy, quiet, and pleasant. There were just the two of them; no lawyers, accountants or financial advisors. Though they were old friends, the meeting was tense, and as Stonecipher recalls, they were too fidgety to sit down, and instead circled each other "like a couple of cats."[4] They both knew a merger made sense. Condit posed the first question.

"Okay," he said "Where are you?"

"I have authority from my board to buy TI or bid on Hughes," Stonecipher said, referring to the defense divisions of Texas Instruments and General Motors—"or do this deal—and I want to do this deal."

"I have authority from my board to try to do this deal," Condit replied.[4]

It took them less than an hour to sketch out a rough agreement. Boeing would acquire McDonnell Douglas for $13.3 billion in Boeing stock. Condit would be Chairman and Chief Executive Officer, and Stonecipher would be President and Chief Operating Officer.

For the next two hours they explored the implications of the deal. By now they were acting like "giddy school kids," recalls Stonecipher. "We got ready to go," he recalls, and Phil said something like, 'Gosh, I guess we ought to shake hands,' So we did."[4]

From that handshake on December 10, 1996, until the deal was formalized, a Boeing transition team under Jerry King worked out the details. King was a Boeing veteran, having joined in 1958 after graduating from New Mexico State University with a bachelor's degree in mechanical engineering. While at Boeing, he completed advanced management programs and the University of Michigan's executive development program. After a number of assignments in command, control, and communication programs, as well as tactical and strategic missiles, he was appointed executive vice president of the Military Airplane Division. In 1993, he was named as Senior Vice President of the Company with the title of President of the Defense and Space Group. The Group comprised five divisions: Helicopters, Military Airplanes, Missiles & Space, Information & Electronic Systems, and Product Support, and also a number of subsidiaries, including Boeing North American.

King was transferred from his position as head of the Boeing Defense and Space Group to the Headquarters Offices, and Alan Mulally was named as his successor.

The Federal Trade Commission (FTC) gave unconditional approval to the merger on July 1, 1997, and on July 25th the stockholders were quick to add their approval, in separate meetings in Seattle and St. Louis.

In an emotional speech at McDonnell Douglas headquarters in St. Louis, John McDonnell—CEO, and son of Mr. Mac—somberly sounded out the words that submerged his beloved company.

"This is John McDonnell calling the McDonnell Douglas team for the last time. For me personally, today fulfills a goal I set for our company when I became chairman, to become the preeminent aerospace company of the world. At the same time, today is a day that is tinged with sadness. To achieve the goal of preeminence, we are giving up our independence to become part of a greater team. Also it is a time for me to personally say goodbye."[2]

It had been forty-three years since John McDonnell started in a summer job in his father's company.

For Airbus Industrie, the merger represented a major concern, and the European Commission (EC) took up the battle. Karel Van Miert, the European commissioner in charge of competition policy, indicated that the EC had "serious reservations" on whether the merger conformed to European rules. He furnished a statement of objections to Boeing and McDonnell Douglas, and noted a formal decision would be made by July 31, 1997.

Specifically, Van Miert criticized contracts in which Delta and American Airlines agreed to buy airplanes exclusively from Boeing for the next twenty years.

Near the end of July, after tough negotiations and compromises by both sides, the European Commission approved the merger, and it became official on August 1, 1997.

The year-end employment of 169,000 in 1995 had increased to 238,000 by year-end 1997, but was destined to be reduced dramatically. The Company was being called the "new" Boeing. The new Boeing had the shared vision of two unusually capable leaders. This new vision enhanced the original version that Condit introduced at the March, 1996 meeting, and Stonecipher, in remarks to *Boeing News*[5], agreed that the concept would help to unite the two companies.

"Right now, this is Phil's vision—as it should be. He's our leader. Ultimately though, it needs to become *our* vision. And by that I don't mean Phil's and mine. I mean it belongs to *all* people of the new Boeing Company.

"The sooner each one of us grabs on to it as our own, the better this Company and everyone associated will be."

Stonecipher recognized the difficulty of changing old mindsets, i.e. the decades-old references to McDonnell Douglas commercial airplanes as "Brand X."

"After a honeymoon period, I expect some people will revert to thinking in the 'us' versus 'them' ways that we did as competitors. I hope that doesn't run very deep or last very long.

"With your help, we can make this vision come alive," he said. "We can build a whole new Company and a common culture that takes us well beyond what we've been able to accomplish separately," he concluded.

Independent experts were quick to note the impact that the merger would have on the launch vehicle business.

"It begins to move them toward the same kind of preeminence in space transportation that they currently enjoy in civil aircraft and military aviation," said Wolfgang Demisch.[6]

Fortune magazine had called it "The Sale of the Century" in February 1997, and in October, created their first "World's Most Admired Companies" ratings, giving Boeing the number one spot in aerospace. Boeing had been number one in the U.S. every year for fifteen years—ever since *Fortune* began the rating.

The most spectacular evidence of change came at St. Louis, Missouri, where Mr. Mac had launched the McDonnell Aircraft Corporation sixty-one years before.

Commuters on Interstate 70 were startled to see a giant, electric-blue neon sign that had apppeared almost overnight on the front of the McDonnell Douglas main hangar, home of the F-15 *Eagles*, the F/A-18 *Hornets* and T-45 *Goshawks*. Gone was the old familiar red landmark McDonnell Douglas sign. The huge letters with the new logo spelling out the word BOEING, were in themselves twelve feet tall. The sign, thirty-three feet above the ground, was 145 feet wide, its 13,694 feet of neon tubes gobbling up 30,000 watts of power. It had been first illuminated in a brief ceremony on April 24, in time for the Annual Meeting of the Stockholders on the 26th. The meeting had never before been held outside of Seattle, Washington.

1. *Annual Report*, The Boeing Company, 1996, 4,5.
2. *Calling All The Team*, John McDonnell reporting to the Stock holders at the 25 July, 1997 Special Meeting.
3. *Fortune*, 17 February, 1997, 98.
4. Ibid., 92.
5. *Boeing News*, 1 August, 1997, 1.
6. *Aviation Week & Space Technology*, 23/30 December, 1996, 14.

Harry Stonecipher 1936–
President 1997–

CHAPTER THIRTY-THREE

Turbulent Skies

Now came the hard part—performing. Even though the transaction was a buyout of McDonnell Douglas by Boeing, both companies wanted desperately for the marriage to become a true merger—from the top all the way to the factory floor. Soon, a complaint, common in the Puget Sound area was, "Boeing bought McDonnell Douglas and now they have taken over." Many of the unhappy workers laid the blame on Harry Stonecipher for everything that went wrong, and the "Stonecipher problem" became widespread. It was not surprising because, as Chief Operating Officer, he had to make the unpopular decisions, and to leave CEO Phil Condit above the fray.

Boeing executives remembered well the 1967 merger of McDonnell and Douglas, which became no more than a knot at the top, and were determined not to see a repeat of that scenario.

On the other hand, the Rockwell International acquisition, creating Boeing North American, resulted in a smoother transition. Old animosities die hard, and the competition with Rockwell International had not been so fierce over the century as that with McDonnell Douglas.

For many diverse reasons—some said preoccupation of the top managers with the merger—earnings took a nosedive, and Boeing reported its first net loss in fifty years, recording $178 million in red ink in 1997.[1] Indeed, performance was so bad that Boeing was the "dog of the Dow" in 1998, with its stock falling more than 33 percent. It seemed that Boeing had lost sight of why it was in business.

The Company, claiming that failing to do a good job in management of the ambitious rampup in production of commercial airplanes was the main problem, promised to do better in 1998, pointing out that the backlog was the highest ever at $121.6 billion.

True, the new Boeing had embarked on a nearly impossible program aimed at more than doubling the number of airplanes coming off the production lines over a period of eighteen months. Many 737 airplanes were rolling out unfinished, sporting a blizzard of "pickup" tags. These "out-of-sequence" airplanes had to be finished on the flight line, incurring inordinate costs of moving people and parts out of the final assembly building.

The Company was forced to take drastic measures—shutting down both the 737 and 747 lines for a month to bring the work back into sequence—the first shutdown since the end of the B-29 program. Deliveries of 747s were delayed once again.

However, the cause of the problem was much more complex than simply the ramp-up decision. Between 1989 and 1995, employment had been reduced from 106,670 to 71,834 in Washington State, which included the 7,000 veteran employees who had taken early retirement in 1995—a wealth of experience that the Company could ill afford to lose in one grand swoop. Then, between 1995 and 1998, employment was increased by 28,000. Many of these new people required extensive training, further stretching the Company's thin line of expertise.

Further adding to the pressure was Boeing's decision in 1996 to focus on market share. With Woodard in the driver's seat, and financial discipline all but abandoned after the retirement of Harold Haynes, an unchecked drive to defeat Airbus Industrie escalated to the point where 737 airplanes were being sold at breakeven prices—in some cases even below cost. In 1997, fixed price contracts were negotiated with American, Continental, and Delta wherein Boeing would be the sole supplier for twenty years.

Woodard believed that the Company could overhaul its antiquated production and inventory control methods in time to recover profits by reducing manufacturing costs by 25 percent, while at the same time delivering a record number of airplanes. He hoped to bury Airbus in an avalanche of orders, predicting confidently, "Our goal is a 67% market share."[2]

On August 25, 1998, British Airways announced it would purchase Airbus Industrie narrow body airplanes in lieu of Next-Generation 737 *airplanes—a shocker for the industry—since the airline had been an exclusive Boeing customer.* By this time, top management at Boeing had recognized they were pursuing a bankrupt course and had decided to draw a line in the sand—refusing to continue the price war.

Wolfgang Demisch had prophesied earlier, that "Boeing will have to take a big hit, with a major carrier, to turn the price war around."[3]

Peter Jacobs of Ragen MacKenzie in Seattle, echoed the same sentiments when the deal was announced. "If Boeing lost the order to British Airways because of being less aggressive in its pricing, so be it. It's a good move. Boeing is starting to get smart," he said.[4]

The "old hands" were less than kind to Boeing management. At the spring banquet of the Gold Card Chapter of the Boeing Management Association (BMA) in 1998, the guest speaker was none other than Jim Dagnon, newly hired with the title of Senior Vice President, People. Dagnon had been active in leading the successful merger of Burlington Northern and Santa Fe railroads, and his experience as a leader in merging corporate cultures was felt to be invaluable. When Dagnon finished his speech, and invited questions, he was verbally attacked from all sides.

"What's all this crap about *people* organizations," one irate retiree wanted to know. "Why don't you just get down to the brass tacks of building airplanes?"

Another veteran leaped up. "What in hell is the matter down at Boeing? We never missed a delivery date in twenty years.[5]

Dagnon, somewhat taken aback by the intensity of the unexpected criticism, attempted to explain, but the audience didn't seem to be listening.

Contributing to the dismay of the old timers was the bewildering new titles for management people. In addition to "People," there was "Workforce Administration," Advertising and Corporate Identity," and Socioeconomic Executive," to name a few.

It even went beyond management. The age-old title of secretary was now "Office Administrator," in deference to the newly elevated philosophy of "personal esteem" as the most important virtue of the work force.

The venerable title of "Public Relations," disappeared when Harold Carr retired in 1997. Larry Bishop, who graduated from the University of Southern California and came to Boeing in 1992 as Vice President of Investor Relations, then took on the task of merging investor relations with the traditional public relations functions, under the new title of Communications and Investor Relations. This proved to be an enormous task, considering the acquisition process then in progress.

There was no simple way to explain to the retirees what was happening at the Company. They represented a radically different Boeing—strongly engineering oriented, where the guys with suits and ties made the decisions, and the people in the factory simply went out and got the job done—no questions asked. The Company was still in the process of reinventing itself to accommodate to the vast cultural shifts in the United States of the last several decades. This "new" Boeing was now being called upon to assimilate two companies, each with a corporate culture of its own.

In a later interview, Dagnon pointed out that Boeing now faced a much different marketplace.

"Just being a great engineering Company is no longer sufficient. Now we are a manufacturing Company facing the pressures from Airbus—a vigorous and competent competitor. Our priorities are how we control our cost, and how we control our inventory."[6]

Dagnon's assignment was to bring together the major elements necessary to achieve the cultural objectives first set forth in the Company's twenty-year vision. He was well prepared for his new assignment. Graduating with honors from the University of Minnesota with a bachelor of science in business, he devoted twenty-five years to managing human resources. He began as a union representative at Burlington Northern and worked up through the ranks to become senior vice president of employee relations. In this capacity he led the successful merger of the two railroads.

For Dagnon, the bottom line was to get the entire human resources of all three companies involved—with decision processes starting as much from the bottom as from the top.

Alan Mulally echoed those sentiments when he said, "We're not going to get there at all unless we get there together." His favorite expression to describe the reinvention goal in two words was "employee involvement."[7]

During the gangbusters sales of the late eighties, organizations began to expand vertically, and new layers appeared all through the Company. *Boeing News,* a bellwether of Company fortunes, showed the trend, when in October 1997, the page count jumped from sixteen to twenty, and occasionally twenty-four during 1998. Indeed, the January 19, 1998 issue revealed a complete overhaul of the newspaper. It was announced that more local news would be included, and more news about people. Thus, separate local editions were introduced for the employees in California, the Northwest States, the Rotorcraft oprations, St. Louis, and Wichita. The new look would include color on all pages. *Boeing News* had come a long way from the "lean and mean" days after the blood bath of 1969-1971. Perhaps it was time for another "ice-water guy."[8]

Paradoxically, in spite of promises to do better, Boeing's *Next-Generation* 737 program became the Company's most financially troubled, while gaining the most early sales of any project the Company had ever undertaken.

In the spring of 1998, Boeing announced it would write-off up to $350 million in the first quarter—related to production and certification delays, parts shortages, and late delivery penalties to customers. That came on top of a similar $700 million write-off against the *Next-Generation* 737 in 1997. Boeing had sold 866 *Next-Generation* 737s by the end of the first quarter, but according to Wall Street analysts, the Company stood to lose $1 billion on the first 400 airplanes.[9]

Boeing began cleaning up its operations. In June the Company announced the end of production of the MD-11 for February, 2000, completing orders on the books. The MD-80/90 programs had already been discontinued in the fall of 1997, with the last unit coming off the line in mid-1999.

Sales of the MD-95—which was destined to be the last "MD" model to go into production—after jetting off to an auspicious start with an AirTran (formerly Valujet) order for fifty, slowed to a trickle. To bolster its image, the MD-95 tag was dropped in favor of a venerable old 700 series number—the Model 717. The designation had been around since the beginning of the commercial jet age, first assigned to the tanker version of the 367-80 prototype, later named the KC-135 by the Air Force, and still

Model 717

The last of the McDonnell Douglas "MD" series, the MD-95, was renamed the Model 717 and became the smallest member of the Boeing family.

later offered to and turned down by United Airlines in favor of the Model 720 designation.

In May 1998, when Boeing revealed a plan to transfer some 737 work to the Douglas Long Beach plant, possibly opening a new final assembly line there, the Seattle local of the International Association of Machinists (IAM) strongly objected, even threatening to take the Company to court.

After intensive negotiations, the union agreed not to fight the Company's plans, in exchange for Boeing's promise to limit production there to five airplanes per month. This agreement was the final hurdle Boeing needed to clear, and the Company finalized plans to implement a production line at Long Beach in the fall.

As a starter, ten "out-of-sequence" 737s were flown to Long Beach to be completed and ready for delivery, thus taking some early pressure off the congested Renton production lines. A cadre of Douglas mechanics were trained by Boeing supervisors from Seattle to complete the installation of galleys, lavatories, and seats, and to finish up other interior work.

Nevertheless, with relentless Wall Street pressure for higher earnings, there seemed to be no doubt that some heads in the Commercial Airplane Group would roll.

Abruptly, on September 2, 1998, Ron Woodard, president of the Commercial Airplane Group, was asked to resign. His top team was swept out with him. In his place came Alan Mulally, only recently having taken charge of the Information, Space, and Defense Group.

The firing of Ron Woodard was made with strong reluctance by both Phil Condit and Harry Stonecipher, since the drive for market share had been fully endorsed by top management. The financial community had essentially demanded that somebody at a high level be thrown to the wolves.

As if to apologize for the firing, Boeing awarded Woodard a handsome separation package. He received $900,000 in cash, and a consulting fee of $19,000 a month through November 2000, or about $450,000. He also received $43,000 to pay taxes on stock options he had recently exercised before he was fired, and matching recent contributions he had made to local charities. The severance totalled about $1.35 million.[10]

Mulally's first action after taking over was to call Bill Johnson, president of the IAM local.

"I called him on my cell phone," he said proudly. When asked what they talked about, he was quick to point out the importance of the Company/IAM relationship.

"Hey, we're not going anywhere without the union. They represent 44,000 people. We need their hearts and minds."[7]

Mulally's candid response demonstrated a genuine effort to improve relations with the Company's largest union. The four-year contract was scheduled to expire on September 1, 1999, and both the union and Boeing management were determined to avoid a strike. Bill Johnson, a veteran Boeing employee who first joined the Company in 1965—painfully aware of the cyclical nature of airplane production—recognized that job security would be one of the strongest concerns of the union. Work outsourced to Chinese factories was a major issue in the 1995 strike. To demonstrate the importance of this practice, Boeing sponsored a joint trip to China in the fall of 1998 to understand first hand why this outsourcing was so important to Boeing sales in the world's largest commercial airplane market. Fifteen members of the union were on the team which visited all the aircraft factories in China.

Of course, there was a militant faction in the union led by David Clay, jig builder at the Everett plant, who was making unrealistic demands, and since Clay was posturing to unseat Johnson as union president, all the elements of confrontation would be on the table. A major hot button issue was medical costs.

Nevertheless—considering the consequences of a strike—both sides began conciliatory moves early in 1999, leading to contract negotiations in August. The negotiated result over the 737 Long Beach production controversy gave cause for optimism.

Following on the heels of the Woodard ouster, came the demise of Larry Clarkson, who headed Boeing Enterprises, a more or less diversification oriented entity. The organization was reduced drastically in scope and the remainder folded into the customer services unit, reporting to Mulally.

Phil Condit had been pointed in emphasizing the Company's key mission when he said, "We see tremendous opportunities in the future of flight. As a result, we are not interested in diversification."[11]

Further, it was announced that Harry Stonecipher would take over as acting financial officer, as Boyd Givan was forced out, retiring early on the first of September, 1998. In November, Deborah Hopkins was introduced as the new chief financial officer for Boeing, the highest ranked woman ever employed by the Company. She came with impeccable credentials, most recently vice president of General Motor's European operations.

Hopkins received a bachelor's degree in business from Walsh College and attended the Wharton School of Business.

Boeing Chairman Phil Condit praised Hopkins for her track record at General Motors, pointing out her leadership in adopting strategies for lean manufacturing processes pioneered by the Japanese.

Hopkins came at a base salary of $450,000 and a guaranteed performance incentive of $360,000 for 1999, which could be significantly higher, depending on business results, as well as a signing bonus of $750,000.[10]

Reorganization continued. The Company had been searching for a "high visibility" person in communications, and in December 1998, Larry Bishop, approaching 62, announced his early retirement. In February 1999, Boeing hired Judith Muhlberg, a twenty-two year veteran of the Ford Motor Company. She brought an impressive curricula vitae to the job, including two years in the White House during the Ford administration. A graduate from the University of Wyoming in communications, Muhlberg was a Fulbright scholar and holds a juris doctorate from the Detroit college of Law.

As Vice President, Communications, Muhlberg was given overall responsibility for the Company's public relations, executive and employee communications, and advertising. In September, the Company announced the appointment of two new vice presidents, reporting to Muhlberg: Anne Toulouse, as Vice President, Advertising and Corporate Identity, and Thomas J. "Tom" Downey as Vice President, Executive and Internal Communications—separating employee communications from the Company's external media and advertising efforts—which are expected to exert a greater global reach in concert with McCann Erickson, its new advertising agency.

Employees in the Seattle area were quick to note—with a tinge of trepidation—that both Toulouse and Downey came from the old McDonnell Douglas organizations. However, it appeared that the Company was responding to both youth and demonstrated leadership talent. Toulouse, after receiving her bachelors degree in science from Florida State University in 1980, and serving as a media specialist for the U.S. Air Force, joined McDonnell Douglas in 1989, and rose to Director of Communications at Huntington Beach. Tom Downey is a graduate of St. Louis University with a degree in English, joining McDonnell Douglas in 1986 as an associate writer on the communications staff. He took a one year leave in 1990 as a Brookings Institute Congressional Fellow. His latest assignment was general manager of Communications and Community Relations for the Military Aircraft and Missile Systems Group at St. Louis.

When Mulally revealed his new organization, it was clear that he would be tightening up. Eliminating several levels of management, he adopted a classic horizontal structure.

In the wake of the management shakeup of Boeing's Commercial Airplane Group, the Company began rethinking its plans to open a new 737 line in Long Beach, and notified factory workers there that startup was being postponed until early 1999—possibly in February.

Kedrick Legg, president of the United Aerospace Workers (UAW) Union at Douglas, toured the Boeing plants in the Seattle area, and was amazed at what he saw. "It was like stepping forward thirty years," he said. "All that new technology and high speed tooling...we have World War II tooling. That's why I always admired Boeing. They were willing to spend money and take chances."[12]

Indeed, the disparity in comparative modernization of airplane manu-facturing plants could be traced to one of Boeing's enduring policies. *The latest in manufacturing technology and equipment, including completely new facilities, had been a hallmark of the Boeing Company from its beginnings, promoted mightily by William M. Allen during his marathon twenty-three years as president.*

When Boeing executives visited the Long Beach plant, they were ap-palled to find how much work and investment would be required to bring it up to Boeing standards, and on December 11, 1998, Boeing announced that all final assembly work for the 737s would remain at Renton—be-cause of "excessive incremental costs for the Long Beach operation."[13]

Foreshadowing the possibility of still another setback to the Long Beach operations, in November 1998, Airbus Industrie revealed it had won a tentative order from International Lease Finance Corporation (ILFC) for as many as thirty A318s, the plane it would build to chal-lenge the Model 717.

Some industry observers were suggesting the 717 program should be abandoned. "It's safe to say there is room in the market for only one plane in this class, and with International Lease Finance Corporations's stamp of ap-proval, it's obvious the A318 is that airplane," said Richard Aboulafia, senior aviation analyst with Teal Group, a closely followed aerospace market research firm. "If I were Mulally, I'd say it's time to pack it in on the 717."[14]

Less than a month later, TWA announced an order for fifty of the new 717 twins with options for fifty more. But to confound both the optimists and the naysayers, TWA also ordered fifty A318 Airbuses, and became the launch customer for that airplane. From the TWA point of view it was an artful decision. With the 717 order, they received almost instant airplanes since it was already flying. On the other hand, they provided the impetus to kickoff the A318, for delivery in the fourth quarter of 2002. TWA could then go straight to the A318, canceling its 717 options.

It was clear that the 717/A318 battle was a long way from being won, and Boeing would need substantial further orders to break even. Never-theless, Mulally was very optimistic.

"The 717 will directly replace the DC-9," he said, "and there's a ton of them out there. Also, the A318 is a double-shrink of the A320 and carries a lot of excess structural weight around."[7]

***Delta II* Rocket**
The highly successful *Delta II* series launching a payload to synchronous orbit.

Boeing received favorable news regarding competitive financing with Airbus on overseas sales in February 1999, when the Export-Import (EX-IM) Bank of the united States announced its support of an arrangement called "Stretched Overall Amortization and Repayment Structure," or SOAR, which allows a carrier to stretch out its payments over a longer period of time, making it easier to finance the purchase of new airplanes. Such a financing structure had been in use for several years by the export credit agencies of the U.K., France, and Germany to support the sale of Airbus airplanes.

On the defense and space sides of the Company, business was proceeding in a more positive fashion.

Boeing was well into its three-year, $1.6 billion contract with the Department of Defense as the lead system integrator for the National Missile Defense (NMD) program, commonly referred to as the "Son of Star Wars." John Winch had been named to head the program. The contract called for leading the development and integration of a system to the point of decision-making for deployment.

On October 24, 1998, a Boeing *Delta II* launched NASA's *Deep Space 1* beyond the Earth-moon system. The mission was to test and validate an ion propulsion engine.

Then, on January 4, 1999, a *Delta II* rocket lifted a robot called the *Polar Lander* with two piggy-back microprobes on a mission to Mars. After an eleven-month journey, the lander will parachute gently to the surface of the red planet and start scooping up dirt in search of evidence of water.

The *Polar Lander* was a companion to the *Climate Orbiter*, a Martian weather satellite, already on its way on a previous *Delta* rocket. *Climate Orbiter* arrived near Mars on schedule in September, but failed to establish an orbit, and the $125 million spacecraft was lost.

On February 8, 1999, a Boeing *Delta II* launched *Stardust*, a spacecraft designed to make a seven-year, three billion mile journey into deep space to capture comet dust and bring it back to Earth in 2006.

At Long Beach, the C-17 was humming along in production and incorporating new advances in materials and structures technology, notably a large, single piece composite horizontal tail.

The new tail is 20 percent lighter and costs 50 percent less than the all-metal construction which it replaces.

The composite tail was an innovation brought to production fruition by the St. Louis based Phantom Works. Beginning at McDonnell Douglas at St. Louis as a laboratory for "black" military programs, Phantom Works was expanded in 1998 to become the "shared resource" for basic technology, manufacturing, prototyping, and laboratories across the Boeing Company, including commercial airplanes. The organization was Boeing's answer to the question of consolidating its internal research efforts along with many technology oriented contracts from the military and NASA which comprise about 75% of the funding. Now, the "black" military programs comprise only about one-third of the total. Phantom Works employs about 4,000 people, with 90% located at the major hubs in St. Louis, Seattle, and Southern California. A scattered, duplicative network of more than 600 general purpose laboratories are being streamlined and cut by one-fourth.

Early in 1999, the F/A-18E/F *Super Hornet* moved into a new addition on the south end of the main assembly building in St. Louis. The additional facilities will accommodate increasing production rates on the *Super Hornet* program.

Overall, the year of 1998 would not be easy to forget. Problems in production were not the only headaches faced by the Company. But happily, the year ended on an upbeat note. Boeing not only met, but exceeded its target and delivered 559 airplanes—and the bottom line showed a profit of $1.12 billion, primarily attributed to strong earnings in defense and space.

Nevertheless, it represented a discouraging 1.95 percent of sales. Boeing predicted an improvement for 1999, projecting a profit of 2.5 to 3 percent, and delivery in the range of 620 commercial airplanes.

In fact, financial performance for the first three quarters of 1999 exceeded analysts' expectations—and were significantly better than the Company's own predictions—promising full year operating margins in excess of 5 percent on total revenues of around $58 billion. Analysts were beginning to describe Boeing's 1999 performance as "robust."

Race discrimination, a national malady, always lurking close beneath a thin veneer of forced regulations, became focused in 1998, when dozens of lawsuits were filed against Boeing. The most visible case was on behalf of Jesse Jones, a black supervisor who claimed to have been passed over for promotion. The Jones case came to national attention in September when the Reverend Jesse Jackson, champion for black American's rights, visited the Company as the case came to trial in federal court in Seattle, Washington.

After hearing the testimony, a jury of four men and eight women found that Jones had not proven his allegations, and the case was closed.

However, there were still two class action lawsuits pending on behalf of black workers throughout the Company. The cases came to a conclusion on January 22, 1999, in an out-of-court settlement, with Boeing agreeing to pay $15 million. Under the terms of the settlement, approximately 20,000 current and former black Boeing employees would share in $7.3 million in payments, with about half of the money going to 264 individually identified plaintiffs. This, after the lawyers share of more than $4 million in fees and expenses.

In fact, Boeing—for most of the century—had pioneered in the cause of equal opportunity for minorities. During World War II, recruiters searched the South, signing up blacks to go to work in Seattle.

"In my view, that was real, hardcore affirmative action, when considered in light of the social mores of the North and South at the time," said Bertram Williams, on the occasion of his retirement in February, 1985.[15] Williams, who joined the Company in 1948—and was promoted to management eight years later—was one of the first two blacks to reach that level.

In a sea of whites, minorities will always stand out, and hardly any will say that they do not harbor a modicum of discrimination—it's a national disease. In the Jones case, had the complainant been a white male, he would most likely have been demoted or fired as a "malcontent"—never to be heard from again.

Throughout its history, Boeing has been an equal opportunity employer, making special efforts to attract qualified women and minorities. In one such program, Boeing is working with eight historically black colleges and universities to provide summer jobs and scholarships.

Since 1972, Boeing has maintained a program to provide minority-owned businesses with an equitable opportunity to compete for contracts. In 1990, for example, Boeing awarded more than $138 million in business to small minority-owned firms.

Further, Boeing is committed to being a corporate good neighbor, supporting a wide range of educational, human service, civic, and cultural programs. The total cash and in-kind contributions for the year of 1998 was

$94.7 million, to almost 400 organizations in twenty-seven States, including employee contributions to the Employee Community Fund (Renamed from the Boeing Employees Good Neighbor Fund—BEGNF)—largest employee-driven fund in the world.

Boeing News had felt the bite. On January 18, 1999, Boeing shifted most of its news to E-Mail—with a daily electronic news digest called *Boeing News Now* delivered to all employees with E-Mail accounts, and featuring three to five brief news items. The future printed versions of *Boeing News* were limited to twelve pages most weeks, with a less expensive paper stock and an ending to the regional inserts. The "ice-water guy"[8] had arrived.

Continuing to consolidate the merger with McDonnell Douglas, Boeing announced the sale of the commercial helicopter business it had inherited to be better able to focus on its more profitable military helicopters, and the Company completed the restructuring that had begun with the new acquisitions. Three major groups were created: Commercial Airplanes under Alan Mulally, Space and Communications under Jim Albaugh, and Military Airplanes and Missile Systems under Michael Sears.

Taking stock of the decade of the nineties, on the plus side, Boeing won the prime contract for the International Space Station, and completed the largest merger in the history of aerospace—bringing into the fold the best in fighters, military transport, and launch vehicles. In the commercial field, the Company maintained its preeminence in commercial airplanes, while bringing out a new line of 737s, and hatching an unbelievable bird—the 777 twinjet—first airplane to be completely designed with computers—without the use of drawings or mockups.

On the minus side, in August 1998, the first *Delta III* rocket went out of control—and to provide further concern, the second launch in May 1999 also failed. On September 2, 1998, Swissair flight 111—an MD-11—went down near Halifax, Nova Scotia, and on October 31, 1999, EgyptAir flight 990—a Boeing 767—crashed into the Atlantic near Nantucket, Massachusetts. Boeing reported its first net loss in fifty years; and announced that 28,000 employees would be laid off by the end of 1999. But for the ultimate disappointment, *Fortune* dropped Boeing from No. 1 as most admired aerospace company—the first time ever. The Company fell to No. 8 in the ranking, five steps below Lockheed-Martin.[16]

Meanwhile Airbus Industrie showed its teeth, improving its market share dramatically—and booking a profit—a result not only attributed to subsidies, but also to expert technology and dedicated determination.

On the international scene, the Asian markets stuttered, stumbled, and crashed. The Russian ruble went into free fall, and the "Asian flu" began to hit the stock markets around the world.

Even the robust U.S. economy was threatened, as the Dow dived 512 points on Monday, August 31, 1998.

On the optimistic side, the Dow reversed itself eight days later, and shot up 330 points, the largest single day rise in history. For the first time since 1966, the federal budget was balanced, even showing a $70 billion surplus—and Mark McGuire hit seventy home runs, shattering Roger Maris' thirty-seven-year-old record of sixty-one.

1. *Annual Report*, The Boeing Company, 1997, 72.
2. *Boeing News*, 19 January, 1996.
3. Private Communication.
4. *Seattle Post Intelligencer*, 25 August, 1998, 1.
5. Private Communication.
6. Jim Dagnon interview by E.E. Bauer, 25 January, 1999.
7. Alan Mulally interview by E.E. Bauer, 27, January, 1999.
8. T. Wilson was the "ice water guy" in the 1969-1971 layoffs.
9. *Aviation Week & Space Technology*, 20 April, 1998, 47.
10. *Seattle Post Intelligencer*, 9 March, 1999, C1.
11. *Annual Report*, The Boeing Company, 1997, 5.
12. *Seattle Post Intelligencer*, 10 June, 1998, A14.
13. Ibid., 12 December, 1998, A6.
14. Ibid., 18 November, 1998, D1.
15. *Boeing News*, 31 January, 1985, 3.
16. *Fortune Magazine*, 1 March, 1999, F-2.

CHAPTER THIRTY-FOUR

The Future

As the twentieth century drew to a close, its echoes were destined to be heard for centuries to come, and historians will view its accomplishments with awe and wonder.

On a growth curve beginning arithmetically with the Bronze Age, technology had entered its exponential phase.

It was the century during which man had finally broken the bonds of gravity that had held him to his native Earth—and freed him to dare the final frontier—the savage, black void of outer space.

Flying machines could rightfully share a prominent place among the leading developments of that magic century.

As the new millennium began, two giant companies were competing for the lion's share of the defense and space business in the United States. With the acquisition of Rockwell and McDonnell Douglas, Boeing had become the largest. Lockheed-Martin, the result of a previous merger, was second.

In some ways they were as much collaborators as competitors, considering their joint roles for the advanced F-22 fighter, and their joint venture in the United Space Alliance (USA), NASA's prime contractor for operating the space shuttle fleet, flying the spacecraft safely, supporting the flight manifest, and lowering processing and shuttle launch costs.

With Boeing in the role of prime contractor for the multibillion dollar international space station, *Freedom*, and Lockheed with the ten-year, $3.44 billion prime contract to run NASA's space operations, the two companies will be working closely together.

When a Russian *Proton* booster rocket lifted off from a launch pad in Kazakstan on November 20, 1998, it was carrying *Zarya*, the 44,000 pound power and propulsion module—the first part of the new international space station—into orbit.

Fifteen days later, on December 4, the United States space shuttle *Endeavor* blasted off a launch pad at Cape Canaveral, Florida, lifting *Unity*— a 25,000 pound connecting node—to be joined to *Zarya*. Measuring eighteen feet long and fifteen feet in diameter, *Unity* was built by a Boeing team in Huntsville, Alabama.

The six astronauts, and one cosmonaut, who had ridden up on the *Endeavor* shuttle, made three space walks to join the two modules.

NASA estimates that forty-three more launches and 159 more spacewalks will be needed to complete the entire complex, which will have a mass of one million pounds, be longer than a football field, house up to seven astronauts and cosmonauts—and not be completed until 2005.

The fourteen year-old station project had been rocked by billions of dollars of overruns, delays, redesigns, and attempts by the U.S. Congress to kill it.

But on December 11, 1998, when the crew entered the joined assembly for the first time and switched on the lights, that event marked the point of no return. An unwritten and unspoken symbolic message was sent to Earth, *there would be no turning back.*

On schedule, in the early morning of May 27, 1999, just as the sun broke over the eastern horizon, the next mission—on *Discovery*—made a flawless liftoff from Cape Canaveral to deliver 5,000 pounds of supplies for future crews, and a Russian-build cargo crane called *Strela*. The crane will be used for construction of the remaining units of the space station. *Discovery* also deployed *Starshine*, a student satellite that will provide educational observations for students around the globe.

The General Accounting Office, the independent watchdog agency of the Congress of the United States, has estimated that it will have cost the nation nearly $100 billion, including $25 billion in operating costs, by the time the station nears the end of its projected 10-year life. Thus NASA's major program for the next fifteen years will be managed by Boeing.

After many years of *ad hoc* planning, NASA, in 1998, celebrating its 40th anniversary, finally introduced a strategic plan for the nation's space programs, revealing a road map for extending man's reach throughout the universe—with clear goals and milestones. Although the space station will continue to occupy center stage, NASA has additional ambitious goals.

The plan builds on NASA's four decades of innovative research, and an unending quest to push back the frontiers of space flight. Heading into the new millennium, the agency has embarked on a three-part mission of (1) scientific research, (2) investigating the solar system and beyond, and (3) technology development and transfer.

The strategic plan, put in place in 1998, spells out the 21st century agenda. The agency's goals have been grouped into three time frames covering a period of twenty-five years, each with a unifying theme. The initial time frame stretches from 1998 to 2002; midterm goals are for the 2003–2009 period; long term goals are within the 2010-2023 time period.

Daniel Goldin, NASA Administrator, announced four basic themes: the Sun–Earth connection, exploration of the solar system, the structure and evolution of the universe, and the astronomical search for origins.

The *Pathfinder*, which dispatched the *Sojourner* to Mars in 1997 on a *Delta II* rocket, was the forerunner of future extensive robotic investigation of the Red Planet. The first "return-sample" mission to Mars is slated for 2008.

According to Goldin, "When we know there's science to be gained and when we can do it for an acceptable cost, we are going to one day crunch our boots on the dusty surface of the Red Planet."[1]

Currently, the *Galileo* spacecraft, launched from the shuttle *Atlantis*, is on a low cost, extended mission around Jupiter and its numerous moons.

The *Explorer* and *Discovery* missions—such as the *Stardust* mission, which is expected to return a sample of comet dust to Earth in 2006—will add to the bounty of scientific discovery. Similarly, between 2002–08 the *Comet Nucleus Tour* will image and spectrally map a trio of very different comets.

Orbiting observatories like the *Hubbell Space Telescope* have taken stunning images of the surrounding cosmos. Joining *Hubbell*—launched on the shuttle *Columbia* on July 23, 1999—was *Chandra*, the *Advanced X-ray Astrophysics Facility (AXAF)*, which will obtain X-ray images of neutron stars, black hole candidates, quasars, and active galaxies. After *AXAF*, will come the *Space Infrared Telescope Facility (SIRTF)*, scheduled for liftoff in 2001–02. *SIRTF* is expected to yield up to ten times the sensitivity of previous infrared observatories.

Boeing, through both hundreds of technology contracts ranging from a few hundred thousand dollars each, to dozens of multi-million dollar contracts, has been a major force for NASA's push into aeronautical and space frontiers. This close association is expected to continue, particularly for launch vehicles.

The *Delta* series, the first commercially financed launch vehicle program in history, should have a bright future. Disappointed, but not diverted by the failure of the first *Delta III* rocket in August 1998, Boeing forged ahead with the program, but in May 1999, the second rocket failed—not only a major setback for Boeing, but a blow to the U.S. efforts to recapture a larger share of the global launch services market. Nevertheless, with a backlog of seventeen launches by 2002, there was no proper course of action except to forge ahead. The *Delta II*, a smaller rocket—which had been highly successful—had thirty-six launches on the books through 2001, and the really big lumber was scheduled for *Delta IV*.

Delta IV will be configured in light, medium, and heavy sizes. All will have the same liquid oxygen-liquid hydrogen first stage, which forms the foundation of the *Delta-IV* series. In the medium size version, the first stage is helped along by small solid fuel rockets. In the heavy version, three first stage cylinders are strapped together. The medium version can lift 9,200 pounds into stationary orbit, while the heavy version can bring up 29,000 pounds.

The Air Force is also a major customer for *Delta IV*, with nineteen launches planned from 2002 through 2006 under a $1.38 billion contract, awarded in October 1998.

Delta IV is Boeing's main bet to acquire a larger share of the world's communications satellite business. In 1999, U.S. companies had about 30 percent of the market, with the remainder divided between Russia and China.

At Decatur, Alabama, near Huntsville, Boeing has invested $450 million in a 1.5 million square foot integrated factory building, sized to turn out forty *Delta IVs* a year. The plant is scheduled to be completed on January 4, 2000, with launch of the first operational rocket in April, 2001.

Jim Albaugh, President of Boeing's Space & Communications Group, predicts great things for *Delta IV*. "It promises to lower the cost of access to space by 50 percent and will become a very profitable program.²"

With the success of *Sea Launch* on October 9, 1999, Boeing consolidated its position in the launch business. This platform in the middle of the ocean is really a commercial spaceport. Boeing will have the advantage of not having to wait in line to launch commercial payloads because of backups at the limited number of ground launch sites around the world. The potential lower costs of *Sea Launch* bodes well for a large market.

Boeing is well positioned to produce fighter airplanes for the Air Force, Navy and Marines at its St. Louis facility. Production is continuing for variations of the F/A-18 *Hornet*, including a *Super Hornet*, however when Greece and Israel chose the Lockheed F-16 over the Boeing F-15, it signaled the end of that program early in 2000. In production since the 1970s, over 1,500 F-15s were built and it ruled the skies for two decades. In terms of manpower, the phase-out was huge—Boeing announced 7,000 layoffs for St. Louis. The early phaseout also impacted long lead time subcontracts, resulting in a $225 million third quarter 1999 pretax charge against earnings. Over the longer term, the *Super Hornet* promises to fill the production gap. The airplane has the Navy's highest acquisition priority, hoping for 548 of the jets at an estimated cost of $46 billion. In October, 1999, a giant step toward that goal was realized when Congress authorized multi-year procurement for 222 of the new jets at an estimated cost of $9 billion.

Also at St. Louis, a major remanufacturing effort is in place for the British AV-8 *Harrier*, and the T-45A *Goshawk*—a key component of the T-45 Training System for the Navy—is still in production. The Lockheed-Martin/ Boeing F-22 *Raptor*, in the engineering and development phase, will replace the F-15 as the next air superiority fighter.

In November 1996, Boeing was awarded a $660 million contract by the Department of Defense to build and flight test two variants of the Joint Strike Fighter (JSF). A single contractor is scheduled to be chosen between Boeing and Lockheed-Martin early in the 21st century to build as many as 3,000 machines.

Potentially adding a large increment to the Company's flying machine family is the new helicopter program, the *Comanche*—a Boeing-Sikorsky design—the U.S. Army's choice for a 21st century, armed reconnaissance helicopter. Also in the helicopter field are two modernization programs; the AH-64D *Apache*, an advanced version of the battle proven AH-64A, for which Boeing has a multi-year contract to remanufacture 232 AH64As into AH64Ds—and the CH-74D fleet of *Chinooks*. This latter modification program is a multibillion dollar commitment covering at least 300 machines and extending to 2013.

After logging more than 1,250 flight hours, the V-22 *Osprey* tilt-rotor craft reached the production stage, when the first low rate production unit flew at the Bell plant in Arlington, Texas, on April 30, 1999. Four units were delivered to the Marine Corps in 1999, and operational evaluations began in October. Boeing/Bell has a contract for 360 units with the Marine Corps. The V-22 is well suited for Army use, and although they backed out of an original program to deliver 231 aircraft, interest continues, and depending upon Marine Corps evaluations, the Army remains as a strong potential for new orders.

In the military transport field, Boeing continues to build the C-17 *Globemaster III,* the most advanced, versatile airlifter ever made—which has become the Air Force's premier transport—contracting for a total of 120 machines through the year 2004. In the fall of 1999, Congress gave the green light to begin negotiations for a multi-year procurement of an additional sixty aircraft. Boeing would be required to reduce the cost to the Air Force by about 25%.

The appealing dream of being whisked across the Pacific in four hours in a supersonic transport seems to be far in the future, unless there is a sudden interest by the U.S. government to subsidize it, an unlikely scenario. Boeing put most of its effort on the shelf in 1998. The technology is in hand, however the economics is far from being competitive. Currently, a production airplane is not expected before 2020.

Now that humanity has become irrevocably wedded to the jet airplane, the preponderance of future business for Boeing in both numbers and revenue will be conventional subsonic jets. The battle between the Airbus A320 and the *Next-Generation 737s* will become even more intense.

The strength of the A320 is showing up in the Asian market as well as in the increasingly important Latin American market. As the 20th century closes, Latin American airlines are facing a host of challenges, as it is now the only region of the world besides the U.S. with no government owned airlines. They have all been privatized after having been subsidized for decades by the public sector. Airports in the region are also being privatized.

It is perhaps prophetic to note that ACES of Colombia, Aeropostal of Venezuela, LanChile, Mexicana, and the TACA Group of El Salvador—most of which began with Boeing products—all have A320 airplanes on order. Of these, the trend in the TACA Group is most significant. In 1976, TACA purchased their first 737-200, sold their BAC-111s and went all-Boeing. In subsequent years they assimilated most of the airlines of the small countries of Central America, building their fleet to twenty-nine 737s and two 767s, and adding six A320s. In 1998, TACA joined LanChile and TAM of Brazil in ordering 90 A319 and A320 airplanes—to be delivered in the following five years—with options to purchase an additional 80 aircraft.

In 1999, the People's Republic of China was mired in overcapacity. Indeed in February, the CAAC imposed a moratorium on commercial aircraft purchases until 2002 and instructed manufacturers to postpone an unspecified number of planes ordered for delivery in 2000 and 2001. The downturn may last longer as a result of the May 8, 1999, bombing of the Chinese Embassy in Yugoslavia. However, in spite of all the negatives, the next wave of demand will be even stronger than previously.

Airbus had 64 airplanes in China's fleet of 477 airplanes in 1999, a miniscule 13 percent share, however the consortium has established China as a high priority target. For example in May 1999, it was reported that Airbus had offered to buy some of Air China's excess capacity in exchange for the future purchase of A318s.[3]

The total world market for jet airplanes is substantial—estimated to require 20,150 new transports by 2018—worth $1.38 trillion.[4]

Overall, Boeing has its destiny in its own hands. With both competitors off to a slow start in 1999—at the Paris Air Show, Boeing announced 139 orders and Airbus 233—the real story lies in production. In 1998, Boeing delivered 550 airplanes, while Airbus delivered 229. In 1999, Boeing will deliver a near record 620 airplanes. (The record is 681—the pre-merger production of both companies in 1968.) Although Airbus had almost as many orders as Boeing in 1998, and appeared to be ahead in 1999, it was far behind in production capacity. Further, Airbus will face major hurdles as it moves toward privatization. On the other hand, privatization may prove to be exactly what Airbus Industrie needs.

As Harry Stonecipher points out, "When they offer an IPO [initial public offering] on the market—in view of their proven success in building and selling airplanes—they should be able to attract enormous amounts of capital."[5] A privatized Airbus could easily be more competitive than the current organization.

On October 14th, 1999, Daimler Chrysler AG, of Germany, and Aerospatiale Matra SA, of France, announced they were merging—viewed as a first step toward privatization of Airbus Industrie.

As the industry continues to fragment and differentiate, with an increasing demand for point-to-point service, capacity and range of subsonic jets will be more closely tailored to the market. Thus, the strongest attribute for success is a large and complete family of airplanes. Boeing is significantly ahead of Airbus in this regard, and is able to offer a specific airplane for every twenty to thirty seat increment.

Indeed, the June, 1999, Paris Air Show provided proof that there is a lot of life left in the *Next-Generation 737* family, when International Lease Finance Corporation ordered fifty airplanes and took options on fifty more. Total deliveries of 737s of all models passed the 3,000 mark in 1998, whereas the A320 did not reach the 1,000 milestone until early 1999.

Nevertheless, considering its much later start, the A320 has proven to be a tough competitor, and it is quite conceivable—indeed probable—that Airbus will be able to maintain a 50 percent share in the medium range market.

Airbus Industrie is on record with an intention to introduce the A3XX—a 550 passenger machine—in 2004. However, the economic equation militates against it. It is doubtful whether the European governments will subsidize such a venture—estimated to cost $15 billion.

Alan Mulally sees a very small market for this airplane.

"We should be able to match Airbus' capacity by improvements in the 747 family—at only a fraction of the cost,"[6] he states flatly.

Boeing has been studying larger versions of the 747 for many years, as a -400X. Early in 1999, the Company seemed to have reduced the possibilities; a forty-eight foot stretch with a larger wing, which would seat 100 more passengers than the dash 400 and have a 500 nautical mile greater range, or a more ambitious design featuring a single deck with three aisles in a 2-4-4-2, twelve abreast cabin, seating up to 550 passengers in a three class configuration.

The real battle will be to reduce the cost of new machines, as refurbishment of older aircraft becomes a stronger economic option.

The *twenty-two inch decision* for the 777 will prove to be Boeing's ace in assuring the airplane a predominant market in the jumbo twin category for the next twenty-five years due to its unmatched—and unmatchable—seat-mile costs, as increased demand continues to fill the seats. With 451 announced orders at the end of 1998, the 777 should soon reach the golden status of *cash cow*. It also seems certain that increased range versions of the 777-200 and -300 are not far in the future, with Boeing having already chosen General Electric for its 115,000 pound thrust engine, in a spirited competition.

With the 777 crossing the line to profitability, Boeing has never had an unprofitable commercial airplane program in its entire history. The closest the Company came to the precipice was the *Stratocruiser*—requiring ten years of spares sales to bring the program into the black.

History has yet to reveal whether the Model 717 can continue this record. When British Airways announced on October 11, 1999, that they were purchasing the A318 instead of the 717, a big question mark overshadowed the program. After more than four years since its inception, the 100-seat twin—a renamed MD-95—still seemed to be an orphan. With firm orders stuck at 115, and yet to get the nod from a top tier airline, it lacks that all-important attribute, commonality. To make matters worse, on October 24, 1999, the Chinese shocked Boeing—ignoring their own declared moratorium—by ordering Airbus planes, including ten A318s.

In spite of these setbacks, Boeing still has high hopes for the 717 in China. Indeed, the Company is expected to escalate its offer of offset business in exchange for a large order. It seems conceivable that even the 717 wing is a candidate for manufacture at the Xian or Shanghai aircraft factories, and a coproduction of complete airframes is not out of the question.

It appears probable that some version of the UnDucted Fan (UDF)—postponed by both Boeing and McDonnell Douglas in the eighties—will return to center stage. Another oil crisis—a future economic certainty, with only the date in question—will trigger Boeing to bring an advanced version of its UDF out of the mothballs.

With the focus on reducing the cost of production, it may very well be that a severely standardized machine will be required to reduce costs to an acceptable level. Customerization has reached an extreme, with manufacturers offering everything the airlines asked for. For the 737 alone there are 280 operators, each with a customized airplane. With so many airplanes in service and in the market, ownership of individual machines is becoming more fluid, militating toward more standardization.

Indeed, the airlines have already begun to address this situation, beginning to study what is called a "no frills" transport. One improvement, for example, could be certifying one engine per aircraft design. The 777X/G.E. decision was a step in that direction. A little farther out is the notion that Boeing and Airbus would only build the airframes, allowing specialized interior and seat outfitters to finish the rest.

Boeing has put major resources into this opportunity with the implementation of its new computerized system for configuring and manufacturing airplanes—DCAC/MRM. Although the ambitious program is behind schedule, Company officials continue to be bullish. "Our next big move will be putting everything in modules," Alan Mulally said recently. "First, the interiors, and then the flight decks,"[6] he continued.

An area of rapid expansion will be the air cargo market. With an increasing number of high capacity airplanes becoming available for conversion to freighters, lower value commodities will become candidates for air transport. The cargo market is forecast to grow about 8.2 percent annually as compared to passenger traffic growth of 4.9 percent. The August 11, 1999, order by China Airlines of Taiwan for thirteen 747 freighters was a strong validation of the cargo forecast. The 747—initially designed as a freighter—will be the prime cargo carrier in the future, as growth versions of the 777 take over much of its passenger market.

In February, 1999, Boeing announced the creation of Boeing Airplane Services, a new business entity dedicated to airplane modification and engineering services, a growing, profitable market. For example, it is predicted that more than 1,500 passenger airplanes will be converted to freighters during the next twenty years. Further, many older passenger airplanes will be modernized.

Rapid delivery of spare parts and field service support of the airlines—*ceteris paribus*—will increase in importance in sales decisions. Boeing had 124 men in the field in 1978, and 324 in 1999. Current practice for spare parts is to notify the customer of the shipping schedule within four hours of the request, and in case of AOG (Airplane On Ground) orders, parts are shipped within two hours. All regular spares are shipped within twenty-four hours.

The most worrisome problem for Boeing as the end of the 20th century approached, was its increasingly critical labor relationships. With most of the many contracts up for renewal in 1999, both sides were working hard, with cautious optimism. In May, a contract was signed—admittedly small—affecting only some 3,500 employees. However, the spirit of the negotiations led Bill Johnson, president of the IAM to hearald it as a "landmark agreement." Then in August, the UAW (United Aerospace Workers)—representing 3,200 employees—reached agreement with Boeing North American on a four-year contract. "This is in keeping with the Company's record of negotiating as many as thirty-five bargaining agreements successfully in the last twenty-four months," said Boeing spokesman Peter Conte.[7]

Talks had been continuing with the IAM since the beginning of June, and hard bargaining for a new contract with the 44,000 machinists began in the last two weeks of August. An aura of optimism prevailed. But by the middle of the second week the climate had changed, as minor items were resolved and the hard issues of pay and benefits came to the table. The existing four-year contract was due to expire on September 1, and the membership had already voted to authorize a strike in the event that a Boeing offer was rejected.

On Friday August 27, 1999, the last day of scheduled negotiations—with a midnight deadline looming—the two sides were still far apart. With the prospect of failure very real, Johnson and chief union negotiator Dick Schneider asked to meet secretly with Phil Condit, Boeing CEO. By 8:00 PM the two sides had reached agreement on most of Boeing's wage and benefits package, but still had to tackle the toughest issue—job security—which seemed to defy resolution.

At the eleventh hour, Bill Johnson met with reporters at the SeaTac Doubletree Inn, where the two sides were negotiating. Weary and frustrated, he had almost given up hope. "At this point I'd predict that on September 2, we would not be building airplanes, but it's not over," he said.[8]

Indeed, both sides were preparing for a strike, with the union collecting wood for barrel burns and the Company painting "no cross" stripes at the plant entrances.

At 12:15 AM, union negotiator Dick Schneider stuck his head in the door of one of the rooms and said the union team was heading to the main table to reject Boeing's "best and final" contract offer, hinting that a strike was imminent.

The final sticking point was job security. The union wanted a guaranteed floor in number of employees, an impossible position for any company.

Phil Condit, remaining optimistic throughout, and determined to avoid a strike, decided it was time to play his last card. Interceding directly, he proposed new words for the sticky issue of job security. The question was what happens to an employee who loses his or her job due to subcontracting? The answer that Boeing provided in the new language was simply that Boeing would agree to retain and retrain that person for a different job. Of course, that would not be the case in the event of dwindling business, or in the case of offsets.

At 1:15 AM, the union signaled that the language was acceptable. Bill Johnson called the agreement a miracle.

With 4, 4, and 3 percent raises over the three-year contract, a ratification bonus of 10 percent of the average worker's yearly salary, a 25 percent increase in monthly pension benefits, and no layoffs due to subcontracting, the union had won handsomely. Additionally, the Company withdrew its demands for employees to share in medical costs, and its proposal for a flexible work week.

The new contract was promptly ratified, with 86 percent voting yes. Boeing workers now stood at the top in the aerospace industry for wages and benefits.

Having seen the handwriting on the wall, Phil Condit had put his personal stamp on the negotiations. The contract won in 1995 had established a more aggressive attitude in the minds of the union members. By rejecting both the first and second of Boeing's offers in that long and bitter strike, the rank and file had rediscovered their power, and would have no hesitation to strike again. Phil Condit was certain of this, and he knew the Company could not afford a strike. There was nothing to be gained by offering less than the maximum the Company could afford—but much to be lost.

True to his management philosophy, perhaps best described as *compassionate pragmatism,* Condit said he believed the pact benefitted both sides. "This is about the future, about going forward, about making Boeing competitive in the world markets," he said. "I believe that by working together with the union, we have a much higher probability of success than working against each other. That's what this agreement is all about," he continued.[9]

The union had reason to be jubilant, however there was no room for complacency or business as usual. There is no free lunch, and it would be incumbent on everyone—working together—to increase productivity. Otherwise, Boeing products would become more costly—and less competitive with Airbus—in the long run a loss for the union.

At least, the stage was set for the opportunity for improved union-Company relations, higher morale, greater worker satisfaction, and increased productivity. Once again, a feeling of peace settled in over the Puget Sound area.

In September, as part of its continuing efforts to improve efficiency and competitiveness, Boeing announced that Phantom Works, its premier research organization, would move its headquarters from St. Louis to Seattle. Executive vice president David Swain was promoted to president, reporting directly to Phil Condit rather than to senior vice president Michael Sears.

Swain joined the McDonnell Aircraft Corporation in 1964 on the Gemini project, after graduating from Purdue University in aeronautical engineering. Surviving two mergers, Swain left an impressive imprint, and as senior vice president and program manager for the C-17, received the Laurel Award from *Aviation Week* for its successful first flight. In his new assignment, he will also be the senior vice president of engineering and technology for the Company.

This reorganization underscores the determinaion of Phil Condit to move the cutting edge of technology to the factory floor in the shortest possible time.

In October, 1999, Boeing announced a major overhaul in its customer financing department. Abandoning its role as "lender of last resort," the Company will henceforth offer its customers "full service financing," taking a significant stride in competing with Airbus Industrie.

It is impossible to visualize most of the new developments that will transpire during the 21st century.

Who would have predicted in 1900—the year when the zeppelin made its first flight near Friedrichshafen—that *heavier-than-air* machines would become one of the principal means of world transportation and commerce before the century was out?

Or, that man would have set foot on the moon and returned safely to Earth?

Or, that manned journeys to near space would have become commonplace, and unmanned satellites would escape our solar system?

No one, before or since, has encapsulated Boeing's philosophy better than Frank Shrontz, when he addressed all employees back in September, 1989:

"The key to the future," he said, *"also lies in our past. Throughout our Company's history, we have achieved success by designing and building quality products with quality service. Our plan for the future is to build on those traditional principles, not replace them."*[10]

It is much too soon for history to judge the Condit years for he will not reach retirement age until 2006. However, his *"Vision for 2016"* has been established—the Company has stopped its dive and has started its climb—and if the past is any indication of the future, one can expect Boeing to achieve it.

The number of deliveries of commercial airplanes is predicted to drop to 490 in the year 2000, fueling a continuing downsizing from the 1997 high of 238,000 employees to about 200,000 at the end of 1999, and a further drop to about 185,000 by the end of 2000, resulting in a much leaner—but more efficient producer. According to Stonecipher, the major growth area will be in space.[5]

Whether the traditional "family culture" of Boeing—where seniority has been more important than performance—will survive, or whether Harry Stonecipher's performance oriented "team culture" will prevail remains to be seen. Indeed, Boeing has an active executive task force seeking to define a culture for the newly merged companies.

Stonecipher will reach retirement age in May, 2001. Boeing has a stable of extremely competent executives prepared to succeed him, including for the first time, a woman—Deborah Hopkins—but Alan Mulally appears to be in line for the presidency. With Mulally, performance will win the battle of cultures. However, he has that rare ability to make people feel comfortable even while swallowing bitter medicine. Following this scenario, Mulally can achieve the post of CEO in 2006, at age 61.

But, in order to reach the goal of Condit's "*Vision for 2016*", the "*Working Together*" philosophy that was born on the 777 program must endure and permeate the entire corporation—*from the factory floor to the highest executive.*

Harking back to December 1986, we are reminded of Mal Stamper's words, when he said, "To succeed, we must out-think our competitors, as well as out-perform them, and out-work them." [11]

A worthy goal, which will call to the heart of every employee, present and future—for dedication, determination and persistence—is to be chosen as the most admired corporation in the United States by its 100th anniversary.

Why not?

1. *Aviation Week & Space Technology,* 28 September, 1998, S3- S20.
2. Jim Albaugh interview by E. E. Bauer, April 27, 1999.
3. Private communication.
4. *Aviation Week & Space Technology,* 21 June, 1999, 40.
5. Harry Stonecipher interview by E. E. Bauer, June 30, 1999.
6. Alan Mulally interview by E. E. Bauer, January 27, 1999.
7. *Seattle Post Intelliggencer,* 22 June, 1999.
8. Ibid., 28 August, 1999.
9. Ibid., 29 August, 1999.
10. Frank Shrontz interview by E. E. Bauer, December 9, 1998.
11. *Boeing News,* Eagle Progress Report, December, 1986.

Earthrise

This historic photograph, taken on August 23, 1966, by *Lunar Orbiter 1*, shows the Earth rising above the moon's cratered surface.

BIBLIOGRAPHY

BOOKS

Allen, S.A. *Revolution in the Sky*. Brattleboro, VT: The Stephen Greene Press, 1964.

Bauer, Eugene E. *China Takes Off*. Seattle: University of Washington Press, 1986.

————. *Boeing in Peace and War*. Enumclaw, WA: TABA Publishing Inc., 1991.

————. *Contrails—A Boeing Salesman Reminisces*. Enumclaw, WA: TABA Publishing Inc., 1996.

Birtles, Philip. *Modern Civil Aircraft, 757/767*. Runnymede, England: Ian Allan Ltd., 1987.

Boulton, David. *The Grease Machine*. New York: Harper and Row, 1978.

Brokaw, Tom. *The Greatest Generation*. New York: Random House, 1998.

Bureau of Aeronautics. *Aircraft Recognition Manual*. Washington, D.C.: Departments of the Army, the Navy and the Air Force, 1959.

Butterfield, Fox. *Chine—Alive in the Bitter Sea*. New York: Times Book Co. Inc., 1982.

Cohn, E.J. Jr. *Industry in the Pacific Northwest and the Location Theory*. New York: King's Crown Press, 1954.

Collison, Thomas. *The Superfortress is Born*. New York: Sloan and Pearce. 1945.

Crouch, Tom D. *The Eagle Aloft*. Washington, D.C.: Smithsonian Institution Press. 1983.

Cunningham, Frank. *Sky Master*. Philadelphia: Dorrance and Company, 1943.

Daley, Robert. *An American Saga*. New York: Random House, 1980.

Dillon, Mary Earhart. *Wendell Willkie*. Philadelphia: J.B. Lippincott & Company, 1952.

Emme, Eugene M. *Two Hundred Years of Flight in America*. San Diego: American Astronautical Society, Univelt, Inc., 1977.

Franz, Anselm and Others. *The Jet Age*. Washington, D.C.: Smithsonian Institution Press, 1979.

General Dynamics Corporation, *Dynamic America*, New York: Doubleday.

Gibbs-Smith, C.H. *A History of Flying*. London: B.T. Batsford, 1953.

Gilbert, James. *The World's Worst Aircraft*. New York: St. Martin's Press, 1975.

Godson, John. *The Rise and Fall of the DC-10*. New York: David McKay, 1975.

Green, William, Gordon Swanborough, and John Mowinski. *Modern Commercial Aircraft*. New York: Portland House, 1987.

Halberstam, David. *The Reckoning*. New York: Avon Books, 1987.

Hardy, M.J. *The Lockheed Constellation*. New York: Arco Publishing Company, 1973.

Hart, Ivor B. *Mechanical Investigations of Leonardo Da Vinci*. London: Chapman & Hall, 1925.

Holmes, Donald B. *Air Mail: An Illustrated History*. New York: Crown Publishers, 1981.

Horwitch, Mel. *Clipped Wings*. Cambridge: The MIT Press, 1982.

Jacoby, N.H., P. Nehemkis, and R. Eells. *Bribery and Extortion in World Business*. New York: MacMillan, 1977.

Khayyam, Omar. *Rubaiyat of Omar Khayyam*. London: George G. Harrap and Company, 1940.

Klass, M.D. *Last of the Flying Clippers*. Atglen, PA: Schiffer Publishing Ltd.,1997

Knight, Geoffrey. *Concorde: The Real Story*. New York: Stein and Day, 1978.

Mansfield, Harold. *Vision*. New York: Popular Library, 1966.

————. *Billion Dollar Battle*. New York: Arno Press, 1980.

Maynard, Crosby. *Flight Plan For Tomorrow*. Santa Monica: Douglas Aircraft Company, 1962.

McArthur, Warren. *Four Miles South of Kitty Hawk*. New York: Warren McArthur Corporation, 1943.

Monteith, Charles N. *Simple Aerodynamics and the Airplane*. Washington D.C.: Office of the Army Air Corps, 1925.

Newell, Gordon. *Ready All!* Seattle: University of Washington Press, 1987.

Petzinger, Thomas Jr. *Hard Landing*. New York: Random House, 1996.

Rice, Berkely. *The C-5A Scandal*. Boston: Houghton Mifflin Company, 1971.

Rodgers, Eugene. *Flying High*. New York: The Atlantic Monthly Press, 1996.

Rosen, Milton W. *The Viking Rocket Story*. New York: Harper and Brothers, 1955.

Schon, Donald A. *Technology and Change*. New York: Delacorte Press, 1967.

Sabbaugh, Karl. *21st Century Jet*. New York: Scribner, 1996.

Schreiber, Servan, J.J. *The American Challenge*. New York: Atheneum, 1968.

Shakespeare, William. *Five Great Tragedies*. New York: Pocket Books, 1939.

Sikorsky, Igor. *The Story Of The Winged-S*. New York: Dodd, Mead, and Company, 1938.

Torres, George. *Space Shuttle: A Quantum Leap*. Novato, CA: Presidio Press, 1986.

————. *Space Shuttle: The Quest Continues*. Novato, CA: Presidio Press, 1989.

Wagner, William. *Reuben Fleet and the Story of Consolidated Aircraft*. Falbrook, CA: Aero Publishers, 1976.

Willkie, Wendell L. *One World*. New York: Simon and Schuster, 1943.

Yenne, Bill. *A Tale of Two Giants*. New York/Avenel New Jersey: Crescent Books, 1989.

THESES

Calkins, K.L. *An Analysis of Labor Relations News Coverage in the Boeing Company Paper and the Union Paper During the Strike of 1948*, Master's Thesis, University of Washington, 1968.

MacDonald, A.N. *Seattle's Economic Development 1880-1910*, Ph.D. Thesis, University of Washington, 1959.

REFERENCE BOOKS

Chronicle of the 20th Century. New York: Chronicle Publications, 1987.

Flight: A Pictorial History of Aviation. 1953.

Space Technology - An Illustrated Encyclopedia. 2nd Edition, New York: Orion Books, 1989.

PERIODICALS

AVIATION WEEK & SPACE TECHNOLOGY
February 9, 1959, Page 39; December 8, 1975, Page 15; December 18, 1978, Page 18; January 8, 1979, Page 25; August 4, 1980, Page 21; June 3, 1991, Page 34; March 16, 1992, Page 14; May 4, 1992, Page 25; March 7, 1994, Page 54; April 11, 1994, Page 36; January 15, 1996, Page 37; December 23/30, 1996, Page 14; April 20, 1998, Page 47; August 10, 1998, Page 17; September 28, 1998, Pages S3-S20.

BOEING NEWS, The Boeing Airplane Company/The Boeing Company
January 1930, Page 1; June 1937, Page 4; April 26, 1945, Page 5; March 21, 1946, Page 1; June 10, 1948, Page 2; August 11, 1960, Page 4; October 5, 1978, Page 3; April 16, 1981, Page 1; June 9, 1983, Page 1; January 31, 1985, Page 3; December 19, 1986, Page 1; August 7, 1987, Page 2; September 20, 1988, Page 1; March 22, 1991, Page 7; July 2, 1993, Page 1; January 19, 1996, Page 1; August 2, 1996, Page 1; August 1, 1997, Page 1.

BUSINESS WEEK
December 18, 1989, Page 47; March 1, 1993, Page 60.

DUN'S REVIEW
December, 1978, Page 36

FORBES
November 26, 1979, Page 42

FORTUNE
January, 1962, Page 65; September 25, 1978, Page 46; September 28, 1987, Page 64; July 17, 1989, Page 44; August 28, 1989, Page 80; February 17, 1997, Pages 92 and 98; March 1, 1999, Page F-2.

INTERNATIONAL HERALD TRIBUNE
December 21, 1981, Page 7; February 27/28, 1982, Page 1; September 12, 1985, Page 20.

NEW YORK TIMES
February 23, 1977, Page A22; February 15, 1979, Page A1; February 16, 1979, Page D5; June 2, 1979, Page 29.

SEATTLE POST INTELLIGENCER
January 1, 1980, Page D11; May 7, 1995, Page F3; June 10, 1998, Page A14; August 25, 1998, Page 1; November 18, 1998, Page D1; December 12,

1998, Page A6; March 9, 1999, Page C1; August 28, 1999, Page 1; August 29, 1999, Page 1.

SEATTLE TIMES
May 27, 1979, Page A7; March 20, 1984, Section D; June 3, 1984, Pacific Section, Page 12; September 2, 1989, Page B8; October 4, 1989, Page A8; October 24, 1989, Page 1; April 11, 1991, Page B2.

TIME
March 15, 1937, Centerfold; January 18, 1943, Page 72; March 1, 1943, Page 56; April 7, 1980, Page 52; March 31, 1967, Cover Story.

WALL STREET JOURNAL
December 4, 1975, Page 1; May 7, 1976, Page 1; February 10, 1979, Page 13; October 9, 1980; September 11, 1981, Page 12; July 1, 1982, Page 40.

WASHINGTON The Evergreen State Magazine
November, 1988, Page 117

SPECIAL REPORTS

ALIGNMENT CHECK—AIRPLANE N712PA, Internal Boeing Communication, CSPR-18, February 10, 1959.

BOEING ARCHIVES, Numerous Historical Details.

CORPORATE STATISTICS, The Boeing Company, 10-00-10, Page 1.

DC-3 DAKOTA NEWSLETTER, McDonnell Douglas, Douglas Aircraft Company, December 17, 1985.

DC-3 FEATS—FACT OR FANCY, McDonnell Douglas *NEWS*, December 17, 1985.

Charles E. Simon and Company Study, 1977.

M. T. Stamper Speech Before the National Contract Management Assn., Los Angeles, California, July 22, 1988.

FIRST ANNUAL REPORT TO THE STOCKHOLDERS, United Aircraft and Transport Corporation, December, 1929.

REPORT TO THE STOCKHOLDERS, The Boeing Airplane Company, 1934, Pages 5 and 6.

REPORT TO THE STOCKHOLDERS, The Boeing Airplane Company, 1942, Pages 6 and 7.

REPORT TO THE STOCKHOLDERS, The Boeing Airplane Company, 1957, Page 19.

REPORT TO THE STOCKHOLDERS, The Boeing Company, 1965, Page 25.

REPORT TO THE STOCKHOLDERS, The Boeing Company, 1975, Page 5.

REPORT TO THE STOCKHOLDERS, The Boeing Company, 1976, Page 4.

REPORTS TO THE STOCKHOLDERS, The Boeing Airplane Company/ The Boeing Company, 1941-1998.

LETTERS

Boeing Letter, J.C. Foley, to Helen Holcombe, August 6, 1917.

INTERVIEWS

Bauer, E.E., with M.T. Stamper, November 13, 1989; George Torres, November 10, 1998; John Winch, December 2, 1998; G. "Mike" Bunney, December 2, 1998; Harry Fachet, December 2, 1998; Volker Roth, December 2, 1998; Lucy Slater, December 2, 1998; Mark Smith, December 2, 1998; Michael Sears, December 3, 1998; Lawrence Merritt, December 3, 1998; Frank Shrontz, December 9, 1998; Jim Jamieson, January 11, 1999; John Cashman, January 12, 1999; Larry Dickenson January 19, 1999; Jim Dagnon, January 25, 1999; Allan Mulally, January 27, 1999; Roger Wynne, March 3, 1999; Jim Albaugh, April 27, 1999; Ray Bracy, May 3, 1999; Steve Morse, May 5, 1999; Latif Rahimane May 6, 1999; L. Norm Yearsley, May 27, 1999; Sherry Nebel, May 28, 1999; and Harry Stonecipher, June 30, 1999.

Schmechel, Donald S., with E.C. Wells, June 1986; M.T. Stamper, October 17, 1986; and M.T. Stamper, November 1, 1986.

Spitzer, Paul, Boeing Archives, with Charlie Thompson.

VIDEOS

KCTS Productions. *21st Century Jet, The Building of the 777.* Seattle and London: 1995/1996.

McDonnell Douglas. *Calling All The Team.* St. Louis: 1997.

PRIVATE COMMUNICATIONS

Countless conversations between the author and other Boeing employees, managers, and executives, over a period of forty-five years.

INDEX

Models are listed by producer in approximate chronological order.

Eugene E. Bauer

ABOUT THE AUTHOR

Eugene "Gene" E. Bauer joined the Boeing engineering department in 1941, went away to war in 1943, and returned to Boeing in 1946. He was appointed to management in 1956, after completing his master's degree in Metallurgical Engineering at the University of Washington. He served on the technical staff for 20 years.

During the 1960s, he earned an MBA in International Business from the University of Washington—stretching his day at work full time while attending school part time. After graduating, he was assigned the Corporate International Desk.

In 1973, he joined the Boeing sales force for Latin America. Mastering both Portuguese and Spanish, he sold commercial airplanes in nine countries for five years.

In 1980, he was sent to the People's Republic of China to reestablish and manage a Customer Support Office, where he remained for five years. Following a similar assignment in Brazil, he retired in 1988.

Boeing

BOEING